SOME SAYINGS OF THE BUDDHA

SOME SAYINGS OF THE BUDDHA

ACCORDING TO THE PĀLI CANON

TRANSLATED BY

F.L. WOODWARD

WITH AN INTRODUCTION BY

SIR FRANCIS YOUNGHUSBAND

MANOHAR

2020

First published 1903
Reprinted 2020

ISBN 978-93-90035-42-7

Published by
Ajay Kumar Jain *for*
Manohar Publishers & Distributors
4753/23 Ansari Road, Daryaganj
New Delhi 110 002

Printed at
Replika Press Pvt. Ltd.

SOME SAYINGS OF THE BUDDHA

ACCORDING TO THE PĀLI CANON

Translated by

F. L. WOODWARD

With an Introduction by

SIR FRANCIS YOUNGHUSBAND

The World's Classics

HUMPHREY MILFORD
OXFORD UNIVERSITY PRESS
London New York Toronto

"Some Sayings of the Buddha" was first published in 1925. In "The World's Classics" it was first published in 1939 and repreinted in 1942 and 1945.

CONTENTS

CONTENTS

CONTENTS

CONTENTS

INTRODUCTION

GAUTAMA, afterwards known as Buddha, was born more than five hundred years before Christ and, like Christ, left no written record. Yet Indian life to-day is not so utterly different from what it was in his time that we are wholly unable to imagine the life he led. From the Hindu sacred books which are still in use to-day as they were in his time we know the kind of spiritual food upon which he was nourished. From the oral tradition of his teaching which was handed down by his disciples we know with a high degree of accuracy the general principles which he sought to inculcate. And from the innumerable figures of him which we see in Buddhist countries, and from the lives of the most saintly of his followers, we can gather the general impression he made upon mankind. With these elements let us create a picture of this great Hindu reformer who unintentionally founded a new religion.

Buddha was born a prince, the son of a King—in other words, of a Maharaja. Living in India to-day are scores of small Maharajas of very much the same type as Buddha's father. They live in palace-fortresses of considerable beauty and keep up much outward state. And despotic though they are on the one side, on the other they are very democratic. They live a public life surrounded by ministers, nobles, and retainers and by ministers' and nobles' retainers. Theoretically they may issue any order. In practice they are curiously hedged in by ancient custom and tradition, by the words, and even looks, of the little public round them, and lastly by their women-folk.

In such-like surroundings Buddha must have been brought up. He would have been utterly spoilt by his mother, the women-folk of the palace, and by the servants, but he would have been sternly repressed by his father. Between these two extremes his life would have developed. And, be it noted, he would have been right in life from the very commencement. It would have been no secluded life he led. The impact upon him of live human beings would have been felt from the first. He would have felt also the pressure of long tradition. Especially would the weight of religious custom have been heavy upon him. The Court Brahmin priest would have ruled his religious life. He would have had to conform to the prescribed religious observances. The customary routine he would have had mechanically to follow. Even his wife would be chosen for him. He would not see her till he was actually married. It is known that Buddha was married when quite a young man and had a son.

There would have been much of routine and convention and stark superstition in the early life of Buddha, yet that would not have been all. Even as far back as his time India possessed a great culture of its own. Centuries before then the Upanishads and the Bhagavad Gita—works revered to this day in Europe as well as India—had been written. There were great oral traditions going back further still. Right in the blood of the

Indian culture of Buddha's time there must have been strains of pre-Vedic culture dating from a time long before the Aryans had arrived in India, strains coming up from the Indus civilisation existing more than three thousand years B.C., and from a Ganges civilisation which must undoubtedly have existed contemporaneously with the Indus. From childhood upward he would every year have seen performances of great sacred dramas ancient even in his time. He would have joined in singing the sacred songs and dancing the sacred dances. From time to time he would have visited the sacred city of Benares, scarcely a hundred miles away on the sacred river Ganges. He would have mingled with the happy crowds at the great religious festivals and thrilled to the spiritual fervour.

Both at his own home and at Benares he would have been struck by the tremendous contrast between the luxury and extravagance on the one side and the utter squalor and poverty on the other. Alongside the riches of his father's palace and of the temples in Benares he would have seen thousands of men, women, and children living just at starvation point. But he would also have seen —and by this his sensitive nature would have been acutely impressed—numbers of holy men who had deliberately forsaken family and friends and comfort in order to lead the holy life. He would have seen men who obviously set their affections on things above. He would have conversed with them, or at least listened to them conversing with others. And far more than from the rigidly meticulous routine of daily worship, far more even than from the sacred dramas,

S.S.B.—I*

he would have caught from them the deep inner essential spirit of the Hindus and yearned to be free from the fetters of his conventional position and like them fare forth into the free world of the spirit. He may have felt even more. We may well surmise that he may have heard a voice within him whispering that he would one day have that to tell the world which even the holiest among them had not yet dreamed of, and that he must forthwith prepare for his mission.

At length the bursting-point must have been reached—the moment when he could contain himself no longer. The bonds which bound him he would have broken asunder. Summoning all his courage, he would have informed his revered father and his clinging wife of his firm intention to lead the solitary life of the spirit. Many an Indian has had this same dread experience. Admired though the lone life of the holy man is by Indians, it is for others than their own sons or husbands that mothers and wives adore it. Always it is a fearful strain on all concerned for him who would venture in the spirit to break with the home. And it must have been the same with Gautama.

But once the ties were sundered, once he was free to give himself entirely to religion, deep holy joy would have been his. Now he could be himself to the full. He would have no money, no house. Even for his bread he would have to beg. But he could call his soul his own and he would have been happy. And in India such a wayfarer in the land of the spirit is never entirely alone. For a space he may go off into the jungles and live by himself. But he need not stay there. And so near Benares Gautama would have been meeting others who had, like himself, broken the bonds and utterly devoted themselves to spiritual things. Surely he would have met men who had followed the sacred river Ganges to the sacred city Hardwar at the spot where it issues from the mighty Himalaya. He might even have met a few who had followed the river further still to its very source in the everlasting snows and found inspiration from the overwhelming grandeur of the mountains and the utter purity of their unsullied summits. From all such he would have imbibed still more of the essential spirit of the Hindus. His religious curiosity would have been yet further aroused. And perhaps, in accordance with Indian custom, he might have gone to one "guru" after another, sitting at the feet of first this master, then that, to learn what he could, and having satisfied himself that he had no more wisdom to gather, asked for the guru's blessing and departed on his way, till at length he would feel that the time had come for himself to assume the rôle of master, gather disciples round him, and deliver his long-pent-up message.

* * * *

All this is mere conjecture. What is certain is that Buddha was brought up in a land steeped in spirituality—in a country with a religious tradition even in his time at least three thousand years old and possessing a great religious literature. It is certain also that he was a man not only of great heart and great soul but great mind, and that he gradually collected round him a band of devoted disciples. He wrote nothing, but he imprinted himself on the plastic, retentive souls of his listeners. And it is from what they have handed down that we have to gather his teaching. In course of generations their oral tradition would be transferred to writing. And the present book is a translation of some of such records.

Yet, in addition to these actual teachings, there must have been about Buddha some subtle, elusive quality, a little of which his disciples may have caught from him but which escaped his disciples' disciples and which the distant disciples of those disciples were not able to convey in the written word. These latter were able to repeat arguments and record rules of conduct but may have been unable to communicate that charm which must surely have captivated those who knew him in his lifetime. May I give an illustration of what I mean ? A Japanese Buddhist, Susuki, attended the World Congress of Faiths in London in 1936. He delivered an excellent address. But it was not the address which impressed the Congress ; it was himself. It was the charm of his personality which captivated his audiences. He had studied the teachings of Buddha. He had taught the teachings of Buddha. But he had gone much further than this. He had saturated his whole life with the teachings of Buddha and in his own way he expressed those teachings so that everyone who saw or heard him was drawn to him and disposed towards Buddhism. Buddha was an Indian and would therefore have been far different from this Japanese. Yet to an even intenser degree he must have had that compelling charm and authority which wins disciples to a master. Undoubtedly he must have schooled himself with the sternest discipline. His disciples must all the time have felt he was master of himself and had himself tautly in hand. But no prim disciplinarian could have exerted the influence which he did. Through the severity of his self-discipline must have shone a sweetness which would make men hang on his words and which would have imprinted itself on their memories. Perhaps we may still detect a remnant of this sweetness in that smile which we see on the features of nearly every representation of Buddha. Of the Prophet Mahomed no picture, statue, or bust is ever made. Christ is usually, but mistakenly, represented as a Man of Sorrows, and nailed to an instrument of torture. But Buddha through the ages has been depicted seated calm and serene, gently smiling upon mankind. He is shown as a man who has attained imperturbable happiness and who was anxious to make all others as happy as he was.

Perhaps, however, these figures of Buddha which one sees set up all over any Buddhist country may in one respect give a false impression of the Great Teacher. As he sits there in such calm repose we are disposed to think of him as the personification of inactive impassivity. Yet, in fact, he led a life of incessant action. He did not with folded arms accept things as they were. He had the insight to see how wrong things were and he had the initiative to set out boldly to put them right. He had to wrestle hard with himself and then with those about him. In accordance with the tolerant spirit of the Hinduism in which he was brought up he neither hurled vituperation on the orthodox nor did the orthodox denounce him and have him tried and tortured. Nevertheless, he displayed extreme audacity in showing the better way which he himself had with such difficulty found. His long life was never one of ease and comfort. Having deliberately given up all worldly things he had to endure great hardships. And, to attract and keep disciples and train them to spread his good news, intense and prolonged activity were required. Buddha was essentially a man of action. He was also a sound practical man of the world.

But, in spite of the care with which he taught his disciples, it may perhaps be only now at this long distance of time that his teachings are beginning to be really understood. His disciples may have been too close to him really to grasp the true significance of his doctrines. For long an impression was created that Buddhism was something negative. Men were not to do this—not to do that. The end of all things was nothingness—as Nirvana was interpreted. And there was no God. Nowadays this is being recognised as an utterly false conception of Buddha's teaching. He could never have made such a mark as he has upon mankind with a negative doctrine. In it there must have been something strong and positive, or so deep an impression could never have been made. But for long the impression prevailed that Buddhism was negative rather than positive.

And to a great extent it certainly was negative. As an instance, we have the not taking of life. Buddhists are taught not to take life and it is a joy to travel in a Buddhist country and see how tame the wild animals are. But these same Buddhists are not taught with equal vigour the positive doctrine of saving life. There were not till recently Societies for the Prevention of Cruelty to Animals. Yet Buddha with his great compassionate heart would surely have pressed this positive side of his doctrine in his lifetime.

It is, however, in his attitude towards the idea of God that Buddha is most misrepresented. Because he refrained from making any sharp definition of God, and especially because he did not define Him as a Person—as a Father, for example—he is put down as an atheist and Buddhism is contemptuously tossed aside as unimportant. But it may have been because Buddha had too great, not too small, an idea of God that he refused to restrict himself to a sharp definition of the Deity. There are certain things which are too great to be put into words. Who, for instance, would care to define love? Buddha did not presume to define God, but both he and his disciples were saturated with the conception of a Power behind the eye that sees and the ear that hears, and behind all the phenomena of Nature. They had no hard, cold, mechanistic, materialistic view of the universe. They never conceived of it as anything else than spiritual. They assumed as a matter of course that there was a great spiritual power driving through all things as through themselves, and making for ever higher perfection. Buddhism cannot therefore be regarded as mere atheism.

This imputation of atheism to Buddhism has indeed aroused much resentment among students of Buddhism. The veteran Buddhist scholar, Mrs. Rhys Davids, especially has vehemently protested and contended that Buddhism is neither antitheistic nor atheistic. "The educated man in Buddha's day," she says, "believed in Deity as immanent in each man, as the Most, the Highest, the Best in that man's spiritual being or self."

It seems, in fact, to have been as much taken for granted that men were imbued with the Spirit of the Universe as nowadays it is assumed that Frenchmen are imbued with the spirit of France. It was taken as a matter of course that man was saturated with the Divine Universal Spirit, but it was thought no more necessary, or indeed possible, to define that Spirit in precise terms than it is for Frenchmen to define what is the spirit of France. That spirit is indeed at times symbolised in a person. In the Rubens Gallery at the Louvre, France is symbolised in the pictures as a glorious personage in a magnificent helmet. She is painted among other persons in groups. But no one would seriously regard her as standing for an actual person like the others. All recognise that the figure merely symbolises the spirit of France. In the same way in other pictures God is represented as a tremendous male figure, but no one would regard that figure as more than symbolical.

Now it would seem that Buddha shrank from giving even symbolical expression to the inexpressibly tremendous Spirit which actuates the Universe and drives through every one of us. To describe It—especially to describe It as a Person—was only to belittle It. He was silent on the Nature of God not from any inadequacy of appreciation, but from excess of reverence. But we can conjecture what was in his mind as to the fundamental nature of things by studying the philosophical writings which were prevalent in his day. Both he and those about him were brought up on the Upanishads and according to those writings, ancient even in Buddha's day, there was one Source, one Power, one Reality, one Being—call It what we may—from which—and from which alone—emanated all our intellectual powers, all our faculties, and all the powers of nature. In that Great Reality we all exist as It exists in us. It permeates us through and through as the spirit of France permeates all Frenchmen. It is the source of all the activity in the world, human or natural, vital or purely physical.

But this Greatest, Highest, Most is not something wholly outside us and apart from us, any more than France is wholly outside Frenchmen. It is an Ideal which is actuating, drawing, compelling, and impelling us. The Upanishads regard It as the true Self in us all. If we could delve deep down within ourselves to the profoundest depths we would find the Supreme Reality. Or occasions may arise when in a flash It is revealed to us. There, in each one of us, is the very essence of the whole Universe—"nearer to us than breathing and closer than hands and feet." There may not be a distant, aloof, Divine Potentate who knows all and can do anything, but working through the world may be an all-pervasive Principle constraining the whole towards an ultimate Perfection.

Somewhat like this was the conception of things in Gautama's time. And it was known that the illumination of men's true inner selves brought to the few who were privileged to experience it a Joy which transfigured their whole lives. They would have touched the Fountain Source of all that is. They would have directly experienced the Joy of Creation—the Joy from which every power and every faculty proceeds. And it was such Illumination that eventually came to Gautama. He reached Nirvana. And thenceforth he became the Buddha, the Enlightened One.

And here we come to the second great misconception of Buddhism. Nirvana is looked upon by Western people as implying a state of Nothingness, extinction, annihilation, whereas it is in fact a state of Somethingness to the *n*th degree. Western writers refer to Nirvana as if it were a state of blank emptiness, when the man's mind would be devoid of all intelligence and all feeling—a complete vacuum. The truth is the precise opposite. One who has attained the state of Nirvana may indeed be motionless and regardless of all sights and sounds. Yet inwardly his soul may be in a condition of intensest activity. He may be utterly absorbed in himself but he may be himself to the fullest stretch of his capacity—infinitely more himself, his real true deep-down self, than he is when moving about in the world, wide-awake, with all his faculties about him. When a man is suddenly faced with a masterpiece, he hears nothing, he sees nothing but the one object. He is absorbed in contemplation of supreme beauty. Yet he is in no state of nothingness, his soul is not empty. Inwardly he is full of activity. He has been stirred to be himself as never before. Lovers still better exemplify the point. In their moment of supreme bliss they may be devoid of all motion, their thinking processes may be in abeyance, their eyes and ears may be closed to all sights and sounds, yet they are not empty: they have reached the very acme of inner activity. Each has stirred the other to be himself to the very full. To an even higher degree is it in regard to Nirvana. He who has entered that state may be oblivious of all around him. All his faculties may for the time be suspended. Yet he may have become so profoundly himself that he may be in contact with the Self which is the ultimate source of all activity, and consequently in a state of such tremendous activity as to appear to be as motionless as a spinning top. This is what is meant by Nirvana. And this is the goal of Buddhism. Not nothingness, but superlative activity.

So Buddha urged each to become what he is—what he really is down in his deepest foundations—what in moments of loftiest exaltation he discovers himself to be. Buddha had lived in life and it was out of his experience of life that he offered his advice, and offered it with all courtesy rather than with any accompanying denunciation of those who differed from him. His advice was very simple—if exceedingly difficult to carry out. Men wanted to be happy. He would make them happy. Let them get rid of all hatred and malice, all indulgence in lower desires, all lying and evil thoughts. For these let them substitute good thoughts and worthy desires, feelings of charity and compassion, and be serene and composed. In each man the mighty Soul of the World, the Self of all selves, is working to achieve the Greatest and the Highest. Let men, therefore, purify their thoughts and desires and so get in touch with that Universal which is operative everywhere and all the happiness they can possibly bear will be theirs.

Such was the gist of Buddha's teaching. Such was his new way of life. It may sound platitudinous and impracticable. But Buddha was a very practical man. And had he himself not practised what he preached, his teaching would have been of no avail. It was because he showed in his life that what he taught was both practicable and reasonable that he has exerted such a mighty influence upon mankind. He sought to put a new temper into men, to imbue them with a new spirit, give them a new heart. It was more than could be achieved in only 2,500 years. But mankind is still young and impressionable. The impression Buddha made was deep. Reinforced by like impressions made in different ways by other religious leaders it will surely work itself out and its effect be felt in ever-increasing degree. The heart of man will indeed be cleansed. From the joy in that heart will spring a compassion fixed as an instinct in the race. All hardness will be melted—conflict turned to composure.

FRANCIS YOUNGHUSBAND.

PREFACE

THIS collection consists of passages from the *Vinaya Piṭaka*, the Four Great Nikāyas (*Dīgha-*, *Majjhima-*, *Saṃyutta-*, and *Anguttara-Nikāyas*), and those parts of the Short Nikāya, such as *Dhammapada*, *Itivuttaka*, *Udāna*, and *Sutta Nipāta* (the last-named contains some of the oldest parts of the Pāli Canon), where the Buddha is represented as speaking, both in prose and verse. I have included the whole of the *Khuddaka-Pāṭha*, which tradition has regarded as containing 'the whole duty' of the Buddhist.

How much of this is the genuine utterance of the Buddha, and how much is worked up and put into the Master's mouth (especially in the case of the verse passages), cannot be accurately decided.

In the use of terms I have generally adopted those evolved, during the labours of many years, by the late Professor and Dr. C. A. Rhys Davids. The references are to the editions of the Pāli Text Society, except in the case of *Vinaya*.

I owe many thanks to my friend Mr. Peter de Abrew, of Colombo, Ceylon, at whose suggestion I started, and by whose support I have been enabled to publish, this little book.

F. L. WOODWARD.

ADYAR, MADRAS.
April, 1925.

NOTE TO THE "WORLD'S CLASSICS" EDITION

In order to avoid alteration of the type yet to bring the book into line with my later translations, I suggest here a few changes I would like to make :

(*a*) For *brother* and *sister* read *monk* and *nun* throughout.

(*b*) For *Tathagata* read *Wayfarer*.

(*c*) Where the Teacher speaks of himself, remove the frequent capital letters which have somehow crept in. I use capitals, however, for technical terms.

F. L. Woodward.

Rowella, Tasmania.
1939.

THE ARAHAT

THRO' MANY A ROUND OF BIRTH AND DEATH I RAN,
NOR FOUND THE BUILDER THAT I SOUGHT. LIFE'S STREAM
IS BIRTH AND DEATH AND BIRTH, WITH SORROW FILLED.
NOW, HOUSE-BUILDER, THOU'RT SEEN! NO MORE SHALT BUILD!
BROKEN ARE ALL THY RAFTERS, SPLIT THY BEAM!
NO MORE COMPOUNDED, MIND HATH CRAVINGS SLAIN.

Dhammapada, 153–4.

BEGINNINGS

HOMAGE TO HIM, THE EXALTED ONE, THE ARAHANT, THE ALL-ENLIGHTENED ONE

THE GOING FORTH OF GOTAMA[1]

'Now I, brethren, before my enlightenment, when I was not yet a perfected Buddha, but was a Bodhisatta, being myself still of nature to be born again,—I sought after things that are of nature to be reborn. Being myself of nature to decay, being subject to disease and death, being myself subject to sorrow, to the impurities, I sought after things of like nature.

Then there came to me the thought: "Why do I, being of nature to be reborn, being subject to death, to sorrow, to the impurities . . . thus search after things of like nature? What if I,

[1] *Note* from *Majjhima Nikāya,* i. 163 (*Ariya-pariyesana-sutta* or The Sutta of the Ariyan Searching).
The popular legend of the Great Renunciation is not in the Pāli Tipiṭaka, but is based on the story of the young noble Yasa (*Vinaya,* i. 7) and is expanded in *Lalita Vistara* and the late *Commentary of the Jātaka Tales.*

being myself . . of such nature, and seeing the disadvantage of what is subject to rebirth, were to search after the unsurpassed, perfect security, which is Nibbāna? Being myself subject to decay, disease, death, sorrow, and the impurities, and seeing the disadvantage (of what is subject to these things), what if I were to search after the untainted, unsurpassed, perfect security, which is Nibbāna?"

Then I, brethren, some time after this, when I was a young lad, a black-haired stripling, endowed with happy youth,[1] in the first flush of manhood, against my mother's and my father's wish, who lamented with tearful eyes, I had the hair of head and face shaved off, I donned the saffron robes, and I went forth from my home to the homeless life.

Thus become a wanderer and a searcher for what is good, searching after the unsurpassed, peaceful state most excellent, I approached Ālāra Kālāma, and drawing near I said to Ālāra Kālāma: "Friend Ālāra, I desire to live the holy life in this Norm-Discipline (of yours) . . ."'

(*He then soon acquired all that Ālāra ālāma had to teach, the path of yoga for reaching in meditation the Realm of the Void, but no further. So leaving him he went to Rāma, who took him a step further, to the realm where there is no more perception of anything. Dissatisfied with this he went to Uddaka, disciple of Rāma, who professed*

[1] This statement about early youth does not harmonize with the account given in the *Mahā-Parinibbāna-Sutta* (see end of this book), where the Buddha says he was twenty-nine years old at the time.

to go a little further, but who, confessing that he could not go beyond a certain point, himself accepted Gotama as his master. So Gotama resolved to struggle on alone to reach the Goal, the 'incomparable security which is Nibbāna.')

THE ATTAINMENT OF NIBBĀNA BY GOTAMA

'So I, brethren, thinking lightly of that teaching (of Ālāra and the others), being averse from that doctrine, went away.

Then I, brethren, in my search for what is good, searching after the unsurpassed state of peace most excellent, while roaming about among the folk of Magadha, came to Uruvelā, a suburb of the Captain of the Host. There I beheld a lovely spot, a pleasant forest grove and a river of clear water flowing by, easy of access and delightful, and hard by was a village where I could beg my food. Then, brethren, I thought thus:

"Delightful in truth is this spot, pleasant this forest grove and this river of pure water flowing by, easy of access and delightful, and this village hard by where I can beg my food! Truly a proper place is this for a clansman bent on striving for his welfare, to strive therein!"

So, brethren, there and then I sat down, saying to myself: "A proper place is this for striving in!"

Then I, being of nature to be reborn, perceived the disadvantage of things of like nature . . . (*as above*) . . . and searching after the unsurpassed state of security, that is Nibbāna, free from the impurities, I did attain unto the utter peace of Nibbāna that is free from the impurities, so that the Knowledge arose in me, the Insight arose in me thus: "Sure is my release. This is my last birth. There is no more birth for me!"'

Majjhima Nikāya, i. 166.

HARD IS THE TRUTH TO DISCERN

'Then, brethren, I had this thought:

"This Reality[1] that I have reached is profound, hard to see, hard to understand, excellent, pre-eminent, beyond the sphere of thinking, subtle, and to be penetrated by the wise alone.

But this world of men is attached to what it clings to, takes pleasure in what it clings to, delights in what it clings to. Since then this world is thus attached (to things) . . . a hard task it is for them (to grasp) . . . namely, the Originating of things by Dependence on Causes.[2] A hard task it is for them to see the meaning of the fact that all activities may be set at rest, that all the bases of being may be left behind, the destruction of craving, Passionlessness, Cessation, which is Nibbāna.

Verily, if I were to teach them the Truth, this Reality, others would not understand, and that would be labour in vain for me, vexatious would it be to me."'

(*Then Brahmā Sahampati, the great Deva, appeared and begged the Buddha to preach the Truth for the sake of a few.*)

[1] *Dhamma*, The Norm, The Law, The Truth.

[2] *Paticca-samuppāda.*

FOR THE SAKE OF A FEW, BUT THE PROFIT OF THE MANY

Then said Brahmā Sahampati:

'Let my Lord the Exalted One teach the Truth: let the Happy One teach the Truth. For there are some creatures whose sight is but little clouded with dust. They are perishing through not hearing the Truth. They will become knowers of the Truth.' So spake Brahmā Sahampati, and so saying added this further:

In Magadha was hitherto a Norm—
A Norm not pure, by minds impure thought out.
Open this Door to what is 'Deathless' called:
Let men hear *this* Norm by the Pure discerned.

As, standing on a rocky mountain-peak,
One may look down upon the folk below:
So, Wise One, climbing up the Norm-built steps,
Do thou, with eye that seeth all around,
Look down upon the folk in sorrow plunged—
Thou who art freed from sorrow—O look down
On folk by birth, age and decay o'erwhelmed.

Rise up, brave heart, victorious in battle,
Debt-freed, Band-Leader, roam through all the world!
Let the Exalted One show us the Norm.
Hearing it, men shall come to understand.

Vin. i, 4 = *M.* i, 168.

Cf. *Dhammapada*, 28:

Lo! the sage that drives away
The cloud of sloth by heedfulness,

SOME SAYINGS OF THE BUDDHA

Climbing up the heights of wisdom
Sorrowless looks down upon
All the miserable beings,
As a hillman on the plains.

ALL SORTS AND CONDITIONS OF MEN

'Then I, brethren, seeing the wish of Brahmā Sahampati, out of compassion for all beings, looked down upon the world with the eye of a Buddha. And as I looked down upon the world with a Buddha's eye, I beheld beings whose eyes were but little clouded with dust, also beings whose eyes were much clouded with dust: beings of sharp wits and beings of dull wits, beings of good and beings of evil natures: beings docile and beings of stubborn sort, and some of these abode in understanding of the danger of lives to come and fear of evil deeds.

As in a pond of lotuses blue and red and white, some plants which spring and grow in the water come not to the surface, but flourish underneath; and some spring and grow in the water and reach up to the surface; and yet others in like manner push up above the surface and are not wetted by the water,—even so, brethren, did I, looking over the world with a Buddha's eye, behold beings whose eyes were but little clouded with dust. . . .

Then, brethren, did I make answer to Brahmā Sahampati in verse:

Open for such is the Door to the Deathless State.
Ye that have ears, renounce the creed ye hold.[1]

[1] *Pamuñcantu saddhaṃ*—a much discussed phrase and wrongly translated by the early Pāli scholars

Conscious of danger, in its depth, Brahmā,
I would not preach the Norm of Norms to men.'[1]

THE FIRST SERMON

Thus have I heard: Once the Exalted One was dwelling near Benares, at Isipatana, in the Deer-Park.

Then the Exalted One thus spake unto the company of Five Brethren:

'These two extremes, brethren, should not be followed by one who has gone forth as a wanderer:

Devotion to the pleasures of sense—a low and pagan practice, unworthy, unprofitable, the way of the world (on the one hand), and on the other hand devotion to self-mortification, which is painful, unworthy, unprofitable.

By avoiding these two extremes He who hath won the Truth (the Buddha) has gained knowledge of that *Middle Path* which giveth Vision, which giveth Knowledge, which causeth Calm, Insight, Enlightenment, and Nibbāna.

by 'give faith,' 'put forth belief,' etc.—but it undoubtedly means 'put away.'

[1] *Note.*—In other passages the Buddha has pointed out that if a Buddha give out occult truth to an unbelieving generation, harm befalls the man who rejects it. E.g. *Saṃyutta Nikāya,* ii. 261: 'I also, brethren, have seen these things before, yet I did not reveal them. I might have revealed it, and others would not have believed it. Now, had they not believed me, it would have been to their loss and sorrow.'

And what, brethren, is that *Middle Path* which giveth Vision, which giveth Knowledge, which causeth Calm, Insight, Enlightenment, and Nibbāna ?

Verily it is this Ariyan Eightfold Path, that is to say :

RIGHT VIEW, RIGHT AIM, RIGHT SPEECH, RIGHT ACTION, RIGHT LIVING, RIGHT EFFORT, RIGHT MINDFULNESS, RIGHT CONTEMPLATION.

This, brethren, is that *Middle Path*, which giveth Vision, which giveth Knowledge, which causeth Calm, Insight, Enlightenment, and Nibbāna.

Now this, brethren, is the Ariyan Truth about *Suffering* :

Birth is Suffering, Decay is Suffering, Sickness is Suffering, Death is Suffering, likewise Sorrow and Grief, Woe, Lamentation and Despair. To be conjoined with things which we dislike, to be separated from things which we like—that also is Suffering. Not to get what one wants—that also is Suffering. In a word, this Body, this fivefold Mass which is based on *Grasping*, that is Suffering.

Now this, brethren, is the Ariyan Truth about *The Origin of Suffering* :

It is that *Craving* that leads downwards to birth, along with the Lure and the Lust that lingers longingly now here, now there : namely, the Craving for Sensation, the Craving to be born again, the Craving to have done with rebirth. Such, brethren, is the Ariyan Truth about *The Origin of Suffering*.

And this, brethren, is the Ariyan Truth about *The Ceasing of Suffering* :

Verily it is the utter passionless cessation of, the giving up, the forsaking, the release from, the absence of longing for, this *Craving*.

Now this, brethren, is the Ariyan Truth about *The Way leading to the Ceasing of Suffering.* Verily it is this Ariyan Eightfold Path, that is:

RIGHT VIEW, RIGHT AIM, RIGHT SPEECH, RIGHT ACTION, RIGHT LIVING, RIGHT EFFORT, RIGHT MINDFULNESS, RIGHT CONTEMPLATION.

At the thought, brethren, of this Ariyan Truth of Suffering, concerning things unlearnt before, there arose in me Vision, Insight, Understanding: there arose in me Wisdom, there arose in me Light.

At the thought, brethren, "this Ariyan Truth about the Origin of Suffering is to be understood," concerning things unlearnt before, there arose in me Vision, Insight, Understanding: there arose in me Wisdom, there arose in me Light.

At the thought, brethren, "this Ariyan Truth of Suffering has been understood," concerning things unlearnt before, there arose in me Vision, Insight, Understanding: there arose in me Wisdom, there arose in me Light.

Again, at the thought, brethren, of this Ariyan Truth of the Origin of Suffering, concerning things unlearnt before, there arose in me Vision, Insight, Understanding: there arose in me Wisdom, there arose in me Light.

At the thought, brethren, "the Origin of Suffering must be put away," concerning things unlearnt before, there arose in me Vision, Insight, Understanding: there arose in me Wisdom, there arose in me Light.

So also at the thought " The Origin of Suffering has been put away " . . . there arose in me Light.

Again, at the thought, brethren, of this Ariyan Truth of the Ceasing of Suffering . . . there arose in me Light.

At the thought, brethren, " the Ceasing of Suffering must be realized " . . . there arose in me Light.

At the thought, brethren, " the Ceasing of Suffering has been realized " . . . there arose in me Light.

Finally, brethren, at the thought of This Ariyan Way leading to the Ceasing of Suffering . . . there arose in me Light.

At the thought, brethren, " the Way leading to the Ceasing of Suffering is to be developed " . . . there arose in me Light.

At the thought, brethren, " the Way leading to the Ceasing of Suffering has been developed " . . . concerning things unlearnt before, there arose in me Vision, Insight, Understanding: there arose in me Wisdom, there arose in me Light.

Now so long, brethren, as my knowledge and my insight of these thrice-revolved twelvefold Ariyan Truths, in their essential nature, were not quite purified,—so long was I not sure that in this world, together with the devas, the Māras, the Brahmas, among the hosts of recluses and brahmi of devas and mankind, there was one enlightened with supreme enlightenment.

But so soon, brethren, as my knowledge and my insight of these thrice-revolved twelvefold Ariyan Truths, in their essential nature, were quite purified,—then, brethren, was I assured what it is to be enlightened with supreme enlightenment with regard to the world and its devas, Māras, and Brahmas, and with regard to the hosts of recluses and brahmins, of devas and mankind.

But now Knowledge and Insight have arisen in me, so that I know, "Sure is my heart's release. This is my last birth. There is no more becoming for me."'

Saṃyutta Nikāya, v. 421–3.

ANALYSIS OF THE EIGHTFOLD PATH

And the Exalted One said:

'Now what, brethren, is RIGHT VIEW?

The knowledge about Ill, the Arising of Ill, the Ceasing of Ill, and the Way leading to the Ceasing of Ill,—that, brethren, is called Right View.

And what, brethren, is RIGHT AIM?

The being set on Renunciation, on Non-resentment, on Harmlessness,—that, brethren, is called Right Aim.

And what, brethren, is RIGHT SPEECH?

Abstinence from lying speech, from backbiting and abusive speech, and from idle babble,—that, brethren, is called Right Speech.

And what, brethren, is RIGHT ACTION?

Abstinence from taking life, from taking what is not given, from wrong-doing in sexual passions, —that, brethren, is called Right Action.

And what, brethren, is RIGHT LIVING?

Herein, brethren, the Ariyan disciple, by giving up wrong living, gets his livelihood by right living,—that, brethren, is called Right Living.

And what, brethren, is RIGHT EFFORT?

Herein, brethren, a brother generates the will to inhibit the arising of evil immoral conditions that have not yet arisen: he makes an effort, he sets energy afoot, he applies his mind and struggles. Likewise (he does the same) to reject evil immoral conditions that have already arisen. Likewise (he does the same) to cause the arising of good conditions that have not yet arisen. Likewise he does the same to establish, to prevent the corruption, to cause the increase, the practice, the fulfilment of good conditions that have already arisen. This, brethren, is called Right Effort.

And what, brethren, is RIGHT MINDFULNESS?

Herein, brethren, a brother dwells regarding body as a compound, he dwells ardent, self-possessed, recollected, by controlling the covetousness and dejection that are in the world. So also with regard to Feelings, with regard to Perception, with regard to the Activities . . . with regard to Thought. This, brethren, is called RIGHT MINDFULNESS.

And what, brethren, is RIGHT CONTEMPLATION?

(*The Four Jhānas*)

Herein, brethren, a brother, remote from sensual appetites, remote from evil conditions, enters upon and abides in the First Musing, which is accompanied by directed thought and sustained thought (on an object). It is born of solitude, full of zest and happiness.

Then, by the sinking down of thought directed and sustained, he enters on and abides in the Second Musing, which is an inner calming, a raising up of the will. In it there is no directed thought, no sustained thought. It is born of contemplation, full of zest and happiness.

Then again, brethren, by the fading away of the zest, he becomes balanced (indifferent) and remains mindful and self-possessed, and while still in the body he experiences the happiness of which the Ariyans aver "the balanced thoughtful man dwells happily." Thus he enters on the Third Musing and abides therein.

Then again, brethren, rejecting pleasure and pain, by the coming to an end of the joy and sorrow which he had before, he enters on and remains in the Fourth Musing, which is free from pain and free from pleasure, but is a state of perfect purity of balance and equanimity. This is called Right Contemplation.

This, brethren, is called the Ariyan Truth of the Way leading to the Ceasing of Woe.' [1]

Dīgha Nikāya, ii. 312.

THE CAUSE OF ILL

Now the Exalted One thus addressed the brethren:

'Through not understanding, through not penetrating the Four Ariyan Truths, brethren, we have run on and wandered round this long, long journey (of rebirth), both you and I. What are those four?

[1] *Note.*—After the Fourth Step, the walker on the Path is termed 'disciple,' and after the Fifth Step, 'brother' (*bhikkhu*), lit. 'beggar,' one who has renounced the world.

S.S.B.—2*

The Ariyan Truth of Ill: the Ariyan Truth of the Arising of Ill: the Ariyan Truth of the Ceasing of Ill: the Ariyan Truth of the Way leading to the Ceasing of Ill.

But, brethren, when these Four Ariyan Truths are understood and penetrated, then is uprooted the craving for existence, cut off is the thread that leadeth to rebirth, then is there no more coming to be.'

Thus spake the Exalted One. When the Happy One had thus spoken, the Master added this further:

Blind to the Fourfold Ariyan Truths of things,
And blind to see things as they really are,
Long was our journeying thro' divers births.
Gone is the cord of life when these are seen.
No more becoming when Ill's root is cut.

D.N. ii. 90.

EARLY STRUGGLES FOR LIGHT

(*Before attaining the Middle Way, Gotama followed every known ascetic practice. In his old age he related his Experiences to Sāriputta.*)

'I can recall, Sāriputta, how I practised the four-square practice of the holy life. Thus: I was a penance-worker, outdoing others in penance: I was a rough-liver, outdoing others in roughing it: I was scrupulous, outdoing others in my scruples: a solitary was I, outdoing others in solitude.

Thus far, Sāriputta, did I go in my penance.

I went without clothes. I licked my food from my hands. I was no complier with invitations of "Come in, your reverence! Stay, your reverence!" I took no food that was brought, or meant specially for me. I accepted no invitations to a meal. I took no alms from pot or dish. I took no food from within a threshold, or through window-bars, or within the pounding-place, nor from two people eating together, nor from a pregnant woman, nor from a woman suckling a child, nor from one in intercourse, nor from food collected here and there; nor food where a dog stood by, nor from places where flies were swarming, nor fish nor flesh, nor drink fermented, nor drink distilled, nor yet sour gruel did I drink.

I ate from just one house, and just one morsel from that. Or else I ate from two houses only and just two morsels thence: or I ate from seven houses only, and just one morsel from each house. I kept myself going on food from just one pot, or just two pots, or just seven pots at a time. I took food only once a day or once in two days or once in seven days. Thus did I dwell given to the practice of taking food by rule, at stated intervals, even to intervals of half a month.

I lived on vegetables, on millet, on wild paddy, on *daddula*, on watercress, on paddy-husk, on scum of rice, on ground sesamum, on grass, on cowdung. I lived on roots and fruits of the forest, on casual fruits [that had fallen] I existed.

I was one who wore coarse clothes, I wore hemp

woven in with other things, grave-cloths, dustheap rags, a dress made of bark : I wore antelope-skin, a dress made of shreds of antelope skin, I wore *kusa* fibre, bark fibre, clothes made of shavings, a hair shirt of human hair, a hair shirt of horse-hair, or made of owl's feathers.

I plucked out hair and beard, and kept the practice up. I stood always, refusing to sit down. I was a squatter on my heels, struggling by the method of squatting. I was a thorn-bed man and lay upon a bed of thorns. I lived given to the habit of bathing thrice a day, going down into the water.

Thus in divers ways did I dwell given to tormenting and again tormenting the body. To that extent, Sāriputta, was I given to penance.

And thus far did I go in roughing it, Sāriputta. —The dirt of many seasons gathered on my body just like the outer crust of tree-bark. Just like the stump of a *tinduka*-tree was I, Sāriputta, covered with the outer crust of bark gathered through countless seasons. But never once did I think to myself : " O to wipe off this dirt and dust with my hand," or " O that others might do so for me ! " I never thought of such a thing. Thus far, Sāriputta, did I go in roughing it.

And thus far, Sāriputta, did I go in scrupulosity. —Mindful was I in going and in coming. Even to a drop of water was charity established in me, thus : " May I not be guilty of violence in harming tiny living things (therein)." Thus far, Sāriputta, did I go in my scrupulosity.

And thus far did I go in solitude.—I used to resort to some forest domain, plunge into it and dwell therein. When I saw a cow-keeper or a herd or a grass-gatherer, or a gatherer of sticks, or a forester, then from forest to forest, from jungle to jungle, from marshland to marshland, from upland to upland I fled away. And why? Lest they should see me or I should see them. Even as, Sāriputta, a wild creature of the forest on beholding man flees away from forest to forest, from jungle to jungle, from marshland to marshland, from upland to upland,—even so did I flee and flee away, lest they should see me, lest I should see them. Thus far did I go in the practice of the solitary life.

Then, Sāriputta, where there were cowpens and cows penned therein, when the cowherds had gone away, I drew near with my water-pot and gathered up the droppings of calves and young calves and sucking calves. So long as my own excrements lasted, Sāriputta, I lived even on mine own excrements. To such extremes did I go, Sāriputta, as to live on filth for food.

Then, Sāriputta, I plunged into a fearsome forest thicket and dwelt therein. Such was the fearsome horror of that dread forest thicket that anyone whose passions were not stilled and entered there,—the very hairs of his body would stand on end.

Then those cold frosty nights between the eighths [of the lunar month], on nights when the snow was falling, those nights did I pass in the open air, and the days I spent in the forest covert. And in the last month of the hot season, by day I dwelt in the open air, by night in the forest covert. So that, Sāriputta, these verses never heard before, these curious verses, occurred to me:

> Scorched, frozen, and alone,
> In fearsome forest dwelling,
> Naked, no fire to warm,
> Bent on the quest is the Sage.

Then again, Sāriputta, in a charnel-field I lay down to rest upon bones of corpses. And the cowherds came up to me, even spat upon me and even made water upon me, spattered me with mud, even poked straws into my ears. Yet, Sāriputta, I cannot call to mind that a single evil thought against them arose in me. Thus far was I gone in forbearance, Sāriputta.'

M.N. i. 77–9.

PANIC FEAR AND DREAD

(*The Master describes his early experiences of the struggles, mentioned above, to the brāhmin Jānussoni.*)

'Then, brāhmin, I thought, "Suppose now that on those nights that are notable and well marked, the fifteenth and eighth (of the lunar month),—suppose I spend them in shrines of forest, park, or tree, fearsome and hair-raising as they are, making such shrines my lodging for the night, that I may behold for myself the panic fear and horror of it all."

So, brāhmin, when the next time came round I did so, and made such shrines my lodging for the night. As I stayed there, a deer maybe came up to me, or a peacock threw down a twig, or else a breeze stirred a heap of fallen leaves. Then thought I, "Here it is! Here comes that panic fear and horror." Then, brāhmin, there came to me this thought: "Why do I remain thus in constant fear and apprehension? Let me bend down to my will that panic fear and horror, just as I am, and just as it has come to be." So as I was walking to and fro that panic fear and horror came upon me. Then I neither stood still nor sat nor lay down, but just walking up and down I bent to my will that panic fear and horror.

Again, as I was standing still, it came upon me. But I neither walked up and down, nor sat nor lay, but just standing bent it down to my will. And yet again, as I was sitting, it came upon me. But I neither stood up nor walked up and down, nor lay down, but, just sitting as I was, I bent it to my will. Then as I lay it came upon me. But I sat not up nor stood up nor walked up and down, but, just lying as I was, I bent that panic fear and horror to my will.'

M.N. i. 20–1.

STRUGGLES MORE TERRIBLE

(*Here He describes to Saccaka, the Jain, whom He calls by His title, His further struggles for the Light.*)

(a) *The Suspension of Breath*

'Then I said to myself: "How now if, setting my teeth and pressing my palate with my tongue, I were to hold down and force down my mind by will and so destroy it?"

So, Aggivessana, I set my teeth and pressing tongue to palate by an effort of will I strove to hold down, to force down my mind and so destroy it. And as I struggled, Aggivessana, with the effort the sweat burst forth from my arm-pits.

Just as if a strong man were to seize a weaker man by head and shoulders, and try to hold him down, press him down and break him in,—even so did I struggle.

Thus, Aggivessana, was my energy strenuous and unyielding. Mindfulness was thus indeed established undisturbed, but my body was perturbed ; it was not calmed thereby, because I was overpowered by the stress of my painful struggling. But even such painful feeling as then arose could not lay hold of and control my mind.

Then, Aggivessana, I said to myself : " Suppose now I practise the musing of breath suppressed."

Accordingly I checked the breathing in and out from mouth and nostrils. Then with mouth and nostrils stopped, in my ears arose a roaring noise of the escaping vital airs. Just as the sound of a smith's bellows being blown, even such was the roaring noise in my ears of the vital airs that struggled to escape when I had stopped mouth and nostrils.

Then, Aggivessana, was my energy strenuous and unyielding indeed. Mindfulness was indeed established undisturbed, but yet my body was perturbed : it was not made calm thereby, because I was overpowered by the stress of my painful struggling. But even such painful feeling as then arose could not lay hold of and control my mind.

Then, Aggivessana, I said to myself : " Suppose

I practise still further the musing of breath suppressed." Accordingly I stopped my breathing in and out from mouth and nostrils, and I closed my ears.

Then, just as if a strong man with a sharp-pointed sword should crash into the brain, so did the rush of air, all outlets being stopped, crash into my brain. Then was my energy strenuous (*as before*). . . . Yet such painful feelings as arose could not lay hold of and control my mind.

Then I thought: "Suppose now I practise the musing of breath suppressed still further." So I closed all outlets of the breath. . . . Then did dreadful head-pains come in my head. Just as if a strong man should twist a stout leathern thong round the head, even so did violent pains assail my head. . . . Yet even so, Aggivessana, could not such painful feeling as then arose lay hold of and control my mind.

Then I thought: "Suppose I practise the musing of breath suppressed still further." So I closed all outlets for the breath. . . . Then just as a skilful butcher or butcher's 'prentice with a sharp butcher's knife might rip up the belly of an ox, even so did violent pains assault my belly. . . . Yet even so did not . . . (*as before*) . . . control my mind.

Then I thought: "Suppose I carry the practice further still." So I closed all outlets (*as before*). . . . Then, just as if two strong men should lay hold of some weaker man, seizing him each by an arm, and scorch and burn him in a pit of glowing charcoal, even so, because of the closing of all outlets of the breath, did a burning pervade my body. . . . Then, Aggivessana, was my energy strenuous and unyielding, and mindfulness was established undisturbed. Yet my body was perturbed. It was not made calm thereby, because I was overpowered by the stress of my painful struggling. Yet even such painful feelings as then arose could not lay hold of and control my mind.

Thereupon certain devas beholding me exclaimed: "Gotama the recluse is dead!" But some devas said, "Gotama the recluse is not dead yet, but he is nearing his end." Yet other devas said, "Gotama the recluse is neither dead nor nearing his end. An Arahant is Gotama the recluse. Such is the way an Arahant doth abide!"'

(b) *Abstinence from Food*

'After that, Aggivessana, I thought to myself: "Now suppose I practise for the utter abstinence from food."

Then certain devas approached me and said: "Do not thou, good sir, practise for the utter abstinence from food. Yet if thou dost so practise, we will pour heavenly sustenance through the body's pores, and by that shalt thou be sustained."

Then thought I: "If I proceed to utter abstinence from food and these devas pour heavenly sustenance through my body's pores and I am sustained thereby, that would be a fraud in me." So I rejected the offer of those devas, saying "Let be."

Then, Aggivessana, I thought thus: "Suppose

I feed myself on just a little food, a mere handful now and then, such as the juice of (chewed) beans or vetch or lentils or peas."

And I did so. And my body reached a state of utter exhaustion. Just like knot-grass or bulrush, so did every several joint of it become, through that lack of sustenance. Just like a bison's hoof became my hinder parts through that same lack of sustenance. Just like a row of reed-knots my backbone stood out through that lack of sustenance. Just as the rafters of a tottering house fall in this way and that, so did my ribs fall in this way and that through that lack of sustenance. Just as in a deep, deep well the sparkle of the waters may be seen sunk in the deeps below, so in the depths of their sockets did the lustre of my eyes seem sunk, through that same lack of sustenance. Just as a bitter gourd, cut off unripened from the stalk, is shrivelled and withered by wind and sun, so was the very skin of my head shrivelled and withered through lack of food.

Then that same I, Aggivessana, saying to myself, "I will touch my belly's skin," I seized instead my backbone. And saying, "I will touch my backbone," I seized instead my belly's skin: for so it was, Aggivessana, that the one clung to the other through that same lack of sustenance.

Then that same I, Aggivessana, saying to myself, "I will go to ease myself," there on the spot I stumbled and fell down for that same want of food. And that same I, Aggivessana, saying to myself, "I will ease my body with my hand," when with my hand I stroked my limbs, rotten at the very roots my body's hairs fell off from my body through that same lack of sustenance.

And those who beheld me said, "Gotama the recluse is a black man." But some said, "Nay, he is dusky-hued." But yet others said, "Not so. Gotama the recluse is neither black nor dusky. Sallow is the skin of Gotama the recluse." Thus were the utter purity and clearness of my complexion spoiled by that same lack of sustenance.

Then thought I: "All the feelings, sharp, painful, grievous, and bitter, that recluses and brāhmins in past times have felt,—surely these pains of mine go far beyond them all. All the feelings to be thus borne in future times, surely these painful feelings of mine go far beyond them all. All the feelings that are now thus borne, surely these of mine surpass them all. Yet by all this bitter, woeful way do I not achieve the truly Ariyan excellence of knowledge and insight surpassing mortal things. Maybe there is some other way to the Wisdom."

(c) *The Saner Way*

'Then, Aggivessana, I thought: "I call to mind how when the Sakyan my father was ploughing I sat in the cool shade of the rose-apple tree, remote from sensual desires and ill conditions, and entered upon and abode in the First Musing, that is accompanied by thought directed and sustained, which is born of solitude, full of zestful ease." And I said then, "Is this, I wonder, the Way to the Wisdom?" And on that occasion there came to me the consciousness that follows thought composed, "Yes, this is the Way to the Wisdom."

Then, Aggivessana, I thought, "Why am I afraid of that state of ease, that ease which is apart from sensual desires and ill conditions?"

Then I thought: "No. I am not afraid of that state of ease." . . . Then I said, "But it is not easy for one to reach that state of ease with a body thus utterly exhausted. Suppose now I take some substantial food, some rice gruel." And so I did, Aggivessana.

Now at that time I had with me five brethren attending me, who thought, "Whatever truth Gotama the recluse shall arrive at, that will he impart to us." But, as soon as I took to eating food substantial, those five brethren were disgusted and went away, saying, "Luxurious is Gotama the recluse become! He wavers in his purpose; he has turned back to the life luxurious."

M.N. i. 242–7.

'Then I, Aggivessana, after taking food substantial got back my strength: and remote from sensual desires, remote from ill conditions, I entered and abode in the First Musing . . . the second Musing . . . the Third Musing . . . the Fourth Musing (*as described above in the section on the Four Jhānas*): but in each case the blissful feelings that arose failed to lay hold of and control my mind.

Then with thought steadied, perfectly purified, and made perfectly translucent, free from blemish, purged of taint, made supple and pliable, fit for wielding, established and immovable, I bent down my mind to the recalling of my former existences. I recalled divers births . . . evolutions and involutions of æons . . . conditions of births . . . and experiences in such . . . the rise and fall of beings and their characteristics in the different worlds with the eye divine.

Then I perceived the Four Ariyan Truths . . . the destruction of the *āsavas* . . . and I knew this : " Destroyed is rebirth for me. Lived is the holy life. Done is my task. For life in these conditions there is no hereafter."

Thus on that night, in the last watch of the night, the Threefold Knowledge was attained by me : knowledge arose, darkness was overcome, light arose, as it does for him that abides earnest, ardent and of set purpose. Yet did not the blissful feeling that arose lay hold of and control my mind.'

M.N. i. 247–8.

ALL THESE THINGS AVAIL NOT

Not nakedness, nor matted hair, nor filth,
Nor fasting long, nor lying on the ground,
Not dust and dirt, nor squatting on the heels,
Can cleanse the mortal that is full of doubt.

But one that lives a calm and tranquil life,
Though gaily decked,—if tamed, restrained he live,
Walking the holy path in righteousness,
Laying aside all harm to living things,—
True mendicant, ascetic, Brāhmin he.

Dhammapada, vv. 141–2.

THE EARLY ORDER

THE FIRST DISCIPLES

Now the venerable Aññāta-Kondañña,[1] having seen the Norm, reached the Norm, understood the Norm, plunged into the Norm; having crossed beyond doubt, having banished questioning of this and that, having reached certainty, depending on no other in his knowledge of the Master's Message,—thus spake unto the Exalted One: 'Lord, may I receive ordination and full orders from the Exalted One?'

'Come then, brother!' said the Exalted One. 'Well taught is the Norm. Live the holy life for the utter destruction of Suffering!'

Such was the manner of taking orders for that brother.

Then the Exalted One exhorted and taught the remaining (four) brethren with pious talk. (And they also won the Insight of the Norm and received ordination and full orders in like manner.)

And the Exalted One, living on food brought to Him by the brethren, exhorted and taught the remaining brethren with pious talk. Thus did the Band of Six live on food begged and brought to them by the three.

Vinaya Piṭaka, i. 6.

[1] So called because he was the first to comprehend the teachings of the First Sermon.

SOME SAYINGS OF THE BUDDHA

FIRST TEACHINGS

Then the Exalted One thus spake unto the Band of Five Brethren :—

'Body, brethren, is without the Self. If body, brethren, were the Self, body would not be involved in sickness, and one would be able to say of body: "Thus let my body be: thus let my body not be."

But, brethren, inasmuch as body is not the Self, that is why body is involved in sickness, and one cannot say of body: "Thus let my body be: thus let my body not be."

So also [1] with regard to feelings, perception, the activities and consciousness . . . they are not the Self.

For if consciousness, brethren, were the Self, then consciousness would not be involved in sickness, and one could say of consciousness: "Thus let my consciousness be: thus let my consciousness not be." But inasmuch as consciousness is not the Self, that is why consciousness is involved in sickness. That is why one cannot say of this consciousness: "Thus let my consciousness be: thus let my consciousness not be."

Now what think ye, brethren? Is body permanent or impermanent?'

'Impermanent, Lord.'

'And what is impermanent, is that weal or woe?'

'Woe, Lord.'

[1] I.e. the fivefold mass or *pañca-kkhandhā*, the *attabhāvo* or person.

'Then what is impermanent, woeful, unstable by nature, is it fitting to regard it thus: "This is mine: I am this: this is the Self of me."?'

'Surely not, Lord.'

'So also is it with feeling, perception, the activities and consciousness. Therefore, brethren, every body whatever, be it past, future, or present: be it inward or outward, gross or subtle, low or high, far or near—every body should be thus regarded, as it really is, by right insight,—"This is not mine: this am not I: this is not the Self of me."

Every feeling whatever, every perception whatever, all activities whatsoever (must be so regarded).

Every consciousness whatever, be it past, future or present, gross or subtle, low or high, far or near,—every consciousness, I say, must be thus regarded, as it really is, by right insight: "This is not mine: this am not I: this is not the Self of me."

So seeing, brethren, the well-taught Ariyan disciple feels disgust for body, feels disgust for feeling, feels disgust for perception, for the activities, feels disgust for consciousness. So feeling disgust he is repelled: being repelled, he is freed: knowledge arises that "in the freed is the freed thing": so that he knows: "Destroyed is rebirth: lived is the righteous life: done is my task: for life in terms like these there is no hereafter."'

Thus spake the Exalted One, and the Band of Five Brethren were pleased thereat and welcomed what was said by the Exalted One.

Moreover, by this teaching thus uttered the hearts of those five brethren were freed from the *āsavas* [1] without grasping.

V.P. i. 6, repeated at *S.N.* iii. 66, etc.

THE FIRST MISSIONARIES

Now at that time there were sixty-one Arahants in the world.

Then the Exalted One said to the brethren: 'I am released, brethren, from all bonds, those that are divine and those that are human. Ye also, brethren, are released from all bonds, those that are divine and those that are human. Go ye forth, brethren, on your journey, for the profit of the many, for the bliss of the many, out of compassion for the world, for the welfare, the profit, the bliss of devas and mankind!

Go not any two together. Proclaim, brethren, the Norm, goodly in its beginning, goodly in its middle, goodly in its ending. Both in the spirit and in the letter do ye make known the all-perfected, utterly pure righteous life. There are beings with but little dust of passion on their eyes. They are perishing through not hearing the Norm. There will be some who will understand. I myself, brethren, will go to Uruvela, to the suburb of the Captain of the Host, to proclaim the Norm.'

[1] *Āsavas,* a word hard to render: lit. 'floods, fluxes, intoxicants.' There are four, viz.: *kāma* (sensuality), *bhava* (lust to live), *diṭṭhi* (view or speculation), *avijjā* (ignorance). To be freed from these makes one an Arahant, Saint, or Superman.

Then Māra, the Evil One, drew near to the Exalted One, and coming to Him addressed Him in verse:

'Thou art bound with every bond, bondage human and divine.
Bound with mighty bonds art thou. Thou shalt not escape from me!'

(*The Exalted One*)

'Freed from every bond am I, bondage human and divine.
Freed from every bond am I. Thou art vanquished, End of All!'[1]

(*Māra*)

'In the very air is bondage, where the mind runs to and fro.
With *that*, O recluse, I'll bind thee. Thou shalt not escape from me!'

(*The Exalted One*)

'Shapes and sounds and scents and savours, all delightful touch of sense,
Wish and will are gone from me. Thou art vanquished, End of All!'

Then Māra, the Evil One, (saying) 'The Exalted One knows me! The Wellfarer knows me!' departed sad and dejected, and vanished right away.

Vinaya, i. 21; cf. *S.N.* i. 111.

[1] *Antaka*, 'end-maker,' a name for Māra, the personification of all perishable things, also the Tempter of passion, Death and the Principle of Destruction.

SOME SAYINGS OF THE BUDDHA

THE LIGHT OF THE WORLD

(The Exalted One said :)

'So long, brethren, as moon and sun have not arisen in the world, just so long is there no shining forth of great light, no shining forth of great radiance. But gross darkness, the darkness of bewilderment, prevails. Neither night nor day is distinguishable, not the month nor the half-month nor the seasons of the year are to be discerned.

But, brethren, when moon and sun arise in the world, then is the shining forth of a great light, of great radiance, and gross darkness, the darkness of bewilderment, is no more. Then are distinguished the night and the day, then are discerned the month and the half-month and the seasons of the year.

Just so, brethren, so long as a Tathāgata arises not, an Arahant, a Buddha Supreme, there is no shining forth of great light, of great radiance, but gross darkness, the darkness of bewilderment, prevails, and there is no proclaiming, no teaching, no showing forth, no setting up, no opening up, no analysis, no making plain of the Four Ariyan Truths.

But, brethren, so soon as a Tathāgata arises, all these things take place, and then there is a proclaiming, a teaching, a showing forth, a setting up, an opening up, an analysis, a making plain of the Four Ariyan Truths.

What Four ? The Ariyan Truth of Ill, the arising of Ill, the ceasing of Ill, and the approach to the ceasing of Ill.

Wherefore, brethren, do ye exert yourselves to realize " This is Ill, this is the arising of Ill, this is the ceasing of Ill, this is the approach to the ceasing of Ill." '

S.N. v. 442.

THE CITY AND THE ANCIENT ROAD

. . . near Sāvatthī . . . (The Exalted One said :)

' Formerly, brethren, before my enlightenment, when I was yet unenlightened but a Bodhisat, there came to me this thought : " Verily this world has fallen upon trouble. There is getting born and growing old, and falling (from one state) and being re-born. And yet from this suffering escape is not understood, even from decay-and-death. O when shall escape from this suffering, even from decay-and-death, be made known ? "

Then to me, brethren, came this thought : " What now being present, is there decay-and-death ? What conditions decay-and-death ? "

Then to me, brethren, by rational thinking and by insight came the comprehension : " Where birth is, there also is decay-and-death : decay-and-death is conditioned by birth."

Then to me, brethren, came this thought : " What not being present, is there birth, becoming, grasping, craving, feeling, contact, the sixfold sphere of sense, mind-and-body ? Conditioned by what is mind-and-body ? "

Then to me, brethren, by rational thinking and by insight came the comprehension : " Where consciousness is, there also is mind-and-body : mind-and-body is conditioned by consciousness."

Then to me, brethren, there came this thought: "What now being present, is consciousness present? What conditions consciousness?"

Then . . . came the comprehension: "Where mind-and-body is, there is consciousness: conditioned by mind-and-body is consciousness."

Then, brethren, to me there came this thought: "This consciousness turns back from mind-and-body: it does not go beyond. To this extent one may be born, perish or die, or fall (from one state) or spring up again: that is to say, conditioned by mind-and-body is consciousness: conditioned by consciousness is mind-and-body: conditioned by mind-and-body is the sixfold sphere of sense, conditioned by the sixfold sphere of sense is contact, etc."

Such, brethren, is the arising of this entire mass of Ill.

"*Coming-to-be. Coming-to-be.*" At that thought, brethren, there arose in me a vision into things not before called to mind, and knowledge arose, insight arose, wisdom arose, light arose.

Then to me, brethren, came the thought: "What now being absent, is there no decay-and-death? From the cessation of what is there ceasing of decay-and-death?" Then, brethren, through rational thinking and insight arose the comprehension: "Where rebirth is not, there also decay-and-death are not. From the cessation of rebirth comes cessation of decay-and-death."

Then to me, brethren, came the thought: "What now being absent, is there no birth, no becoming, grasping, craving, feeling, contact, sixfold sphere of sense, mind-and-body: by the cessation of what is there cessation of mind-and-body?"

Then, brethren, through rational thinking and insight arose the comprehension: "Consciousness not being, mind-and-body is not: by the cessation of consciousness comes the cessation of mind-and-body."

Then, brethren, the thought arose in me: "Now, what not being, is there no consciousness? By the cessation of what is there cessation of consciousness?"

Then, brethren, through rational thinking and insight arose the comprehension: "Mind-and-body not being, there is no consciousness: by the cessation of mind-and-body comes the cessation of consciousness."

Then to me, brethren, came the thought: "I have won to the Path of enlightenment, to wit, by the cessation of mind-and-body (is) the cessation of consciousness. By the cessation of consciousness (comes) the cessation of mind-and-body: by the cessation of mind-and-body (comes) the cessation of the sixfold sphere of sense: by the cessation of the sixfold sphere of sense (comes) the cessation of contact, etc. Such is the cessation of this entire mass of Ill."

"*Ceasing to be. Ceasing to be.*" At that thought, brethren, there arose in me a vision into things not before called to mind, and knowledge arose, insight arose, wisdom arose, light arose.

Just as if, brethren, a man travelling in a forest, along a mountain height, should come upon an ancient road, an ancient track, traversed by men of former days, and should proceed along it: and as he went should come upon an old-time city, a royal city of olden days, dwelt in by men of bygone ages, laid out with parks and groves and water tanks, and stoutly walled about—a delightful spot.

Then suppose, brethren, that this man should tell of his find to the king or royal minister, thus: "Pardon me, sire, but I would have you know that while travelling in a forest, along a mountain height, I came upon an ancient road . . . (*as above*) . . . a delightful spot. Sire, restore that city."

Then suppose, brethren, that king or royal minister were to restore that city, so that thereafter it became prosperous, fortunate, and populous, crowded with inhabitants, and were to reach growth and increase.

Even so, brethren, have I seen an ancient Path, an ancient track traversed by the Perfectly Enlightened ones of former times. And what is that Path? It is this Ariyan Eightfold Path.'[1]

S.N. ii. 103–4.

[1] In this *sutta* it is noteworthy that Ignorance and Activities (*kamma*), the first two *nidānas*, are not mentioned: because (says Comy.) these two always belong to a former birth: that is, they are the *fons et origo* of the whole world and of each succeeding life-personality.

THE LAW OF CAUSATION[1]

Thus have I heard: The Exalted One was dwelling near Sāvatthī at Jeta Grove in Anāthapindika's Park. There the Exalted One addressed the brethren, saying, 'Brethren!' 'Yes, Lord!' replied those brethren. The Exalted One said: 'I will teach you, brethren, the Law of Causation. Do ye listen to it. Apply your minds. I will speak.' 'Even so, Lord,' replied the brethren. Then thus spake the Exalted One:

'What is the Law of Causation, brethren? (It is this):—

Actions are determined by Ignorance: by Actions is determined Consciousness: by Consciousness are determined Name-and-Shape: by Name-and-Shape are determined Sense: by Sense is determined Contact: by Contact is determined Feeling: by Feeling is determined Craving: by Craving is determined Grasping: by Grasping is determined Becoming: by Becoming is determined Birth: by Birth is determined Age-and-Death, Sorrow and Grief, Woe, Lamentation, and Despair. Such is the arising of all this mass of Ill.

But from the utter fading out and ending of Ignorance comes also the ending of Actions: from the ending of Actions comes the ending of Consciousness: from the ending of Consciousness comes the ending of Name-and-Shape: from the ending of Name-and-Shape comes the ending of Sense: from the ending of Sense comes the

[1] *Paṭicca-samuppāda.*

ending of Contact: from the ending of Contact comes the ending of Feeling: from the ending of Feeling comes the ending of Craving: from the ending of Craving comes the ending of Grasping: from the ending of Grasping comes the ending of Becoming: from the ending of Becoming comes the ending of Birth: from the ending of Birth comes the ending of Age-and-Death, Sorrow, and Grief, Woe, Lamentation, and Despair. Such is the ending of all this mass of Ill.'

ANALYSIS OF THE LAW OF CAUSATION

(*The Exalted One continued:*)

'And what, brethren, is Age-and-Death?

It is the decay, the ageing, the breaking up, the getting grey, the wrinkling, the life-shortening, the ripening-to-their-fall of the faculties, of such and such beings, of such and such a species. That is called Age.

The vanishing and falling away, the scattering, the disappearance, the mortality and dying out, the coming to an end, the break-up of the factors, the rejection of the body, of such and such beings, of such and such species. That is called Death. This decaying, then, this dying out is that which is called Age-and-Death.

And what, brethren, is Birth?

It is the being born, the origination, the descent, the reproduction, the manifestation of the factors, the seizing hold of the spheres of sense, of such and such beings, of such and such species. This is called Birth.

And what, brethren, is Becoming?

There are these three Becomings: Becoming in the desire-worlds, Becoming in the worlds of visible form, Becoming in the invisible worlds. This is called Becoming.

And what, brethren, is Grasping?

There are these four Graspings: the Grasping of desires, the Grasping of view, the Grasping of rite and ceremony, the Grasping of view about the self. This is called Grasping.

And what, brethren, is Craving?

There are these six groups of Craving: Craving for shape, Craving for sound, Craving for scents, Craving for savours, Craving for tangibles, Craving for ideas. This is called Craving.

And what, brethren, is Feeling?

There are these six groups of Feeling: Feeling born of eye-contact: Feeling born of ear-contact: Feeling born of nose-contact: Feeling born of tongue-contact: Feeling born of body-contact: Feeling born of mind-contact. This is called Feeling.

And what, brethren, is Contact?

There are these six groups of Contact: eye-, ear-, nose-, tongue-, body-, mind-contact. This is called Contact.

And what, brethren, is the sixfold Sense?

The Sense of eye, ear, nose, tongue, body, mind. This is called the sixfold Sense.

And what, brethren, is Name-and-Shape?

Feeling, perception, will, contact, work of mind.[1] This is called Name. The four great elements and the body based on them. This is

[1] *Manasikāro.*

called Shape. This is the Name, and this is the Shape. This is called Name-and-Shape.

And what, brethren, is Consciousness ?

There are these six groups of Consciousness : eye-, ear-, nose-, tongue-, touch-, mind-consciousness. This is called Consciousness.

And what are the Actions ?

There are these three Actions : body-, speech-, mind-action. These are Actions.

And what is Ignorance ?

Not knowing about Ill, the arising of Ill, the ceasing of Ill, the Way leading to the ceasing of Ill. This is called Ignorance.

So then, brethren, Actions are determined by Ignorance, Consciousness by Actions, and so on . . . such is the arising of all this mass of Ill.

But from the utter fading out and ending of Ignorance comes also the ending of Actions ; from the ending of Actions comes the ending of Consciousness, and so on. . . . Such is the ending of all this mass of Ill.'

S.N. ii. 3–4.

ENTANGLEMENT

Conception, Birth, Infancy, Childhood, Manhood, Death, and Birth

'Now by the combining of three, brethren, the development of an embryo is brought about. In this matter there is the coming together of parents : but if the mother be not pregnable and if no gandharva [1] be at hand, then there is

[1] A class of devas said to preside over the processes of conception.

no development of an embryo. Again in this matter, if there be the coming together of parents, and the mother be pregnable, but no gandharva be at hand, then there is no development of an embryo. But when, brethren, there is the coming together of parents, and the mother is pregnable, and a gandharva is at hand, then by the combining of these three there is development of an embryo.

This embryo the mother bears about for nine or ten months in her womb, with great anxiety, a heavy burden. Then at the end of nine or ten months she brings it forth, with great anxiety, a heavy burden. When it is born, she feeds it on her own blood: for "blood," brethren, is mother's milk called in the discipline of the Ariyan.

Well, that child, following on his growth, following on the ripening of his faculties, plays with the toys of boyhood, such as ploughing with a bent stick, the game of two sticks, turning somersaults, toy-windmills, pots and pans, go-carts, bow and arrows.

Then that child, following his growth, following the ripening of his faculties, now roams about possessed of, equipped with the five pleasures of sense, (susceptible to) the forms cognisable by eye, ear, nose, tongue, and tangibles by body, all of them longed for, alluring, delightful, dear, inviting to sensual delight.

Seeing a shape with the eye, he is enamoured of enticing shapes, is repelled by repellent shapes, and dwells with mindfulness not established and has but little thought. He knows not that release of mind and release by wisdom, as it really is, that by which those ill, unprofitable things come to cease without remainder.

Thus he comes to know satisfaction and dissatisfaction: whatever feeling he feels, be it pleasant, painful, or neutral, he welcomes it, greets it, and clings fast to it. Thereby arises the lure. That lure in feelings is the grasping of them. Conditioned by grasping is coming-to-be. Conditioned by coming-to-be is birth. Conditioned by birth are decay-and-death, grief, sorrow, woe, lamentation, and despair. Such is the arising of this whole mass of Ill.

So also with the ear-, nose-, tongue-consciousness: so also with things tangible by body, and being conscious of a thing by means of mind. He is enamoured and repelled thereby, and dwells (as before) ignorant of release.'

Release

(Then a Tathāgata arises in the world, an Arahant, a supreme Buddha, perfect in the knowledge and the practice, a wellfarer, world-knower, Charioteer unsurpassed of men to be tamed, Teacher of devas and mankind, Awakened Exalted One . . . and He preaches the Norm. The man hears the Norm, forsakes the world, and enters upon the Ariyan self-training.)

'Then he, become master of this Ariyan group of virtues, master of this Ariyan restraint of faculties and this Ariyan mindful self-possession, seeks out some secluded lodging, a forest, the foot of a tree, a mountain, a cave, a mountain grotto, a charnel-field, a lonely grove, the open air, a heap of straw.

There, when he has begged his food and eaten it, he sits down crosslegged and holds his body straight, setting mindfulness before him, and, rejecting the covetousness that is in the world, he abides in thought that is freed from dejection. He puts away the taint of malevolence, and abides in the thought of harmlessness. With kindly thought for every living thing and creature he cleanses his heart of the taint of malevolence. Casting away sloth and torpor, he abides free from these. Conscious of illumination, mindful and self-possessed, he cleanses his heart from sloth and torpor. Abandoning flurry and worry, unshaken he abides, inwardly calm in thought he cleanses his heart of worry and flurry. He abandons wavering, and having passed over wavering so abides ; no more a questioner of the how and why of things that are good, he cleanses his heart of wavering.

Thus abandoning the Five Hindrances, wearing down by wisdom the impurities that still remain, aloof from sensual desires, aloof from evil things, he enters upon the Four Musings (as before described).

Then, when he sees a shape with the eye, he is no longer enamoured of enticing shapes. He is not repelled by repellent shapes, but dwells with mindfulness established. Boundless is his sphere of thought. He knows that release of heart, that release by wisdom, as it really is, and by which those ill unprofitable things come to cease without leaving anything behind.

He rejects satisfaction and dissatisfaction. Whatever feeling he feels, be it pleasant, painful, or neutral, he welcomes it not, greets it not, clings not fast to it. Thereby ceases the lure. By the ceasing of the lure ceases grasping. By the ceasing of grasping ceases coming to be . . . and so is the ceasing of all this mass of Ill.

This release by the destruction of craving, brethren, which I have thus succinctly given you, do ye bear it in mind.'

M.N. i. 265–71.

MAN AND HIS BODIES

The Exalted One said:

'There are these three ways of getting a self, Potthapāda, namely: the getting of a physical-body self, the getting of a mind-made self, and the getting of a formless self.

And what, Potthapāda, is the getting of a physical-body self? It is that which has a form, is composed of the four great elements, and it is fed on material food. That is the physical-body self.

And what, Potthapāda, is the getting of a mind-made self? It also has a form and is made of mind, complete in all its limbs, possessed of the super sense-organs. That is the mind-made self.

And what, Potthapāda, is the getting of the formless self? It is that which has no form, but it is made of consciousness. That is the getting of the formless self.

Now I, Potthapāda, teach you a teaching for the rejection of the getting of any self: a way by practising which impure conditions can be put away by you and pure conditions brought to increase, and by which one, even in this very life, may attain unto the fulfilment and perfect growth of the wisdom, realizing it by his own abnormal powers, so as to abide therein.

Now it may well be, Potthapāda, that this thought might come to you: "Yes, impure conditions may be put away: pure conditions may be brought to increase and one may even in this life attain these things and abide therein. But yet one remains sorrowful!"

But that, Potthapāda, is not the way to look at it. For when these things are done . . . there will be, as result, Joy, Zest, Calm, Mindfulness, Self-possession, and the Happy Life.

(And the same may be said of the getting of the mind-made self and of the formless self.)

And if, Potthapāda, others should ask us this question: "But what, friend, is that getting of a physical-body self, a mind-made self, and a formless self, (about which you say all this)?" then we should thus reply:

"It is this same self[1] of which we speak. . . . for at the time when any one of these three modes of self is going on, it is not reckoned as one of the other two. It is only reckoned by the name of that particular personality that prevails. . . ."

For all these are merely names, Potthapāda, terms, ways of speaking, definitions of every-day use. . . . These the Tathāgata uses (when He speaks), but He is not deceived by them.'

D.N. i. 194–202 (*repetitions omitted*).

[1] *Ayaṃ vā so,* that is, the *attabhāva,* or *pañca-kkhandhaka,* or fivefold personality, consisting of body, feelings, perception, activities, and consciousness . . . all of which are impermanent.

THE PARABLE OF THE LOG

Once the Exalted One was staying at Kosambi, on the bank of the River Ganges.

Now the Exalted One saw a great log being carried down Ganges' stream, and on seeing it He called to the brethren, saying: 'Brethren, do ye see yonder great log being carried downstream?' 'Yes, Lord.'

'Now, brethren, if a log does not ground on this bank or the further bank, does not sink in midstream, does not stick fast on a shoal, does not fall into human or non-human hands, is not caught in an eddy, does not rot inwardly,—that log, brethren, will float down to ocean, will slide down to ocean, will tend towards ocean. And why? Because, brethren, Ganges' stream floats down to ocean, slides down to ocean, tends towards ocean.

In like manner, brethren, if ye do not ground on this shore or that shore, if ye sink not in midstream, if ye stick not fast on a shoal, if ye fall not a prey to beings human and non-human, if ye be not caught in an eddy, if ye rot not inwardly—then, brethren, ye shall float down to Nibbāna, ye shall slide down to Nibbāna, ye shall tend towards Nibbāna. And why? Because, brethren, perfect view floats, slides, tends toward Nibbāna.'

At these words a certain brother said to the Exalted One:

'What, Lord, is this bank, what is the other bank, what is sinking in midstream? What is sticking fast on a shoal? What is falling a prey to beings human or non-human? What is being caught in an eddy? What is rotting inwardly?'

'"This bank," brother, is a name for the six personal spheres of sense-action.

"That bank," brother, is a name for the six external spheres of sense-action.

"Sinking in midstream" is a name for the lure and lust.

"Sticking fast on a shoal" is a name for the conceit of self.

And what, brother, is "being caught by humans"?

In this matter, brother, a householder lives in society, rejoices with them that rejoice, sorrows with them that sorrow, takes pleasure with them that take pleasure, suffers with them that suffer, makes a link with all manner of business that befalls. This, brother, is "being caught by humans."

And what, brother, is "being caught by non-humans"?

In this matter, brother, such and such a brother lives the holy life with the wish to be reborn in the company of some class of devas, with the thought "May I by virtue or by practice or by some austerity or holy living become a deva or one of devas." This, brother, is "being caught by non-humans."

"Being caught in an eddy," brother, is a name for the pleasures of the five senses.

And what, brother, is "rotting inwardly"?

Herein, brother, a certain one is immoral, an evil-doer, impure, of suspicious behaviour, of covert deeds: he is no recluse, though a recluse in vows; liver no of the holy life, though vowed thereto: rotten within and full of lusts, a son of filth is he. Such, brother, is "rotting inwardly."'

Now on that occasion Nanda the cowherd was standing not far from the Exalted One. Then Nanda the cowherd exclaimed to the Exalted One:

'I, Lord, am one who is grounded on this bank. I am not stranded on the further bank. I shall not sink in midstream. I shall not run aground on a shoal. I shall not be caught by humans or non-humans. No eddy shall catch me. I shall not rot inwardly. Lord, may I gain ordination at the Exalted One's hands? May I gain full ordination?'

'Then, Nanda, do you restore the kine to their owners.'

'Lord, the kine shall go back. They are longing for their calves.'

'Restore the kine to their owners, Nanda.'

Thereupon Nanda the cowherd, having restored the kine to their owners, came to the Exalted One and said: 'Lord, the kine are restored to their owners. Lord, may I gain ordination at the hands of the Exalted One? May I gain full ordination?'

So Nanda the cowherd gained ordination, gained full ordination at the Exalted One's hands. And not long after, the venerable Nanda, living solitary and remote, ardent and intent . . . won the Goal.

And the venerable Nanda was yet another of the Arahants.

S.N. iv. 179–81.

NO MORE THE SPORT OF EVERY WIND THAT BLOWS

As many divers winds blow through the sky,
East and West and North and South they go,—
Winds dusty, dustless, cool and hot at once,
Winds boisterous and soft, of many kinds,—
So in this body many feelings rise,
Easeful and painful, neither one nor other.

A brother who is ardent, self-possessed,
And from the substrate free, well understands
In his ripe wisdom feelings of all kinds.
He, understanding feelings, in this life
Is drug-immune, and when the body dies
He is a saint, lore-perfect, past our ken.

S.N. iv. 218.

THE ARIYAN DISCIPLE

'But inasmuch, brethren, as the Ariyan disciple by right insight has well seen, in their true nature, this Law of Causation and that all these things have come to be through that Law of Causation, of course (you will say) he will run back to things past, saying, "Was I in the past? Or was I not? What was I in the past? How was I in the past? Having been what, what then did I come to be in the past?"

Or he will run on to the future, saying, "Shall I be in the future, or shall I not be? What shall I be in the future? How shall I be in the future? Being what, what shall I come to be in the future?"

Or else now he will be inwardly a doubter

about things present, saying, "Am I indeed? Or am I not? What indeed am I? How indeed am I? This I, whence did he come and whither will he go?"

Not at all! The thing is impossible! And why not?

Because the Ariyan disciple, brethren, has by right insight seen, in their true nature, both this Law of Causation and that things have come to be through this Law of Causation.'

S.N. ii. 26.

DONE WITH IT ALL

'. . . Now, brethren, inasmuch as the Ariyan Disciple knows the Law of Causation thus, knows the arising of causal relation thus, knows the ceasing of causal relation thus, knows the Way leading to the ceasing of causal relation thus, . . . this one is called, brethren, the Ariyan Disciple who has attained View, who has attained Insight, who has reached the Good Norm, who sees this Good Norm, who has become possessed of the knowledge of the Trained Disciple,[1] who has attained the Norm-Stream, who is an Ariyan fastidious in his wisdom, who stands having reached the Threshold of the Deathless.'[2]

S.N. ii. 41.

STREAM-CLIMBER[3]

In whom is longing for the Nameless born,
Whose mind it hath enthralled,

[1] *Sekho.* [2] *Amata-Nibbāna.* [3] *Uddhaṃ-soto.*

Whose thoughts no longer are by passion torn,—
  That man 'a Climber of the Stream' is called.

As when a dweller in some far-off land
  Safe home returns at last,
Kin, friends, and lovers waiting to greet him stand:
So, when a man on earth good deeds hath done,
  When he hath passed beyond,
All his good deeds, like kin, await that one.

Dhammapada, vv. 218–20.

THE MASTER DELEGATES THE CONFERRING OF ORDERS

Brethren, I grant you this permission. Hereafter do you yourselves give ordination and full orders in such and such districts, and in such and such countries. And ye must do it in this manner:

Let the one to be ordained get the hair of head and face shaved off. Let him get the saffron robes put upon him. Let him put the upper robe over one shoulder, salute the feet of the brethren, sit down in squatting posture, stretch out his folded palms, and let him thus say:

"To the Buddha I go for refuge.
To the Norm I go for refuge.
To the Order I go for refuge."

(*Thrice.*)

I enjoin, brethren, that ordination and full orders do consist in going to these Three Refuges.'

V.P. i. 12.

A LATER WAY

On a certain occasion the Exalted One said:

'Henceforth, brethren, I do abolish the giving of full orders by (the method of) going to the Three Refuges, formerly enjoined by me.

I enjoin, brethren, that ye give full orders by an act of proclamation, together with three questions.'

V.P. i. 27.

SPECIAL RULES

'Let no one, brethren, give full orders, if he knows it, to one under twenty years of age. He who does so must be dealt with in the usual way.[1]

One under twenty years, brethren, cannot bear cold and heat, hunger and thirst, the bite of flies and gnats, the touch of wind and sun and creeping things: cannot bear outspoken offensive speech, nor bodily feelings that arise, painful, bitter, sharp, grievous, unpleasant, life-destroying —he cannot bear them.'

V.P. i. § 47.

ORDINATION FOR CHILDREN

'I allow you, brethren, to give ordination[2] to lads (able to get their living by) scaring crows, even under the age of fifteen years.'

[1] *Yathā-dhammo.* [2] *Pabbajjā.*

THE SHORT SECTION[1]

THE FAITH AND PRECEPTS

HOMAGE TO HIM, THE EXALTED ONE, THE ARAHANT, THE ALL-ENLIGHTENED ONE

To the Buddha I go for refuge.
To the Norm I go for refuge.
To the Order I go for refuge.

(*Thrice.*)

The charge to avoid the taking of life.[2]

The charge to avoid taking what is not given.

The charge to avoid unchastity.

The charge to avoid falsehood.

The charge to avoid fermented liquor, distilled liquor, intoxicants giving rise to sloth.

The charge to avoid unseasonable meals.

The charge to avoid dancing, song, playing music, and seeing shows.

[1] *Khuddaka-Pātha.* This might be called 'the Buddhist Layman's Prayer-book.' I have translated the whole of this little book (except a short section on the parts of the body, which occurs elsewhere), which extends to page 66.

[2] *Sikkhāpadaṃ* (way of training, a lesson, a charge), but not a command. The word *samādiyāmi* (I undertake) does not occur in this early formula, which is from the *Khuddaka-Pātha,* and consists of the Ten Charges observed by the Disciples (*bhikkhus*). A concession was made to the layman by altering the third charge to suit the layman's life. Laymen observe the first five ; devotees the first eight.

The charge to avoid the use of flowers, scents, and unguents, wearing ornaments and decorations.

The charge to avoid the use of raised beds, of wide beds.

The charge to avoid the accepting of gold and silver.

THE NOVICE'S CATECHISM

What is 'the one'?

All sentient beings are supported by food.

What are 'the two'?

'The two' are mind-and-body.

What are 'the three'?

'The three' are the three feelings.

What are 'the four'?

The Four Ariyan Truths.

What are 'the five'?

The five grasping-elements.

What are 'the six'?

The six personal spheres of sense.

What are 'the seven'?

The seven factors of wisdom.

What are 'the eight'?

The Ariyan Eightfold Path.

What are 'the nine'?

The nine abodes of sentient beings.

What are 'the ten'?

The ten qualities, with which endowed one is called Arahant.

[1] Food (*āhāra*) is (*a*) solid food which we eat, (*b*) contact (*phasso*) in the world of sense-feeling, (*c*) mental food, 'thought-stuff,' (*d*) mind-consciousness.

[2] *Nāma-rūpa*. *Nāma* (name) is the four constituents of the fivefold mass or body (*attabhāvo*, *sakkāya*), personality. *See* No. 5.

THE SHORT SECTION

[3] *Tissavedanā*, feelings pleasant-painful-neutral (*sukha dukkha-sadukkhamasukhā*).

[4] Suffering (*dukkha*), its arising (*dukkha-samudayo*), its ceasing (*dukkha-nirodho*), the way leading to its ceasing (The Path).

[5] *Pañca-upādāna-kkhandhā*, the five constituents of a person, or 'the factors of the fivefold clinging to existence'; body-form (*rūpa*), feeling (*vedanā*), perception (*saññā*), activities which make karma (*saṅkhārā*), and consciousness (*viññāna*).

[6] The five sense organs (eye, ear, nose, tongue, skin) and mental faculty (*mano*).

[7] Mindfulness (*sati*), searching the Norm or Scriptures (*dhamma-vicaya*), energy (*viriya*), zest (*pīti*), calm (*passaddhi*), contemplation (*samādhi*), equanimity (*upekkhā*) or 'the higher indifference.'

[8] See above, p. 7, *The First Sermon*.

[9] The spheres of existence: (*a*) Where minds and bodies differ: e.g. as in the case of human beings, some devas, and dwellers in the purgatories. (*b*) Where bodies differ, but minds are the same: e.g. Brahma-loka devas; a stage to be reached by the first *jhāna*. (*c*) Where bodies are the same, but minds differ: e.g. the shining devas of the Brahma world of Form. (*d*) Where both minds and bodies differ: e.g. the all-resplendent devas of the Brahma world of Form. (*e*) Where consciousness of form has disappeared, and only consciousness of infinite space remains. (*f*) Where infinite space is transcended, but there is infinite consciousness. (*g*) Where is consciousness of the Void, or realm of nothingness. (*h*) The previous seven are called 'stations' of consciousness (*ṭhiti*): the next two are 'spheres' where there is no awareness of externals. (*i*) Where is what may be described as neither consciousness nor lack of it, but an alternating state between the two. Nibbāna is beyond all these stages.

[10] The Four Paths and the Four Fruits of the Paths of (*a*) the Stream-winner (*sotāpanno*), (*b*) the Once-returner (*sakad-āgāmi*), (*c*) the Never-returner (*anāgāmī*), and (*d*) the Arahant, together with (*a*) Realization of the *Dhamma* (Law, Norm, Truth,

Doctrine) and (*b*) the attainment of *Nibbāna*, which is perfection.

[These notes are condensed from Buddhaghosa's Commentary on *Khuddaka-Pātha.*]

BLESSINGS

Thus have I heard : Once the Exalted One was dwelling near Sāvatthī, at Jeta Grove, in Anāthapindika's Park. Now when the night was far spent a certain deva of wondrous beauty lit up the whole Jeta Grove, and coming to the Exalted One saluted Him and stood aside. So standing that deva spoke unto the Exalted One in verse :

Many devas and many men have pondered on blessings,
Longing for goodly things. O tell me Thou the greatest blessing !

(*The Lord replied :*)

Not to follow after fools, but to follow after the wise :
The worship of the worshipful,—this is the greatest blessing.

To dwell in a pleasant spot, to have done good deeds in former births,
To have set oneself in the right path,—this is the greatest blessing.

Much learning and much science, and a discipline well learned,
Yea, and a pleasant utterance,—this is the greatest blessing.

THE SHORT SECTION

The support of mother and father, the cherishing of child and wife,
To follow a peaceful livelihood,—this is the greatest blessing.

Giving of alms, the righteous life, to cherish kith and kin,
And to do deeds that bring no blame,—this is the greatest blessing.

To cease and to abstain from sin, to shun intoxicants ;
And steadfastness in righteousness,—this is the greatest blessing.

Reverence, humility, content, and gratitude,
To hear the Norm at proper times,—this is the greatest blessing.

Patience, the soft answer, the sight of those controlled,
And pious talk in season due,—this is the greatest blessing.

Restraint, the holy life, discernment of the Ariyan Truths,
Of one's own self to know the Goal,—this is the greatest blessing.

A heart untouched by worldly things, a heart that is not swayed
By sorrow, a heart passionless, secure,—that is the greatest blessing.

Invincible on every side, they who do these things
On every side they go to bliss,—theirs is the greatest blessing.

Khuddaka-Pātha and
Sutta-Nipāta, vv. 258–69.

THE GEM

All creatures that be gathered here, whether of earth or air,
May all be happy—Let them give good heed to what I say.

Attend ye all, and bear good-will to all the human race:
For day and night they offerings bring. Protect them zealously.

Whatever treasure in this world or in the world to come,
Or in the heaven worlds whatever precious gem there be—
None like unto Tathāgata—(He is beyond compare)—
This Gem pre-eminent, 'tis in the Enlightened One.
By virtue of this truth—Good Luck!

Destroying sin, the passionless, deathless, pre-eminent—
For that the Sakyan Sage was calmed and won the Peace thereby—

Naught like unto the Holy Norm—(it is beyond compare)—
This Gem pre-eminent, 'tis in the Holy Norm.
By virtue of this truth—Good Luck!

This Doctrine pure taught by the Best of all the Enlightened Ones—
This peace of mind, of which men tell, that comes without delay—
Naught like unto that peace of mind—(it is beyond compare)—
This Gem pre-eminent—'tis in the Holy Norm.
By virtue of this truth—Good Luck!

Those Beings Eight, by sages praised—they are those Fourfold Pairs,
The worshipful disciples they, of Him the Happy One,
Mighty the fruit of offerings that unto them are given—
This Gem pre-eminent—'tis in the Brotherhood.
By virtue of this truth—Good Luck!

They who with stout and steadfast heart are firm establishèd
In Gotama's Good Tidings, who have laid their lusts aside—
They who have entered on the Way and won the Deathless State,
And having won it without price enjoy the utter peace—
This Gem pre-eminent—'tis in the Brotherhood.
By virtue of this truth—Good Luck!

Just as the threshold of a gate, deep fixed into the ground,
Cannot be shaken by the winds from the four quarters blowing,
Like unto that do I declare the righteous man to be,
Who hath beheld the Ariyan Truths by plunging into them.
This Gem pre-eminent—'tis in the Brotherhood.
By virtue of this truth—Good Luck!

They who by their own knowledge can the Ariyan Truths discern—
The Ariyan Truths so well proclaimed by Him of wisdom deep—
Tho' they be swayed to sluggishness by worldly things, yet these
After the seventh birth from now shall come to birth no more.
This Gem pre-eminent—'tis in the Brotherhood.
By virtue of this truth—Good Luck!

He who hath glimpsed the Goal and these three things hath laid aside,—
Belief in body-self, and doubt, and all rites whatso'er—
From the four states of woe is freed, and the six great misdeeds—
Such is the nature of him now—he never can commit.
This Gem pre-eminent—'tis in the Brotherhood.
By virtue of this truth—Good Luck!

If one do any wrongful deed by act or speech or thought,
Incapable is such an one of covering his sin:
'Incapable' is he declared, for he hath seen the Path.
This Gem pre-eminent—'tis in the Brotherhood.
By virtue of this truth—Good Luck!

As in the forest-glades the tree-tops blossom forth again
In the first month of summer's heat—so did the Lord proclaim
For profit of the world His Norm that to Nibbāna leads.
This Gem pre-eminent—'tis in the Enlightened One.
By virtue of this truth—Good Luck!

He is the Best, and knows the Best, the Giver of the Best.
He brought the Best, most Excellent, and taught the Best of Norms.
This Gem pre-eminent—'tis in the Enlightened One.
By virtue of this truth—Good Luck!

The old is rooted out, no more fresh deeds can come to be:
Cleansed are their hearts from longing for any birth to come:
Their seed of birth is rooted out, desire for growth is gone:

Quenched are those sages, even as this lamp ye see is quenched.[1]
This Gem pre-eminent—'tis in the Brotherhood.
By virtue of this truth—Good Luck!

(*Here Sakka, king of the devas, appears and sings three more verses, bidding all creatures worship the Triple Gem.*)

K.P. and *S.N.* vv. 222–36.

THE EARTH-BOUND GHOSTS[2]

Outside the walls they stand, at the crossways and outside doors, to their own home returning.

But when a plenteous meal is spread, of food and drink, no man remembers them (the dead). Such is the way of things.

Wherefore do those who have pity on their kin make offerings due, of choice food and drink at seasonable times, saying: 'Be this a gift to kinsmen—may our kinsmen be well pleased thereat!'

Then do those earth-bound kinsmen gather there where a plenteous meal is spread of food and drink, and fail not to render thanks, saying:

'Long live our kinsmen, thanks to whom we have this gift! To us this offering is made: not without fruit are they who give!'

For there (in ghostland) no cattle-keeping, no ploughing of fields is seen. There is no trading

[1] The Commentator says that the Master here pointed to a lamp which flickered out as He was preaching.

[2] *Petā.* This is the *Tiro-kuḍḍa-sutta* of *Khuddaka-Pātha.*

there, as on earth, no trafficking with gold. We ghosts that have departed there exist on what is given here.

Even as water gathered on high ground flows down into the marsh, so are offerings given here on earth of service to the ghosts.

Just as the rivers are filled and fill the sea, even so are offerings given here on earth of service to the ghosts.

'He gave me gifts, he did things for me. They were my kinsmen, friends, and intimates'—thus mindful of past deeds let a man give unto the ghosts in charity.

Of a truth, wailing and grief and all manner of lamentation avail not anything. It helps not the ghosts that kinsmen stand lamenting thus.

Moreover, this gift of charity bestowed on the Order is bound to be of service for a long, long time.

Thus this duty done to kinsmen hath been declared: unto the ghosts it is no mean offering of worship: unto the Brethren of the Order it is strength conferred [1]: unto yourselves no small merit hath been won.

THE HIDDEN TREASURE

In a deep-dug pit a man buries a treasure with this thought: 'In time of need 'twill be a help to me, or if the rājah speak ill of me, if by a robber I am plundered, or to pay my debts, or when food is hard to get, or when ill-luck befalls.'

[1] The offering generally accompanies a meal to the Order.

Such are the reasons in this world for burying a treasure.

Yet all this treasure thus well concealed in its deep hiding-place—it profits the owner not at all.

For either it vanishes away from its hiding-place, or his wits go wandering (so that he forgets where it is laid), or the nāgas convey it away, or the goblins filch it.

Or his foes or even his kinsmen carry it off when he watches not. For when one's merit is used up, all that treasure perishes.

But by charity, by righteousness, by self-restraint and taming of the self, there is a treasure well concealed for woman or for man.

It is a treasure incommunicable to others, that robbers cannot steal away. LET THE WISE MAN DO GOOD DEEDS : that is the treasure that follows after one!

This is a treasure that gives all manner of delights to devas and to men. With it may be won whatsoever things they aspire for.

A fair face, a sweet voice, beauty and grace, pomp and circumstance,—all these this treasure can obtain.

Sovereignty and lordship, the bliss of universal rule that is so dear to man : yea, rule in heaven among the devas,—all these things this treasure can procure.

Worldly prosperity and heaven's delights, the winning of Nibbāna,—all these things are by this treasure won.

He who hath attained a goodly fellowship, by cleaving thereto can win knowledge, release, and self-control :—all these are won thereby.

THE SHORT SECTION

Clear insight, freedom of mind, all the perfections of the Disciple, the enlightenment of self by self, yea, even the state of Buddhahood,—all these are by this treasure to be won.

Such mighty magic power hath the treasure of good deeds. Wherefore are good deeds done by wise and learned men.

Khuddaka-Pātha.

GOODWILL

This must be done by him who is wise to know what is good for him, by him who hath grasped the meaning of the Place of Peace.

He must be able and upright and truly straight: gentle of speech and mild, not having vain conceit of self.

And he should be content, soon satisfied, with but few wants, of frugal appetites: with faculties of sense composed, discreet, not insolent, nor greedy after gifts.

He should do no mean thing for which other men who are wise may censure him.

Now may every living thing, feeble or strong, omitting none, or tall or middle-sized or short, subtle or gross of form, seen or unseen, those dwelling near or far away,—whether they be born or yet unborn—may every living thing be full of bliss.

Let none deceive another, nor think scorn of him in any way whate'er. Let him not in anger or ill-will desire another's ill-fare.

Even as a mother, as long as she doth live,

watches over her child, her only child,—even so should one practise an all-embracing mind unto all beings.

And let a man practise a boundless goodwill for all the world, above, below, across, in every way, goodwill unhampered, without ill-feeling or enmity.

Standing or moving, sitting or lying down, howe'er he be, provided he be freed from sloth, let a man establish this mindfulness of goodwill. For this is what men call 'the highest state.'[1]

Thus shall a man, by passing over wrongful view, by walking righteously, be gifted with insight and conquer greed for sense-desires. Of a truth such an one shall come no more to birth in any womb.

Metta-Sutta of *Khuddaka-Pātha* and
Sutta Nipāta, v. 143.

THE CAR OF THE NORM[2]

Whoso the Faith and Wisdom hath attained—
His states of mind, well-harnessed, lead him on.
Conscience the pole, and Mind the yoke thereof,
And Heedfulness the watchful charioteer:
The furnishments of Righteousness, the Car:
Rapture the axle, Energy the wheels,
And Calm, yokefellow of the Balanced Mind:
Desirelessness the drapery thereof:
Goodwill and Harmlessness his weapons are,
Together with Detachment of the mind.

[1] *Brahma-Vihāra.*
[2] *Dhamma-ratha,* from *Saṃyutta Nikāya,* v. p. 6.

THE SHORT SECTION

Endurance is the armour of the Norm,
And to attain the Peace that car rolls on.
'Tis built by self, by one's own self becometh—
This chariot, incomparable, supreme :
Seated therein the sages leave the world,
And verily they win the victory.

TEACHINGS

TEACHER AND PUPIL

'THE teacher, brethren, should regard the pupil as his son. The pupil should regard the teacher as his father. Thus these two, by mutual reverence and deference joined, dwelling in community of life, will win increase, growth, progress in this Norm-Discipline.

I do enjoin, brethren, that ye live ten years in charge of a teacher. Then he who has completed his tenth year of discipleship may have a charge himself.'

Vin. Pit. Mahāvagga, iii. 1.

KEEPING THE RAINY SEASON

Now at that time the Exalted One dwelt near Rājagaha, in the Bamboo Grove, at the Squirrels' Feeding-Ground. And at that time the Retreat during the rainy season was not yet appointed for the brethren by the Exalted One. So the brethren went a-roaming in the cold, the hot, and the rainy season alike.

Thus folk were vexed and murmured angrily, saying: 'What! Are the recluses who are the sons of the Sakyan to roam about in the cold, the hot, and the rainy season alike? They tread down the green grass, they crush the living thing that has one sense,[1] they trample to death many a tiny life.

Are the recluses of the heretical sects, who follow a Norm ill-preached—are they to settle down and live retired during the rains? Are birds to build their nests on the tree-tops and take shelter in the rains and live retired, and yet are the recluses who are the sons of the Sakyan to go a-roaming in the cold, the hot, and the rainy season alike, treading down the green grass, crushing the living thing that has one sense, trampling to death many a tiny life?'

Now some brethren heard those folk who were vexed and murmured angrily thus, and they told the thing to the Exalted One.

Therefore in this connexion and on this occasion, the Exalted One, after a pious talk, thus spake unto the brethren:

'I enjoin on you, brethren, that ye observe the retreat during the rains.'

Vin. Pit. Mahāvagga, iii. 1.

RULES OF ETIQUETTE

'Brethren, I appoint this rule for the guidance of newly arrived brethren.

A newly arrived brother, brethren, with the thought "I will now enter the residence," having

[1] The vegetable world.

In North India the rainy seasons were two, an early and a late. The early date for keeping *Vassa* (the rainy season) was the day after the *Āsāḷhā* (June–July) full moon, the date of the first Sermon: the later, a month after the same full moon. Probably these were the dates of the ancient Vedic festivals.

S.S.B.—4

taken off his sandals, should turn them down, beat them together, take them up again, lay down his umbrella, uncover his head, put his upper robe over one shoulder, then enter the residence heedfully and without undue haste.

On entering he should consider where the resident brethren have retired, and, wherever they have gone, whether to the service-hall or to the pavilion or to the foot of a tree, thither going let him lay aside bowl and robe, select a proper seat, and so sit down.

Then let him ask about water for drinking and water for use, and inquire which is which. If he need drinking water, let him take and drink it. If he need water for use, let him take and wash his feet therewith.

In washing his feet, let him hold the water with one hand and rub down his feet with the other hand. Let him not do so with the hand that holds the water.

Then let him ask for rags to wipe his sandals, and do so. In wiping his sandals let him first dust them with a dry cloth, and then wipe them with a damp cloth. Then he should rinse the rags and lay them aside.

If the resident brother be an elder, let him salute him. If he be a junior, he should salute the newcomer.[1] Then let him ask about lodging, saying, "What lodging is allotted me? Is it occupied or unoccupied?" And he must ask about his district for begging food, and what

[1] Doubt about seniority is solved by asking 'How many *vassa* (rainy seasons) has your reverence kept?' . . . that is, 'How long have you been in the robes?'

district is out of bounds, what families are to be considered as educated. He should inquire where are the privies and urinals, about drinking water and water for use, about walking staves, the meeting halls of the Order, about time to go in and time to go out.

If (when he arrives) there is no one at home, let him knock on the door, then wait a while, then slip the bolt, open the door, and look in while he still stands outside.'

Vin. Piṭ. ii. 8.

CONVERSION, ORDINATION, ATTAINMENT OF THE GOAL

Thereupon (when the Master had spoken) Sabhiyo, the Wanderer, bowed his head at the feet of the Exalted One and said: 'Excellent, O Lord! Excellent, O Lord! Even as one raises what is overthrown or shows forth what is hidden, or points the way to him that wandereth astray, or holds up a light in the darkness that they who have eyes may see objects,—even so in divers ways hath the Norm been set forth by the venerable Gotama. To the venerable Gotama I go for refuge, to the Norm and to the Order of Brethren. I would take ordination at the hands of the Exalted One, I would take full orders at the hands of the Exalted One.'

(The Master said:)

'He who, formerly being of another faith, Sabhiya, desires ordination, desires full orders[1]

[1] *Mahāvagga* of *Sutta Nipāta*, and *Majjhima Nikāya*, i. 391. *Pabbajjā* and *upasampadā*.

in this Norm and Discipline,—he remains on trial for four months. At the end of four months brethren of established heart give him full ordination in the Brother's Rule. Yet do I recognize a difference of persons.'

(*Sabhiya said :*)

'If it be so (even as the Exalted One hath said), then I too will remain on trial for four months; and, when they are past, let brethren of established heart give me ordination, give me full orders in the Brother's Rule.'

So Sabhiya, the Wanderer, received ordination and full orders from the hands of the Exalted One; and the venerable Sabhiya, not long after taking orders, living alone, remote, earnest, ardent, and resolute, in no long time came to realize for himself in that very life, by his own powers of mind, that Goal unsurpassed of holy living, to win which the clansmen duly wander forth from home; so that he knew for sure: 'Destroyed is rebirth (for me), lived is the holy life, done is my task: there is no more life for me on terms like these.'[1]

And the venerable Sabhiya was yet another of the Arahants.

THE ONLY WAY

(i) The Contemplation of Body

Thus have I heard:

Once the Exalted One was staying among the Kurus,—there is a suburb of the Kurus called

[1] I.e. rebirth in every conceivable condition.

Kammāssa-dhamma. There the Exalted One called to the brethren and said, 'Brethren!' 'Yes, Lord!' replied those brethren to the Exalted One. Then the Exalted One thus spake:

'This is the Only Way, brethren, that leads to the purification of beings, to passing beyond sorrow and lamentation, to the destruction of grief and despair, to the attainment of the Method, to the realizing of Nibbāna, thus: The Four Ways of Establishing Mindfulness.[1] What are the four?

Herein, brethren, a brother abides regarding Body (as a compound); he is ardent, self-possessed, and concentrated by controlling the covetousness and dejection that are in the world. So also with regard to Feelings, and Thought, and Mental States (Ideas).

And how, brethren, does a brother abide regarding body (as a compound)?

In this method, brethren, a brother goes to the forest or to the foot of a tree or to a lonely place, and there sits down cross-legged, and holds his body straight, establishing concentration in front of him.[2] Then he breathes in mindfully, and mindfully breathes out. As he draws a long breath he knows, "A long breath I draw in." As he breathes out a long breath he knows, "A long breath I breathe out." As he draws in a short breath he knows, "A short breath I draw in." As he breathes out a short breath he knows, "A short breath I breathe out."

With the thought "In full body-consciousness

[1] *Cattāro Satipatthānā.*

[2] Concentrating between the eyebrows.

will I breathe in" he trains himself. With the thought "In full body-consciousness will I breathe out" he trains himself. With the thought "Calming down my body-compound I will breathe in" he trains himself. With the thought "Calming down my body-compound I will breathe out" he trains himself.

Just as, brethren, a clever turner or turner's 'prentice, when he gives a long pull [to his lathe-string] is aware "I am giving a long pull," or when he gives a short pull is aware "I am giving a short pull,"—even so does a brother train himself (by conscious in-breathing and out-breathing).

Thus he abides regarding body either in its inner or in its outer state or in both. He abides observing either the rise or the fall of things in body, or the rise-and-fall of things in body. Or else, with the thought "It is body," his mindfulness of body is established, just sufficiently for him to know its existence and to become concentrated. Thus he abides detached, and he grasps at nothing at all in the world.

Thus, brethren, does a brother abide in the Contemplation of Body.

Then again, brethren, a brother when he walks is conscious "I am walking," or when he stands still he is conscious "I am standing still." When he sits, or lies, he is conscious of so doing: and whatever the posture of the body he is aware of it. Thus he abides in Contemplation of Body, inwardly or outwardly or both . . . and grasps at nothing at all in the world. . . .

Then again, brethren, both in advancing and

retreating he acts mindfully. In looking forward or backward, in bending or straightening, in wearing his robes or carrying bowl and robe, he acts mindfully. In eating, drinking, chewing, or tasting, in his bodily functions, he acts mindfully. In going, standing, sitting, sleeping, waking, speaking, or keeping silence he acts mindfully. Thus does he contemplate body, inwardly or outwardly or both . . . and grasps at nothing at all in the world. Thus does a brother dwell in the Contemplation of Body.

Then again, brethren, a brother examines this same body upwards from the soles of his feet to the top of his head. He regards it as something enclosed by skin, and filled with contents of divers kinds, as a thing impure: saying, "Here in this body are hairs of the head, hairs of the body, nails, teeth, skin, flesh, sinews, bones, and marrow: kidney, heart, liver, tissue, spleen, lungs, stomach, bowels, intestines: excrement, bile, phlegm, matter, blood, sweat, fat, tears, serum, saliva, mucus, lubricants, and urine." Just as if, brethren, there were a bag of samples, open at each end, full of grains of divers sorts, such as rice, paddy, beans, pulse, sesamum, or husked rice: and a sharp-sighted man were to loose the ends and examine the contents, saying, "This is rice, this is paddy," and so on. Even so, brethren, does a brother examine the body, from the soles of the feet upwards to the top of the head: regards it as enclosed with skin, and filled with contents of divers kinds, as something impure. . . . Thus does he dwell in Contemplation of Body.

Then again, brethren, a brother considers this same body, however placed or however disposed, by way of its essential properties, thus: "There are in this body the elements of earth, water, heat, and air."

Just as if, brethren, a clever butcher or butcher's 'prentice, on slaying a steer, cuts it up bit by bit and sits with it at the four crossways. Even so does a brother consider this same body, however placed and however disposed, by way of its essential properties of earth, water, heat, and air. . . . So does he abide in the Contemplation of Body.

Then again, brethren, suppose a brother sees a dead body, thrown away in a charnel-field, one day or two days or three days dead,—bloated, black and blue, decomposing: and he compares his own body with that, saying to himself: "Here is this body of mine, it is of such a nature as that, it has come to be like that, it has not gone beyond that!" And so does he consider body inwardly or outwardly or both . . . and grasps at nothing at all in the world. So does he abide Contemplating Body.

Then again, brethren, a brother might see a dead body thrown away in the charnel-field, being devoured by crows, devoured by kites, by vultures, or dogs or jackals or divers sorts of worms. Then he compares this body of his with that, saying (as before). . . . Thus does he abide Contemplating Body.

Then again, brethren, suppose a brother sees a body thrown away in the charnel-field, just a chain of bones, with flesh and blood, and held together by tendons: or else just a chain of bones with the flesh gone, blood-bedabbled and held together with tendons: or else just a chain of bones, with flesh and blood both gone, just held together with tendons. Or he sees bones only, without any connecting links, bones scattered in all directions: here lies a foot-bone, there a leg-bone, here a thigh-bone, there a hip-bone or a backbone or a skull. Then he compares his own body with those, thinking: "Here is this body of mine: it is of such a nature as that, it has come to be like that, it has not gone beyond that!" And so does he consider body inwardly or outwardly or both . . . and abides Contemplating Body.

Or again, brethren, a brother might see a body thrown away in the charnel-field,—just whitened bones, something like sea-shells, or just bones in a heap, over a year old, or bones that are crumbling away to dust. Then he compares his own body with that, saying: "This body of mine is just of such a nature, thus come-to-be, not gone beyond that!"

Thus inwardly contemplating body, or outwardly or both, does he abide. He abides contemplating the rise of things, or the fall of things, or the rise-and-fall of things in body. With the thought "It is body" his mindfulness of body is established, just sufficiently for him to know its existence and to become concentrated. Thus he abides detached, and he grasps at nothing at all in the world.

That, brethren, is how a brother abides in the Contemplation of Body.'

(ii) The Contemplation of Feelings

'In this method, brethren, a brother when feeling a pleasant feeling is aware "I feel a pleasant feeling": or when feeling a painful feeling is aware "I am feeling a painful feeling": or when the feeling is neither pleasant nor painful is aware "I am feeling a neutral feeling."

Or in the same way, when affected by a pleasant or painful or neutral feeling regarding material things, or when so affected by a feeling regarding immaterial things, he is aware of his feelings in like manner.

Thus, inwardly or outwardly or both, he abides contemplating his feelings. He abides contemplating the rise of things in feelings or the fall of things in feelings or the rise-and-fall of things in feelings. He says to himself, "It is feeling," and thus his mindfulness of feelings is established, just sufficiently for him to know their existence and to become concentrated. Thus he abides detached and he grasps at nothing at all in the world.

That, brethren, is how a brother abides in the Contemplation of Feelings.'

(iii) The Contemplation of Thought

'And how, brethren, does a brother abide in the Contemplation of Thought as such? In this method, a brother is aware of a passionate thought that it is passionate: of a dispassionate thought that it is dispassionate. Of a hateful thought he is aware that it is hateful; of a thought free from hate he is aware that it is so.

Of a confused thought he is aware that it is confused, and of a clear thought he is aware that it is clear. Of a concentrated thought he is aware that it is concentrated, and of a diffuse thought he is aware that it is diffuse. Of a lofty thought he is aware that it is lofty, of a low thought he is aware that it is low. Of a thought concerned with the higher he is aware that it is so: of a thought concerned with the lower he is also aware. Of a thought composed or discomposed, of one that is liberated or bound, in each case he is aware that it is so.

Thus, either inwardly or outwardly or both inwardly and outwardly, he abides contemplating thought. He contemplates the rise of things in thought or the fall of things in thought, or the rise-and-fall of things in thought. Thinking "It is thought" his mindfulness about thought is established, just sufficiently for him to know its existence and to become concentrated. Thus does he abide detached and he grasps at nothing at all in the world.

That is how, brethren, a brother abides, as regards thought, in the Contemplation of Thought.'

(iv) The Contemplation of Ideas

'And how, brethren, does a brother, as regards ideas, abide in the Contemplation of Ideas?

In this method, brethren, a brother abides in the Contemplation of Ideas by way of the Five Hindrances.

And how does he so contemplate Ideas?

In this method, brethren, a brother is aware of

an inner sensual desire that it is sensual, and when he has no inner sensual desire he is aware of it. When there arises in him a sensual desire not felt before, he is aware of it. When there is a rejection of a sensual desire that has arisen, he is aware of it. Also he is aware that when he has rejected such a desire it will not rise up again.

So also with regard to Ill-will, Sloth and Torpor, Excitement and Worry, and Wavering. Of each of these he is aware in the same way, that it is present or absent, of the arising of such when not felt before, of its rejection when felt, and of its never rising again when once rejected.

Thus, inwardly or outwardly or both, he abides in the Contemplation of Ideas . . . and grasps at nothing at all in the world.

That, brethren, is how a brother abides in the Contemplation of Ideas by way of the Five Hindrances.'

The Five Grasping-groups

'Then again, brethren, as regards Ideas, a brother abides in the Contemplation of Ideas by way of the Five Grasping-groups. And how does he so abide?

In this method, brethren, a brother reflects: "Such is body, such is the arising of body, such is the passing away of body. Such are feelings, such is the arising of feelings, and so forth. Such is perception, such is the arising of perception, and so forth. Such are the activities. . . . Such is consciousness, such is the arising of consciousness, such is the passing away of consciousness."

Thus inwardly or outwardly (as before) . . . does a brother abide in the Contemplation of Ideas by way of the Five Grasping-groups.'

The Six Spheres of Sense

'Then again, brethren, as regards Ideas, a brother abides in the Contemplation of Ideas by way of the Six Inner and Outer Spheres of Sense. And how does he so abide?

In this method, brethren, a brother is aware of the eye and objects of the eye: and whatsoever fetter is effected by the conjunction of these two, he is aware of that. He is aware how a fetter arises that has not arisen before: how he rejects a fetter which has already arisen: how there is no more arising again in the future of a fetter which he has rejected.

The same with regard to ear and sound: with regard to nose and scent: with regard to tongue and taste: with regard to body and tangibles: with regard to mind and mental images. . . . Thus, brethren, does a brother abide in the Contemplation of Ideas by way of the Six Inner and Outer Spheres of Sense.'

The Seven Factors of Wisdom

'Then again, brethren, with regard to Ideas, a brother abides in the Contemplation of Ideas by way of the Seven Factors of Wisdom. How does he so abide?

In this method, brethren, if in a brother there exist Inner (subjective) Mindfulness as a Factor of Wisdom, he is aware of it: if such be absent, he is aware of it. He is (as before) aware of the arising of such mindfulness not hitherto arisen, and of its perfect development when it has arisen. And in the same way as regards the other Factors of Wisdom, namely: Searching of the Norm, Energy, Zest, Serenity, Concentration, and Mental Balance (or Equanimity) as Factors of Wisdom.

In each case he is aware of their inner or subjective presence or absence, of the arising of each one of them which has not arisen before, and of the perfect development of each one of them when arisen.

That is how, brethren, a brother abides in the Contemplation of Ideas by way of the Seven Factors of Wisdom.'

The Four Ariyan Truths

'Then lastly, brethren, with regard to Ideas, a brother abides in the Contemplation of Ideas by way of the Four Ariyan Truths. And how does he so abide?

In this method, brethren, a brother is aware, as it really is, "This is Ill. This is the arising of Ill, as it really is. This is the Ceasing of Ill, as it really is. This is the Way to the Ceasing of Ill, as it really is." '

(*The* Dīgha Nikāya *account then proceeds with the analysis of Ill, described elsewhere. The* Majjhima Nikāya *account ends as follows:*)

'Now whosoever, brethren, shall thus practise these Four Ways of Establishing Mindfulness for seven years (at most), may look to win one of two fruits: either in this very life he wins the

Knowledge, or, if there be still a residue of him, he wins the Fruit of Not-returning.

But let alone seven years, brethren, whosoever shall thus practise the Four Ways of Establishing Mindfulness for six years, for five, four, three, two, one year,—nay, whosoever shall thus practise them for seven months, for even one month, for half a month, nay, even for seven days,—he shall win one of two Fruits: either in this very life he shall win the Knowledge, or, if there be still a residue of him, he shall win the Fruits of Not-returning.

This, brethren, is what I meant when I said before, "This is the Only Way that leads to the purification of beings, to passing beyond sorrow and lamentation, to the destruction of grief and despair, to the attainment of the Method, to the realizing of Nibbāna, namely: The Four Ways of Establishing Mindfulness."'

Thus spake the Exalted One. And those brethren were pleased with what was spoken by the Exalted One and took delight therein.

D.N. ii. 314–15; *M.N.* i. 62.

THE ELEMENTS

Thus have I heard. Once the Exalted One was dwelling near Sāvatthī, in Jeta Grove, at Anāthapindika's Park. Then the Exalted One, robing himself early, and taking bowl and robe, went forth to Sāvatthī to beg. And the venerable Rāhula [1] also, robing himself early, and taking

[1] The Master's own son.

bowl and robe, followed after the Exalted One, keeping close behind Him.

Then the Exalted One, looking behind, said to the venerable Rāhula: 'Whatsoever form, Rāhula, be it past, future, or present, inward or outward, gross or subtle, low or high, whether far or near, every form must be regarded thus, as it really is, by perfect insight: "This is not mine: not this am I: herein is not the self of me."'

'Is it just form only, Exalted One? Is it just form only?'

'Nay, Rāhula: form and feeling too, Rāhula: and perception, Rāhula: the activities, Rāhula: and consciousness too, Rāhula.'

Then thought the venerable Rāhula: 'Who could go to a village in quest of alms to-day, after being given a warning face to face with the Exalted One?'

So thinking, he turned back again and sat down at the root of a certain tree crosslegged, and holding his body straight set mindfulness before him as his task.

Now the venerable Sāriputta saw the venerable Rāhula so seated, and called to him: 'Practise the practice of mindfulness by breathing in and out, Rāhula: for that practice, if made to grow, is of great fruit and profit.'

Now the venerable Rāhula, rising from his solitude at eventide, went to the Exalted One and, coming into his presence, saluted Him and sat down at one side. So seated, the venerable Rāhula thus addressed the Exalted One: 'Lord, pray how is the practice of mindfulness by breathing in and out of great fruit and profit, when enlarged ?'

'Whatsoever hard, solid matter, Rāhula, has gathered in yourself, personally, such as, the hair of the head, the hair of the body, nails, teeth, skin, flesh, sinews, bones, marrow, kidneys, heart, liver, pleura, spleen, lungs, intestines, mesentery, stomach, excrements, that, Rāhula, is called the personal element of earth. Both that personal earth-element and the external earth-element are called by that name of "earth-element." That you must regard thus, as it really is, by perfect insight: "This is not mine: not this am I: herein is not the self of me." So regarding it one is repelled by the earth-element, and cleanses his heart of it.

And what, Rāhula, is the Element of Water ?

It may be the personal element of water, and it may be the external element of water. But what, Rāhula, is the personal element of water ?

Whatsoever water, whatsoever fluid, has gathered in yourself personally, such as bile, phlegm, pus, blood, sweat, lymph, tears, lubricant, saliva, mucus, oil, urine,—whatsoever of a liquid nature has gathered in yourself personally, Rāhula,—that is called the personal element of water. Both that personal element of water and the external element of water are called by the name water-element, and it must be regarded (as I have told you) in the same way as the earth-element. So regarding it one is repelled by the water-element, and cleanses his heart of it.

And what, Rāhula, is the Element of Heat ?

It may be the personal element and it may be the external element of heat.

Now what, Rāhula, is the personal element of heat ?

Whatsoever heat, or whatsoever is of the nature of burning, has gathered in yourself personally, such as that by which there is warming, digesting, consuming: that by which what is eaten, drunk, chewed, tasted goes to perfect digestion,—whatsoever else of like nature is gathered in yourself personally, that, Rāhula, is called the personal element of heat. That and the external element of heat go by the same name of heat-element. That also is to be regarded as I have told you.

And what, Rāhula, is the Element of Air ?

It may be the personal or the external element of air.

And what, Rāhula, is the personal element of air ?

Whatsoever air, whatsoever is of a windy nature, is gathered in yourself personally, such as, the upgoing and down-going breath, the wind of the belly, wind of the intestines, the vital airs that pervade the limbs, air inbreathed and outbreathed,—all such are called by the name of personal air-element. Both this and the external air-element are called by the same name of air-element. That also must be regarded as I have shown you.

And what, Rāhula, is the Element of Space ?

It may be the personal or the external element of space.

Now what, Rāhula, is the personal element of space ?

Whatever empty space or what is of the nature of void is included in yourself personally, such as, the cavities of ear and nose and mouth, the cavities by which food enters, wherein food is stored, the cavities by which it is extruded,—all such cavities are called by the same name of element of space. Both these and the external element of space are called by the same name of element of space. That also must be regarded as I have shown you.

Now, Rāhula, make your practice of meditation like the earth. If you so practise, all delightful contacts will not seize hold of and be established in your mind. Just as on the earth men throw down what is fair and foul alike, all excrements of dung and urine, saliva, pus, and blood : and yet earth is not worried or troubled or disgusted thereat,—so also do you make your practice like unto the earth, Rāhula. So practising all delightful contacts will not seize hold of and be established in your mind.

And so with water : make your practice of meditation like water. For just as in water men wash things fair and foul alike (as before stated with regard to earth), yet water is not worried or troubled or disgusted thereat. So also do you make your practice like water.

And so with fire. . . . For just as fire burns up fair and foul alike, but is not worried or troubled or disgusted thereat (but burns up all alike), so do you make your practice like fire.

And so with air. . . . For just as the wind carries away things fair and foul alike, but is not worried or troubled or disgusted thereat . . . so do you make your practice like the air.

And so with space. . . . For just as space is not established anywhere, so [unattached] do you make your practice. . . . So practising, Rāhula, all delightful contacts will not seize upon or be established in your mind.

Practise the practice of kindliness, Rāhula, for by so practising all enmity will be abandoned. Practise the practice of compassion, Rāhula, for so will all vexation be abandoned. Practise the practice of sympathy, Rāhula, for so will all aversion be abandoned. Practise the practice of equanimity, Rāhula, for so will all repulsion be abandoned. Likewise meditate on the ugly, for so will lust be abandoned. Meditate on the impermanent, for so will pride-of-self be abandoned.'[1]

M.N. i. 420–5 (*condensing repetitions*).

TO THOSE OF OTHER FAITHS

(*Nigrodha, the ascetic, thinks that the Master wishes to overthrow the views and practices of other sects. He is shown that the Norm is of universal application.*)

'Now this is what I say to you, Nigrodha: "Let any intelligent man come to me, any man who is also without guile, not a deceiver, but an upright man. I will teach him. I will show him the Norm. And if he practises according to my instructions, to know and realize for himself even in this very life that unsurpassed holy life

[1] The further section on breathing, about which Rāhula asks, is given on p. 73.

for the sake of which clansmen go forth from home to the homeless in its perfection, he too shall know and realize in seven years. Do I say seven years? Why, Nigrodha, even if he do so, as I have said, for six, five, four, three, two years, even one year, half a year; five, four, three, two months, even one month . . . nay, if he so practise for seven days, Nigrodha . . . such a man coming to me shall so realize. . . .

Now this I say, Nigrodha, not desiring to win pupils, not wishing to make others fall from their religious vows, not wishing to make others give up their ways of life, not wishing to establish you in wrong ways or to make you give up ways that are good. Not so!

But, Nigrodha, there are bad things not put away, things that have to do with corruption, things that draw one down again to rebirth, things causing suffering, having Ill for their fruit, things concerned with rebirth, decay, and death in time to come. It is for the rejection of these things that I teach you the Norm, walking according to which these things that are concerned with corruption shall be put away by you, and wholesome things shall be brought to increase; by which even in this present life by his own abnormal powers a man shall realize and abide in the full knowledge and realization of perfect wisdom.'"

D.N. iii. 56–7.

THE TONGUE

UNPROFITABLE TALK

Now at that time the brethren of the Band of Six had a habit of rising up in the night before it was dawn. Then, donning wooden slippers, they used to parade up and down in the open air, chattering in shrill loud tones, hawking and spitting, and talking all manner of idle babble, such as: talk about kings and robbers and ministers of state: talk about armies and of fear, tales of fights: talk about food, drink, clothes, beds, lodgings, flower-garlands, scents, kinsfolk, and carriages: about villages, suburbs, towns, provinces, women, and soldiers: gossip of the streets and wells, and tales of ghosts: all sorts of talk: about the world and the Ocean: of things existent and non-existent.[1] And while so doing they trampled to death all sorts of insects. Moreover, they distracted the brethren from their meditation.

[1] This list of idle talks is in *Dīgha Nikāya*, iii. 36–7. Here it is used to give graphic effect to the wooden-slipper incident, for which these brethren were duly rebuked by the Master and forbidden to wear such. These brethren, of the Six, were followers of Assaji and Punnabasu and were afterwards expelled from the order.

THE TONGUE

THE ARIYAN SPEECH

They who talk angrily, full of wrath and proud,
Carp at each other's failings when they meet,
And take delight in blame and finding fault,
And in their rival's fall. But Ariyans
Will never follow practices like these.
If there be one, a wise man, fain of speech,
He knows the proper time, and speech concerned
With righteousness and practice of right talk.
Thus speaks a sage, not angry, well-restrained
With humble mind, not laying down the law,
Not curious ; but wisely speaks fair speech,
Welcomes the kindly word, rejects the cruel,
Knows no resentment, does not carp at faults,
Does not retort nor crush his rival down,
Nor from the issue speak. O true it is
That Ariyans' words alike instruct and please !
Thus Ariyans speak, such is the Ariyan talk :
And knowing this the wise should humbly speak.

Anguttara Nikāya, i. 199.

SILENCE (i)

(*Ajātasattu, rājah of Magadhā, is taken at night by Jīvaka, the child-doctor, to see the Master.*)

Then Jīvaka got ready five hundred she-elephants and the royal elephant ridden by his majesty, and sent word to him, saying : 'The elephants are already decked. Let your majesty do what he thinks seasonable.'

Then Ajātasattu, the rājah of Magadhā, son of the Videha-princess, set five hundred of his women on the she-elephants, one on each, and himself mounted the royal elephant, and with torches borne along went forth from Rājagaha in all his royal magnificence, towards the Mango Grove of Jīvaka (where the Exalted One was residing).

Now when His Majesty Ajātasattu was close upon the Mango Grove, there came upon him fear and trembling, so that every hair upon his body stood on end, and he exclaimed to Jīvaka: 'Surely, master Jīvaka, you are deceiving me! Surely, master Jīvaka, you are playing a trick on me! Are you not delivering me into the hands of mine enemies, Jīvaka?'

(Being reassured by Jīvaka he went on) 'How is it, then, that there is not a sneeze, not a clearing of the throat, not a single sound to be heard in all this company of brethren, numbering (as you say) twelve hundred and fifty?'

'Fear not, Mahārājah. Fear not, Mahārājah. I am not deceiving your Majesty, nor playing you a trick, nor am I delivering your Majesty into the hands of your enemies. Go right on, Mahārājah! Go right on, Mahārājah! See! yonder in the pavilion the lamps are burning.'

Then the rājah went on, riding his elephant as far as the path allowed, then went on foot to the pavilion door. Then he said to Jīvaka: 'Where, master Jīvaka, is the Exalted One?'

'Yonder, Mahārājah, is the Exalted One! Yonder, Mahārājah, is the Exalted One, sitting up against the midmost pillar, facing east and surrounded by the brethren.'

Then the rājah of Magadhā, Ajātasattu, drew near to the Exalted One and stood aside. So standing he gazed upon that company sitting there in perfect silence, calm as a translucent pool. And he exclaimed: 'O that my boy Prince Udayi,[1] The Lucky Lad, may be blessed with the peacefulness wherewith this company of brethren is now blessed!'

D.N. i. 49.

SILENCE (ii)

Once the Exalted One was dwelling at Sāvatthī in East Park, at the storeyed house of Migāra's mother. Then on that occasion the Exalted One was sitting surrounded by the Order of Brethren, and it was the Sabbath. Then the Exalted One, scanning the Order of Brethren as they sat there in perfect silence, thus addressed the brethren:

'Brethren, this company is established in the Reality, in utter purity, with all idle chatter laid aside. Such an Order of Brethren as this, and such a company as this, brethren, is hard to come to behold in all the world.

Such an Order of Brethren, such a company as this is worthy of honour, worthy of reverence, worthy of gifts, worthy of hands lifted in worship, a field of merit unsurpassed in all the world.

To such an Order of Brethren, to such a company as this, even a slight gift is great, and a great gift is greater still.

To behold such an Order of Brethren, to behold such a company as this, brethren, one might well

[1] According to *Anāgata-vaṃsa*, 'the story of the Future,' a late non-canonical work, this lad was the Bodhisatta Metteyya.

start off on a journey of many a long mile, with a satchel on one's back to carry one's food.

Of such a sort, brethren, is this Order of Brethren.'

(*The Master then proceeds to tell how that company contained all the grades of great ones who had attained, some the deva-world, some the Brahma-world, some the Imperturbable, and some the Perfection of Nibbāna.*)

Ang. Nik. ii. 190.

THE ARIYAN SILENCE (iii)

Thus have I heard. On a certain occasion the Exalted One was staying near Sāvatthī at Jeta Grove in Anāthapindika's Park.

Then the venerable Moggallāna the Great said to the brethren: 'Friends and brethren!'

'Yes, friend,' replied those brethren to the venerable Moggallāna the Great.

Then said the venerable Moggallāna the Great: 'Here, friends, when I was secluded and living all alone, this discursive thought occurred to me: "The Ariyan silence! The Ariyan silence! they say. Now what means this Ariyan silence?"

Then, friends, I thus thought: "Herein a brother, by the suppression of discursive thought and investigation, enters on and abides in the Second Trance, a state of internal calm of heart, concentrated on its object, free from discursive thought and investigation, born of mental balance, a state of zest and ease. This is called *the Ariyan silence.*"

So I, friends, by the suppression of discursive

thought and investigation, entered on and abode in the Second Trance . . . a state of zest and ease: and, friends, as I was abiding in that state, there came to me ideas, workings of mind, accompanied by discursive thought.

Thereupon, friends, the Exalted One by magic power came to me and thus spake: "Moggallāna, Moggallāna! desert not the Ariyan silence! In the Ariyan silence establish thy mind! In the Ariyan silence make thy mind sole arbiter! In the Ariyan silence balance thy mind!" '

S.N. ii. 273.

THE ARIYAN SILENCE (iv)

Now on that occasion a number of brethren were assembled in the hermitage of Rammaka, the brahmin, and were occupied in pious talk.

Then the Exalted One stood in the porch outside the door, waiting for the talk to come to an end. Then the Exalted One, seeing that the talk was over, coughed and rattled the door-bar. And those brethren opened the door to the Exalted One.

Then the Exalted One entered the hermitage of Rammaka, the brahmin, and sat down on a seat made ready. So seated He thus addressed the brethren:

'What was it, brethren, that ye were talking of, assembled here, and what was the subject of the talk just broken off?'

'It was about the Exalted One, Lord, that we were talking, and had just left off when the Exalted One arrived.'

'Well said, brethren! It is fitting, brethren, for you, as clansmen who have in faith gone forth from home to live the homeless life, thus to assemble and engage in pious talk. When ye meet together, brethren, ye should do one of two things : engage in pious talk or keep the Ariyan silence.'

M.N. i. 161, cf. *Udāna*, p. 11.

RESENTMENT

Now the venerable Tissa, nephew to the Exalted One's father, went into the presence of the Exalted One, saluted Him, and sat down at one side, woeful, dejected, and shedding a flood of tears.

Then said the Exalted One to the venerable Tissa : 'How now, Tissa ? Why sit you here beside me woeful, dejected, and shedding a flood of tears ?'

'Lord, it is because the brethren with one accord have been mocking me and teasing me.'

'Then, Tissa, that is because you yourself have a tongue and cannot endure the tongue of others. Now, Tissa, it is not seemly that you, a clansman, who gave up your home and went forth to the homeless life, should have a sharp tongue and not endure the tongue of others. One who, like you, has a tongue should also endure the tongue of others.'

Thus spake the Exalted One. When the Wellfarer had thus spoken the Master added this yet further :

Why art thou angry ? Be not angry, Tissa.
Meekness is best for thee ; and to restrain
Anger, conceit, hypocrisy is best.
It is for this we live the righteous life.

S.N. ii. 280.

ENDURANCE OF ABUSE

(*The brother Phagguna had been abused by others. The Exalted One said:*)

'Wherefore, Phagguna, if anyone to thy face should abuse thee . . . if he were to strike thee with fist or hurl clods of earth at thee, or beat thee with a stick, or give thee a blow with a sword, —yet must thou set aside all worldly desires, all worldly considerations, and thus must thou train thyself: "My heart shall be unwavering. No evil word will I send forth. I will abide compassionate of others' welfare, of kindly heart, without resentment." Thus must thou train thyself, Phagguna.'

M.N. i. 124.

RETURN GOOD FOR EVIL

The Parable of the Saw

'Brethren, there are these five ways of speech which other men may use to you:—speech seasonable or unseasonable: speech true or false: speech gentle or bitter: speech conducive to profit or to loss: speech kindly or resentful.

When men speak evil of ye, thus must ye train yourselves: "Our heart shall be unwavering, no evil word will we send forth, but compassionate of others' welfare will we abide, of kindly heart without resentment: and that man who thus speaks will we suffuse with thoughts accompanied by love, and so abide: and, making that our standpoint, we will suffuse the whole world with loving thoughts, far-reaching, wide-spreading, boundless, free from hate, free from ill-will, and so abide." Thus, brethren, must ye train yourselves.

Moreover, brethren, though robbers, who are highwaymen, should with a two-handed saw carve you in pieces limb by limb, yet if the mind of any one of you should be offended thereat, such an one is no follower of my gospel. But thus (as I have shown ye) must ye train yourselves. . . .

And this parable of the Saw which I have taught ye, do ye bear it in mind again and yet again. Do ye not see, brethren, that there is no syllable thereof, either small or great, but ye must agree thereto ?'

'Surely, Lord.'

'Wherefore, brethren, bear in mind this parable of the Saw that I have now taught ye, for it shall be to your profit and welfare for many a long day.'

M.N. i. 128–9.

'This man abused me : he beat me and conquered,
Conquered and plundered.' Wrapped up in such
thoughts,
Never appeased is the hatred of such men.

'This man abused me, he beat me and conquered,
Conquered and plundered.' Stripped bare of such
thoughts,
Quickly appeased is the hatred of such men.

Never by hatred is hatred appeased,
Nay ! but by not-hate : that's the old-time Law.

Dhammapada, vv. 3–4.

THE TONGUE

WRONG SPEECH

(The Exalted One said to the Brahmin housefathers of Sāla of the Kosalans :)

'Now, housefathers, what are the four unrighteous practices in speech ?

In this matter, housefathers, a man is a liar. When he goes to the court of justice or the assembly, or goes amongst the company of relatives or the folk, or to the royal ministers, being brought up and forced to give evidence (they say to him) : "Now, good fellow, say what you know."

Then he, though not knowing, says, "I know" : or knowing he says, "I know not." Or not having seen he says, "I saw" : or having seen he says, "I saw not." Thus to save himself or others, or for the sake of some trifling gain, he deliberately utters lies.

Or else he is a backbiter in words. What he gathers here he spreads abroad to cause disruption there. What he gathers there he spreads abroad to cause disruption here. Thus is he a breaker-up of fellowships, no reconciler of those at strife, finds pleasure and delight in quarrels, revels therein and utters words inciting to quarrels.

Or else he is one of harsh speech. His words are insolent and rude, bitter to others, scolding others, bordering on abuse, not making for balance of mind. Such is the speech to which he is given.

Or else he is an idle babbler, speaking out of season, of things non-existent and irrelevant. A speaker is he of things unrighteous and unrestrained. He utters speech not worth treasuring up, unseasonable, out of place, without discrimination and not concerned with profit.

Such, housefathers, are the four unrighteous practices in speech.'

M.N. i. chap. 41.

WORDY WARFARE

'And how is one no wager of wordy warfare with people ?

Herein, housefather, a brother makes not talk like this : "You know not about this Norm-Discipline. I do know about this Norm-Discipline. How could you know about it ? You have fallen on wrong views. I have come by right views. You speak last what should come first, and first what should come last. I am speaking to the point : you are not. What you have thought out so long is quite upset. Your view is confuted. Go, explain yourself. You are shown up. Clear yourself if you can !" That, housefather, is how one is a wager of wordy warfare with people.'

Home he abandons : homeless wandering
The Sage with folk no longer maketh ties.
Empty of Lusts, showing no preference,
With no man wageth wordy warfare more.

S.N. iii. 11.

THE TONGUE

QUARRELS

At Sāvatthī. . . . Then the Exalted One said:

'I quarrel not with the world, brethren. It is the world that quarrels with me. No preacher of the Norm, brethren, quarrels with anyone in the world.

That which is not upheld, brethren, in the world of Sages, of that I declare "It is not." What, brethren, is upheld in the world of the Sages, of that I declare "It is so."

And what, brethren, is *not* upheld in the world of the Sages, of which I declare "It is not"? That body is permanent, stable, eternal, not subject to decay. *That* is not upheld in the world of the Sages, and of that I declare "It is not." "Feeling, perception, the activities, consciousness is permanent, stable, eternal, not subject to decay." *That* is not upheld in the world of the Sages, and of that I declare "It is not so." '

S.N. iii, § 94.

THE STABILITY OF SOCIETIES

CONDITIONS OF COMMUNAL STABILITY

Now at that time the venerable Ānanda was standing behind the Exalted One and fanning Him. And the Exalted One said to the venerable Ānanda :

'How now, Ānanda ? Have you ever heard that the Vajjians repeatedly assemble together and in large numbers ? '

'I have heard so, Lord.'

'Well, Ānanda, so long as the Vajjians shall assemble repeatedly and in large numbers, just so long may the prosperity of the Vajjians be looked for and not their decay.

. . . So long, Ānanda, as the Vajjians assemble in harmony and disperse in harmony : so long as they do their business in harmony : so long as they introduce no revolutionary ordinance, or break up no established ordinance, but abide by the old-time Vajjian Norm, as ordained : so long as they honour, reverence, esteem. and worship the elders among the Vajjians and deem them worthy of listening to : so long as the women and maidens of the families dwell without being forced or abducted : so long as they honour, revere, esteem, and worship the Vajjian shrines, both the inner and the outer : so long as they allow not the customary offerings, given and performed, to be neglected: so long as the customary watch and ward over the Arahants that are among them is well kept, so that they may have free access to the realm and having entered may dwell pleasantly therein: just so long as they do these things, Ānanda, may the prosperity of the Vajjians be looked for and not their decay.'

D.N. ii. 73.

CONDITIONS OF THE STABILITY OF THE ORDER

1

Then the Exalted One addressed the brethren, saying:

'I will teach you, brethren, seven things that prevent decay. Do ye listen to it carefully. Apply your minds, and I will speak.'

'Even so, Lord,' replied those brethren to the Exalted One, who then said:

'So long. brethren, as the brethren shall assemble repeatedly and in large numbers, the prosperity of the brethren may be looked for and not their decay. So long as the brethren assemble in harmony and disperse in harmony, so long as they do the business of the Order in harmony. So long as they introduce no revolutionary ordinance, break up no established ordinance, but live in accordance with the appointed charges,—

So long as the elder brethren, men of many days and long ordained, fathers of the Order, men of standing in the Order,—so long as these are honoured, reverenced, esteemed, and deferred to,—

So long as brethren do not fall subject to that craving which arises and leads back to rebirth,—

So long as there shall be brethren who are fond of the forest life and lodging,—

So long as brethren shall establish themselves in mindfulness, with this thought, "Let goodly co-mates in the righteous life come hither in the future, and let those that have already come live happily,—"

So long, brethren, as these seven things that prevent decay shall stand fast among the brethren, so long as the brethren shall be instructed therein, —just so long may the prosperity of the brethren be looked for, and not their decay.'

2

'Brethren, I will teach you seven other conditions that prevent decay. Do ye listen to it. Apply your minds carefully. I will speak.'

'Even so, Lord,' replied those brethren to the Exalted One. The Exalted One said :

'So long as the brethren do not delight in (worldly) activities, are not busybodies nor devoted to activities,—

So long as the brethren are not gossipers, not delighting in gossip, not devoted to gossip,—

So long as the brethren are not sluggish, not delighting in sleep, not given to somnolence,—

So long as the brethren are not given to company, not delighting in company, not devoted to company,—

So long as the brethren are not slaves of evil desires,—

So long as the brethren are not the friends, comrades, and associates of men of evil ways,—

So long as the brethren shall not come to a stop upon the Way by the attainment of lesser excellence,—

Just so long, brethren, as these seven conditions that prevent decay shall be established and the brethren are instructed in them,—so long may the prosperity of the brethren be looked for, not their decay.'

3

'I will teach you, brethren, seven other conditions that prevent decay. . . .

So long as the brethren are faithful, modest, and conscientious, of wide knowledge, of ardent energy, of steady mindfulness, and full of wisdom,— —just so long may the prosperity of the brethren be looked for and not their decay.'

4

'Seven[1] other (like) conditions will I teach you, brethren. . . .

So long as the brethren shall practise the limb of wisdom which is mindfulness, the limb of wisdom which is searching into things, energy, zest, calm, contemplation, and equanimity . . . so long may their prosperity and not their decay be looked for.'

[1] These are the Seven Limbs of Wisdom or the *Satta-bojjhanga*.

5

'Seven other conditions, brethren, will I teach you that prevent decay. . . .

So long as the brethren shall practise the perception of Impermanence, of the Unreality of Self, of Impurity, of the Besetting Dangers, of Abandonment, of Passionlessness, of Cessation,—just so long may their prosperity be looked for, not their decay.'

6

'I will teach you six conditions, brethren, which prevent decay. . . .

So long as brethren shall provide themselves with (the habit of) kindly deeds, kindly words, and kindly thoughts, whether in secret or openly,—

So long as the brethren shall be impartial sharers and dividers of whatsoever lawful gains and profits may accrue to them,—even to the mere contents of the begging-bowl,—and shall share them with their virtuous co-mates in the righteous life,—

So long as the brethren shall dwell keeping unbroken, undivided, unvaried, and unsoiled those practices which set one free, which are praised by the wise, which are not used for a wrong purpose, which conduce to contemplation,—so long as they shall dwell endowed with the virtue of such practices along with their co-mates in the righteous life, whether in secret or openly,—

So long as the brethren shall dwell endowed with right views, that is, the Ariyan View which leads to salvation, which leads one who acts accordantly to the utter destruction of Ill,—along with their co-mates in the righteous life, whether in secret or openly,—

So long may the prosperity of the brethren be looked for, not their decay.'

D.N. ii. 79–80.

Now when the Exalted One was dwelling near Rājagaha on the Hill called Vulture's Peak, he gave to the brethren this pious talk about things that include each other:

'Such is Right Practice, such is Contemplation, such is Insight.

Contemplation when compassed about by Right Practice is of great fruit, of great profit.

Insight compassed about by Contemplation is of great fruit, of great profit.

The Mind when compassed about by Insight is utterly freed from the *āsavas*, namely, the *āsava* of sensual lust, wrong views, and ignorance."

D.N. ii. 81.

INSTRUCTIONS TO THE BRETHREN

Then the Exalted One said:

'Wherefore, Cunda, do ye to whom have been shown the things that I have penetrated, do ye one and all meet together and rehearse them together, comparing meaning with meaning and expression with expression, not wrangling over them: so that this way of holy living may be lasting and long-standing, for the profit of many, for the bliss of many, out of compassion for the

[1] A fourth *āsava* (Taint or Intoxicant or Drug) is sometimes added, viz. *bhav'āsava*, desire for continued existence.

world, for the use, for the profit, for the bliss of devas and mankind.

And what, Cunda, are those things which I have penetrated and shown unto you, and which ye should so rehearse together . . . ?

They are The Four Ways of Establishing Mindfulness, The Four Best Efforts, The Four Ways of Will, The Five Controlling Faculties, The Five Powers, The Seven Factors of Wisdom, and The Ariyan Eightfold Path.

These, Cunda, are the things that I have penetrated and shown unto you, which ye should rehearse together . . . as I have said . . . for the bliss of devas and mankind.'

D.N. iii. 127.

EXCESS OF MERRIMENT

'In the Ariyan discipline, brethren, music is lamentation. In the Ariyan discipline, dancing is sheer madness. In the Ariyan discipline, laughing that displays the teeth is childishness.

Wherefore, brethren, do ye break down the bridge that causes music, dancing, laughter. Enough for you just to smile if you have any cause to show your pleasure.'

Ang. Nik. i. 261.

MINDFUL AND SELF-POSSESSED

Now at Vesāli the Exalted One was staying in Ambapāli's Grove. On that occasion the Exalted One called to the brethren and said:

'Brethren, let a brother dwell mindful and self-possessed. This is my advice to you. And how, brethren, is a brother mindful?

Herein, brethren, a brother, realizing body as a compound, remains ardent, composed, mindful, by controlling that covetousness and discontent that are in the world. That, brethren, is how a brother is mindful.

And how, brethren, is a brother self-possessed ?

Herein, brethren, a brother, both in his going forth and in his home-returning, acts composedly. In looking forward and in looking back he acts composedly. In bending or stretching (arm or body) he acts composedly. In wearing his robes and bearing bowl and robe : in eating, drinking, chewing, swallowing : in relieving nature's needs : in going, standing, sitting, sleeping, waking, speaking, keeping silence, he acts composedly. That, brethren, is how a brother is self-possessed.

Then let a brother dwell mindful and self-possessed. This is my advice to you, brethren.'

D.N. ii. 94–5.

By faith and virtue, energy and mind
In perfect balance, searching of the Norm,
Perfect in knowledge and good practices,
Perfect in concentration of your thoughts,
Ye shall strike off this multitude of woes.

Dhammapada, v. 144.

CONFESSION OF FAULTS

(*Certain brethren had expelled another wrongfully, and came to the Master to confess their fault.*)

Then those brethren rising from their seats threw their robes over one shoulder, fell at the feet of the Exalted One, and said to him:

'Transgression, Lord, overcame us : such was

our folly, such was our stupidity, such was our wrong-doing, in that we expelled a brother who was pure and faultless without ground and without reason. May the Exalted One, O Lord, accept this (our confession of) guilt as such, for our self-restraint in future.'

'Truly, brethren, transgression overcame you, such was your folly, such was your stupidity, such was your wrong-doing, in having expelled a brother who was pure and faultless, without ground and without reason. Nevertheless, brethren, as you have seen your transgression as transgression, and have made confession as is fit and proper, I do accept it from you. For this, brethren, is growth in the Ariyan Discipline when, having seen our transgression as such, we make confession as is fit and proper, for the future practice of self-restraint.'

Vinaya. Mahāvagga, 9. 1.

FALLING AWAY

(The Exalted One said :)

'Once upon a time, brethren, a cat was standing in a dust-bin, on a dust-heap, watching for a mouse (and said), "As soon as a mouse comes out in search of food, I will catch and swallow it."

Well, brethren, that mouse came out in search of food, the cat pounced suddenly upon it, caught and swallowed it. But the mouse gnawed away at his inside and gnawed his bowels, as a result of which the cat came by his death and mortal pain.

Even so, brethren, such and such a brother

rises up at an early hour, robes himself, and, taking bowl and robe, enters a village or suburb to beg for alms, with bodily senses unguarded, with mindfulness unsteadied, and senses unrestrained.

There he catches sight of some womenfolk, lightly clad or incompletely clad, and on seeing womenfolk thus clad passion torments his mind. With his mind thus tormented by the stings of passion, he comes by his death or else by mortal pain.

Now, herein, brethren, "death" means to desert the training of the Ariyan discipline and to return to the lower life (of the world): "mortal pain," brethren, means to fall into some grievous offence, (but) an offence of such a sort that recovery from it can be made.

Therefore, brethren, thus must ye train yourselves: "Guarded in body-senses, in speech and in mind, with mindfulness established and senses restrained will we enter a village or suburb to beg for alms."

Even so, brethren, must ye train yourselves.'

S.N. ii. 123.

THE SIMPLE LIFE

The Exalted One said:

'A new teaching, Cunda, do I show you for the control of the *āsavas* which belong to this life. Nay, I do not show you a teaching for the prevention of the *āsavas* of some future life, but for the control of them here and now, as well as for the prevention of them in the future.

Wherefore, Cunda, as to the robe I have permitted you,—let that be enough for you to keep off cold, to keep off heat, to prevent the touch of gnats and stinging flies, of wind and sun and snakes, and for modesty.

As to the food you beg, permitted by me,—let that be enough for the setting up, for the keeping up, for the safeguarding of the body, and for the adoption of the holy life, bearing this in mind: "Thus do I destroy my old feeling and produce no new feeling, so that I shall be blameless and may live at ease."

And as to the lodging that I have permitted, let that be enough to keep off cold, to keep off heat, to keep off the touch of gnats and stinging flies, and wind and sun and bite of snakes,—just enough to provide shelter from the stress of seasons and for solitude.

And as to the supply of drugs and requisites in case of sickness, which I have permitted,—let those be enough to keep off the pains of sickness that have arisen and as a bare sufficiency of relief.'

D.N. iii. 130.

THE PITH OF THE MATTER

'Suppose, brethren, a man in need of sound timber, in quest of sound timber, going about searching for sound timber, should come upon a mighty tree, upstanding, all sound timber, and pass it by; but should cut away the outer wood and bark and take that along with him, thinking it to be sound timber.

Then a discerning man might say thus: "This

fellow surely cannot tell the difference between sound timber and outer wood and bark, branch-wood and twigs: but being in need of sound timber . . . he passes it by and goes off with the outer wood and bark, thinking it to be sound timber. Now such a way of dealing with sound timber will never serve his need."

Thus, brethren, the essentials of the holy life do not consist in the profits of gain, honour, and good name: nor yet in the profits of observing moral rules: nor yet in the profits of knowledge and insight: but the sure heart's release, brethren, —that, brethren, is the meaning, that is the essence, that is the goal of living the holy life.'

M.N. i. 194.

HOW TO REPRIMAND A BROTHER

'First, a brother must be warned (if he be a wrong-doer): and when he has been duly warned, let him again be reminded: and when he has been reminded, let him be definitely charged with wrong-doing. When he has been charged with wrong-doing, let some discreet and able brother bring the matter before the Order.

A brother, Upāli, who is about to admonish another must realize within himself five qualities before doing so, (that he may be able to say), thus: "In due season will I speak, not out of season. In truth will I speak, not in falsehood. Gently will I speak, not harshly. To his profit will I speak, not to his loss. With kindly intent will I speak, not in anger."'

Vinaya, ii. 9.

TREATMENT OF A BROTHER

'Now when ye have thus met together, Cunda, in friendly guise one to another and without wrangling, ye should practise yourselves in these things.

If a co-mate in the holy life should say a thing in the Company, then, if ye think thus: "This venerable one has wrongly grasped the meaning (of the Norm) and wrongly interpreted the letter of it," yet ye should not agree with him nor yet think scorn of him therefor. But without agreement with him or thinking scorn of him, thus should be your speech to him: "Of this meaning, friend, the letters are either these or those. Which is the better of the two?" or "Of these letters either this or that is the right meaning. Which is the better meaning of the two?"

And if he should say: "Of this meaning, friends, it is exactly these renderings (of mine) which are the better: and of these expressions, exactly this meaning (which I give) is the better": then in such case ye should not wave him aside nor yet abuse him: but without rejection or abuse, he must carefully be made to understand by paying attention to that meaning and those expressions.

And again, if a co-mate in the holy life should say a thing in the Company, and if ye judge thus: "This venerable one has wrongly grasped the meaning, but he is right in the expression," then ye should neither agree with him nor yet think scorn of him therefor. But without agreement with him or thinking scorn of him, thus should be your speech to him: "Of these expressions, friend, either this or that is the meaning. Now which is the better of the two?"

Then if he reply, "Of these expressions it is exactly this (one of mine) that is the better meaning," then he should not be waved aside nor yet abused, but without doing either ye must carefully make him to understand by paying attention to that meaning.

But if, on the other hand, he rightly grasp the meaning but give a wrong expression to it, in the same way . . . ye must set him right in the expression of it.

But if he be right in both meaning and letter (of expression), then should ye say: "Well said!" and so agree with him and be pleased with what he says. And with the words "Well said!" and so forth, ye should say thus: "It is a gain for us, friend: it is a thing well gotten by us, that we behold such a venerable one as our co-mate in the holy life, one thus well versed both in the spirit and in the letter (of the Norm)." '

D.N. iii. 127–8.

THE MASTER'S ROBES OF RAGS

Then the venerable Kassapa the Great said to the venerable Ānanda: . . . 'I, friend, am one who has shaved his head and beard, donned the saffron robes, and gone forth from the household to the homeless life. . . . I do not admit to acknowledge any other teacher save that Exalted One, the Arahant who is perfectly enlightened.

In former days, friend, when I was still living the household life, this thought occurred to me: "Oppressive is the household life, a path for the dust of passion[1]: an open-air life is the wanderer's: not easy is it for him who dwells in a house to live the holy life in its entire fulfilment, in its entire purity, made clean and white. What if I get my hair and beard shaved off, don the saffron robes, give up my home, and go forth to the homeless life!"

Well! Some time later I made me an under-robe of rags, and, taking as my pattern those Noble Ones in the world, I had my hair and beard shaved off, donned the saffron robes, left my home, and went forth to the homeless life.

Thus become a wanderer, as I tramped along the high road, I saw the Exalted One,—between Rājagaha and Nāḷanda it was,—seated by a wayside shrine,[2] and when I saw him I thought: "To think that I should behold the Teacher, that I should behold the Exalted One, the Happy One, who is the Exalted One, that I should behold the fully-enlightened One, the Exalted One!"

Thereupon, friend, I fell with my head at the Exalted One's feet and said to him: "The Exalted One is my teacher, Lord! I am the Exalted One's disciple!"

At these words of mine, friend, the Exalted One thus spake: "Whosoever, Kassapa, not

[1] *Rajāpatha*—so explained by Buddhaghosa: but it may mean simply 'a stuffy life.'

[2] *Bahuputte cetiye*—it was called 'the Shrine of the Many Children.'

knowing a disciple thus fully endowed with the power of will should say 'I know,' or not seeing such an one should say 'I see,' his head would split asunder. Now I, Kassapa, knowing such, say 'I know'; seeing such, I say 'I see.'

Therefore, Kassapa, thus must you train yourself: 'There must be the strictest conscientiousness and discretion present in senior brethren, in novices, and in those of medium standing.' Even so must you train yourself.

Therefore, Kassapa, thus also must you train yourself: 'Whatever teaching of the Norm I hear which is attended by profit, realizing that and paying attention to it, considering it with my mind, I will listen to that teaching with a ready ear.' Even so, Kassapa, must you train yourself.

Therefore also, Kassapa, thus must you train yourself: 'Heedfulness and cheerfulness as regards body shall never desert me.' So must you train yourself."

Then, friend, the Exalted One, having thus exhorted me, rose from his seat and went away.

For seven days, friend, I ate the country food and was still in bondage to the flesh: but on the eighth day insight arose in me. After that, when the Exalted One, stepping off the high-road, was approaching the root of a certain tree, folding my under-robe of rags in four, I said to the Exalted One: "Let the Exalted One be seated here, Lord, that it may be for my profit and happiness for many a day."

So, friend, the Exalted One sat down upon the seat I had prepared, and so seated he thus spake:

"Soft, indeed, Kassapa, is this your under-robe of rags."

"May the Exalted One deign to accept this under-robe of rags out of compassion for me."

"Then, Kassapa, will you wear my coarse patchwork cast-off robes?"

"I will indeed, Lord, wear the Exalted One's coarse patchwork cast-off robes."

So, friend, I gave the Exalted One my under-robe of rags, and I myself put on the Exalted One's coarse patchwork cast-off robes.

Therefore, friend, if one would say the truth of me, with truth might he say of me that I am a true son of the Exalted One, born of his lips, born of the Norm, begotten by the Norm, a kinsman of the Norm, one who accepted His coarse patchwork cast-off robes.

I, friend, when I so desire, remote from passions can reach and dwell in each of the nine *jhānas* and I have the five supernormal powers.

And I, friend, by the destruction of the *āsavas*, have entered on and abide in that emancipation of mind which is free from the *āsavas*, having realized it by mine own super-knowledge even in this present life.

Wherefore, friend, he who should think that I can conceal the six supernormal powers might just as well think that an elephant, seven or eight cubits high, could be hidden by a bit of palm-leaf.'

S.N. ii. 220.

THE ADMISSION OF WOMEN TO THE ORDER

Now at that time the Exalted One, the Buddha, dwelt among the Sakyas at Kapilavatthu, in the Banyan Park.

Then did Mahā-Pajāpati, the Gotamid, go to where the Exalted One was, and coming there she bowed before the Exalted One and stood at one side. As she thus stood, she said unto the Exalted One: 'Well were it, Lord, if women were permitted to go forth from the home unto the homeless life under the Norm-Discipline set forth by the Tathāgata.'

'Enough, O Gotamid! Long not that women be permitted to go forth from the home unto the homeless life under the Norm-Discipline set forth by the Tathāgata.'

Then a second and yet a third time did Mahā-Pajāpati, the Gotamid, make the same petition and get the same reply from the Exalted One.

Then did Mahā-Pajāpati, the Gotamid, at the thought: 'The Exalted One permits not that women should go forth' . . . sad, sorrowful tearful, and wailing, saluted the Exalted One by the right and went away.

Then the Exalted One, when he had dwelt at Kapilavatthu as long as it pleased Him, set out on a journey towards Vesāli, and wandering on from place to place he came unto Vesāli. And there at Vesāli the Exalted One dwelt in Great Grove, at the Hall of the Peaked Gable.

Now Mahā-Pajāpati, the Gotamid, got her hair cut off, donned saffron robes, and started off with a number of women of the Sakyan clan to Vesāli: and wandering on from place to place, she drew near to Vesāli, to Great Grove and the Hall of the Peaked Gable. And there she took her stand outside the porch, her feet all swollen and dust-begrimed, sad, sorrowful, tearful, and wailing.

Now the venerable Ānanda beheld her so standing, and he said unto her: 'Wherefore, O Gotamid, dost thou stand there outside the porch with feet all swollen and dust-begrimed, sad, sorrowful, weeping, and wailing?'

'O my lord Ānanda, it is because the Exalted One permits not that women go forth from the home unto the homeless life under the Norm-Discipline set forth by the Tathāgata.'

Thereupon the venerable Ānanda went unto the place where the Exalted One was, bowed down before Him and sat down at one side. So seated the venerable Ānanda said unto the Exalted One: 'Lord, here is Mahā-Pajāpati, the Gotamid, standing outside the porch . . . weeping and wailing . . . because women are not permitted by the Exalted One to go forth . . . under the Norm-Discipline set forth by the Tathāgata. Well were it, Lord, if women were permitted so to do!'

'Enough, Ānanda! Long not that women be permitted so to do.'

Then a second and yet a third time did the venerable Ānanda make the same request and get the same reply from the Exalted One.

Then the venerable Ānanda thought: 'The Exalted One permits not that women go forth . . . to the homeless life. . . . How now if by some other method I were to request the Exalted One to grant permission . . . so to do ?' Then the venerable Ānanda said to the Exalted One :

'Lord, are women capable, after going forth from the home unto the homeless life under the Norm-Discipline set forth by the Tathāgata,—are they capable of realizing the Fruit of Stream-winning, of Once-returning, of Never-returning, of Arahantship ?'

'Women are capable . . . of doing so, Ānanda.'

'Then, Lord, if women are capable . . . of so doing, inasmuch as Māha-Pajāpati, the Gotamid, was of great service to the Exalted One,—for she was aunt, nourisher, and milk-giver, on the death of His mother she suckled the Exalted One,—well were it, Lord, if women were permitted to go forth from home unto the homeless life under the Norm-Discipline set forth by the Tathāgata.'

'Well then, Ānanda, if Mahā-Pajāpati, the Gotamid, will undertake to keep Eight Important Rules, let that be reckoned unto her as full ordination. Those rules are these :

A sister, even if she be an hundred years in the robes, shall salute, shall rise up before, shall bow down before, shall perform all duties of respect unto a brother, even if that brother have only just taken the robes. Let this rule never be broken, but be honoured, esteemed, reverenced, and observed as long as life doth last.

Secondly, a sister shall not spend the rainy season in a district where there is no brother residing. Let this rule never be broken, but be honoured, esteemed, reverenced, and observed as long as life doth last.

Thirdly, at the half-month let a sister await two things from the Order of Brethren, namely, the appointing of the Sabbath and the coming of a brother to preach the sermon. Let this rule never be broken. . . .

Fourthly, at the end of keeping the rainy season let a sister, in presence of both Orders, of Brethren and of Sisters, invite inquiry in respect of three things, namely, of things seen, heard, and suspected. Let this rule never be broken. . . .

Fifthly, a sister guilty of serious wrong-doing shall do penance for the half-month to both Orders. Let this rule never be broken. . . .

Sixthly, when a sister has passed two seasons in the practice of the Six Rules she may ask full orders from both Orders. Let this rule never be broken. . . .

Seventhly, a sister shall not in any case abuse or censure a brother. Let this rule never be broken. . . .

Eighthly, henceforth is forbidden the right of a sister to have speech among brethren, but not forbidden is the speaking of brethren unto sisters. Let this rule never be broken, but be honoured, esteemed, reverenced, and observed as long as life doth last.

Now, Ānanda, if Mahā-Pajāpati, the Gotamid, will undertake to keep these Eight Important Rules, let that be reckoned unto her as full ordination.'

Then the venerable Ānanda, having received from the Exalted One these Eight Important Rules, went to Mahā-Pajāpati, the Gotamid [and told her all that the Exalted One had said], and she replied :

'Just as, lord Ānanda, a woman or a man, youthful, of tender age, fond of self-adornment, having washed the head and gotten a wreath of blue lotus or of jasmine or of scented-creeper flowers, should take it with both hands and place it atop of the head,—even so do I, lord Ānanda, take upon me these Eight Important Rules, never to be broken so long as life doth last.'

Thereupon the venerable Ānanda went back to the Exalted One, bowed down before Him, and sat down at one side. So seated, the venerable Ānanda said to the Exalted One: 'Lord, Mahā-Pajāpati, the Gotamid, has undertaken the Eight Important Rules. Fully ordained is the sister of the Exalted One's mother.'

(Then the Master replied :)

'Ānanda, if women had not been permitted to go forth from the home unto the homeless life under the Norm-Discipline set forth by the Tathāgata, then would the righteous life last long, the Good Norm would last, Ānanda, a thousand years. But now, Ānanda, since women have been permitted to go forth from the home unto the homeless life . . . not for long will the righteous life prevail; only for five hundred years, Ānanda, will the Good Norm stand fast.[1]

Just as, Ānanda, whatsoever families have many women and few men are easily molested by robbers and pot-thieves, even so, Ānanda,

[1] After the Master's death, the Order charged Ānanda with this offence, among others, of introducing women to the Order, and so causing its decay.

under whatsoever Norm-Discipline womenfolk get permission to wander forth from the home unto the homeless life, not for long does that righteous life prevail.

Just as, Ānanda, when the blight called mildew falls upon a blooming paddy-field, that paddy-field does not last for long, even so, Ānanda, under whatsoever Norm-Discipline womenfolk get permission to wander forth from the home unto the homeless life, not for long does that righteous life prevail.

Just as, Ānanda, when the blight called red-rust falls upon a blooming field of sugar-cane, that field of sugar-cane does not last long,—even so, Ānanda, under whatsoever Norm-Discipline . . . that righteous life does not long prevail.

Now just as, Ānanda, a man should cautiously build an embankment to a great waterwork, to prevent the water from flowing out,—even so, Ānanda, have I cautiously proclaimed these Eight Important Rules, not to be broken as long as life shall last.'

Vinaya, ii. x.

WHY THE GOOD NORM WILL NOT ENDURE

Thus have I heard. Once the Exalted One was staying at Kimbili in Bamboo Grove. Then the brother Kimbila came to the Exalted One, sat down, and said:

'What, Lord, is the reason, what is the cause why, when the Tathāgata has finally passed away, the Good Norm lasts not for long?'

'With regard to this, Kimbila, when the Tathāgata has finally passed away, the brethren, the sisters, the lay-brethren and lay-sisters dwell regardless of the Master, and disobedient to him, regardless of the Norm do they dwell and disobedient to the Norm, regardless of the Order do they dwell and disobedient to the Order: they dwell regardless of the Training and pay no attention to it, and so also with regard to concentration of mind, earnestness, and friendly feeling.

That, brethren, is the reason, that is the cause why, after the final passing away of the Tathāgata the Good Norm does not last for long.'

Ang. Nik. iv. 84.

IN TIME OF SICKNESS

THE INCOMPARABLE PHYSICIAN

Thus spake the Exalted One, thus spake the Arahant (as I have heard):

'Brethren, I am a brāhmin given to begging, my hands are ever pure, I am wearing my last body, Incomparable Physician and Surgeon am I.

Ye are mine own true sons, brethren, born of my mouth,[1] born of the Norm, heirs of the Norm, not heirs of worldly things.'

Iti-vuttaka, § 100.

TEND THE SICK

Now at that time a certain brother was suffering from dysentery and lay where he had fallen down in his own excrements.

And the Exalted One was going His rounds of the lodgings, with the venerable Ānanda in attendance, and came to the lodging of that brother.

Now the Exalted One saw that brother lying where he had fallen in his own excrements, and seeing him He went towards him, came to him, and said: 'Brother, what ails you?'

'I have dysentery, Lord.'

[1] Referring to the claim of brāhmins to have been born of Brahmā's mouth.

'But is there anyone taking care of you, brother ?'

'No, Lord.'

'Why is it, brother, that the brethren do not take care of you ?'

'I am useless to the brethren, Lord: therefore the brethren do not care for me.'

Then the Exalted One said to the venerable Ānanda: 'Go you, Ānanda, and fetch water. We will wash this brother.'

'Yes, Lord,' replied the venerable Ānanda to the Exalted One. When he had fetched the water, the Exalted One poured it out, while the venerable Ānanda washed that brother all over. Then the Exalted One taking him by the head and the venerable Ānanda taking him by the feet, together they laid him on the bed.

Then the Exalted One, in this connexion and on this occasion, gathered the Order of Brethren together, and questioned the brethren, saying:

'Brethren, is there in such and such a lodging a brother who is sick ?'

'There is, Lord.'

'And what ails that brother ?'

'Lord, that brother has dysentery.'

'But, brethren, is there anyone taking care of him ?'

'No, Lord.'

'Why not ? Why do not the brethren take care of him ?'

'That brother is useless to the brethren, Lord. That is why the brethren do not take care of him.'

'Brethren, ye have no mother and no father to

take care of you. If ye will not take care of each other, who else, I ask, will do so? *Brethren, he who would wait on me, let him wait on the sick.*

If he have a teacher, let his teacher take care of him so long as he is alive, and wait for his recovery. If he have a tutor or a lodger, a disciple or a fellow-lodger or a fellow-disciple, such should take care of him and await his recovery. If no one take care of him, it shall be reckoned an offence.'

Vinaya. Mahāvagga, viii. § 26.

VISITING THE SICK

Thus have I heard: Once the Exalted One was staying near Rājagaha in Great Grove, at the Squirrels' Feeding-ground.

On that occasion the venerable Vakkali was staying in the Potter's shed, being sick, afflicted, stricken with a sore disease.

Now the venerable Vakkali called to his attendants, saying: 'Come hither, friends! Go ye to the Exalted One, and, in my name worshipping at the feet of the Exalted One, say unto Him: "Lord, the brother Vakkali is sick, afflicted, stricken with a sore disease. He worships at the feet of the Exalted One." And thus do ye say: "Well were it, Lord, if the Exalted One would visit brother Vakkali, out of compassion for him."'

The Exalted One consented by His silence. Thereupon the Exalted One robed Himself, and, taking bowl and robe, went to visit the venerable Vakkali.

Now the venerable Vakkali saw the Exalted One coming, while yet He was far off, and on seeing Him he stirred upon his bed.

Then said the Exalted One to the venerable Vakkali: 'Enough, Vakkali! Stir not on your bed! There are these seats made ready. I will sit there.' And He sat down on a seat made ready.

So the Exalted One sat down and said to the venerable Vakkali:

'Well, Vakkali, I hope you are bearing up. I hope you are enduring. Do your pains abate and not increase? Are there signs of their abating and not increasing?'

'No, Lord, I am not bearing up. I am not enduring. Strong pains come upon me. They do not abate. There is no sign of their abating, but of their increasing.'

'Have you any doubt, Vakkali? Have you any remorse?'

'Indeed, Lord, I have no little doubt. I have no little remorse.'

'Have you not anything, Vakkali, wherein to reproach yourself as to morals?'

'Nay, Lord, there is nothing wherein I reproach myself as to morals.'

'Then, Vakkali, if that is so, you must have some worry, you must have something you regret.'

'For a long time, Lord, I have been longing to set eyes on the Exalted One, but I had not strength enough in this body to come to see the Exalted One.'

'Hush, Vakkali! What is there in seeing this vile body of mine? *He who seeth the Norm, he seeth me : he who seeth me*, Vakkali, *seeth the Norm.* Verily, seeing the Norm, Vakkali, one sees me : seeing me, one sees the Norm.'

(*And when the Master had discoursed on the impermanence of all things, He went away.*)

S.N. iii. 120.

PATIENT AND NURSE [1]

'There are five characteristics, brethren, possessed of which a sick man is hard to nurse.

He will not take remedies, or he observes no moderation in taking remedies, or he does not follow the drugs prescribed, does not disclose the real nature of his ailment to the nurse who desires his welfare, (nor does he tell him) whether his sickness wanes or waxes or stands still : lastly, when he is impatient of his bodily feelings that arise, painful, sharp, cutting, bitter, grievous, unpleasant, life-destroying.

Such, brethren, are the five characteristics possessed of which a sick man is hard to nurse.

And the five characteristics (which make him easy to nurse) are the opposites of these.

There are five characteristics, brethren, possessed of which one is of no use as a nurse. One is incapable of prescribing medicine ; one does not know the proper remedies, what is good and what is bad ; one administers what is unfit and does not administer what is fit : one nurses the patient out of greed and not out of charity : one is squeamish about the removal of excrements,

[1] *Vinaya Piṭaka. Mahāvagga*, viii. § 26.

saliva, or vomit : one is incapable of teaching the patient from time to time with pious talk, incapable of cheering him, of stirring him, and comforting him.

Such, brethren, are the five characteristics possessed of which one is of no use as a nurse.

And the five characteristics (which make one a good nurse) are the opposites of these.'

TYPES OF SICK MEN[1]

There are these three sorts of sick men, brethren, to be found in the world. What three ?

Herein, brethren, a sick man, whether he obtain proper diet or not, whether he obtain proper medicines or not, whether he obtain proper nursing or not, does not recover from his sickness.

Herein, brethren, a sick man, whether he obtain all these things or not, nevertheless recovers from his sickness.

Herein, brethren, a sick man, though he receive not any of these things, recovers from his sickness.

In like manner, brethren, there are three sorts of men to be found in the world who may be compared to these three sorts of sick men. What are the three ?

Herein, brethren, one gets the chance or does not get the chance to see the Tathāgata ; gets or does not get the chance of hearing the Norm-Discipline proclaimed by the Tathāgata : does not enter upon the way of life that is perfect in good deeds.

Herein, brethren, one may or may not get the

[1] *Anguttara Nikāya*, i. 120.

chance of seeing the Tathāgata ; may or may not get the chance of hearing the Norm-Discipline proclaimed by the Tathāgata ; but does (nevertheless) enter upon the way of life that is perfect in good deeds.

Herein, brethren, one gets the chance, does not fail to get the chance of seeing the Tathāgata ; gets the chance, does not fail to get the chance of hearing the Norm-Discipline proclaimed by the Tathāgata ; and does enter on the way of life that is perfect in good deeds.

. . . Now, brethren, it is on account of this last that the preaching of the Norm is enjoined. It is on this account that the Norm should be preached to others.

COMFORTABLE WORDS

Thus have I heard : The Exalted One was once staying among the Bhaggi, at Crocodile-Haunt in Bhesakala Grove in the Deer-Park. Then the housefather Nakulapitar came to the Exalted One, saluted Him, and sat down at one side.

As he sat there, the housefather Nakulapitar addressed the Exalted One, saying : 'Master, I am a broken-down old man, aged, far-gone in years, I have reached life's end, I am sick and always ailing. Moreover, Master, I am one to whom rarely comes the sight of the Exalted One and the worshipful brethren. Let the Exalted One cheer and comfort me, so that it be a profit and a blessing unto me for many a long day.'

'True it is, true it is, housefather, that your

body is weak and cumbered! For one carrying this body about, housefather, to claim but a moment's health would be sheer foolishness. Wherefore, housefather, thus should you train yourself: "Though my body is sick, my mind shall not be sick." Thus, housefather, must you train yourself.'

Then Nakulapitar, the housefather, welcomed and gladly heard the words of the Exalted One, and rising from his seat he saluted the Exalted One by the right, and departed.

S.N. iii. **1.**

COMFORT THE SICK

Once the Exalted One was staying among the Sakyans at Kapilavatthu, in Figtree Park.

Then on that occasion a number of brethren were busied with making robes for the Exalted One, 'for,' said they, 'when the three months are over, the Exalted One, His robes being complete, will go forth on His rounds.'

Now Mahānāma, the Sakyan, heard it said, 'A number of brethren are busied with making robes,' and so forth . . . and he went to the Exalted One, saluted Him, and sat down at one side. So seated, Mahānāma, the Sakyan, said:

'I hear it said, Lord, that a number of the brethren are busied with making robes for the Exalted One, saying, "When the robes are complete, at the end of the three months, the Exalted One will go forth on His rounds." Now, Lord, we have never heard from the Exalted One's own lips how a discreet layman who is sick, in pain, grievously afflicted, should be cheered by another discreet lay-brother.'

'A discreet lay-brother, Mahānāma, who is sick . . . should be cheered by another discreet lay-brother with the Four Comfortable Assurances, thus: "He it is, the Exalted One, the Arahant, Buddha Supreme" . . . and so forth: and "Take comfort, good sir, in the Norm, and in the Order of Brethren: likewise in the virtues dear to the Ariyans, kept unbroken and unsoiled . . . which tend to balance of mind."

Then, Mahānāma, when a discreet lay-brother who is sick has thus been cheered with the Four Comfortable Assurances by another lay-brother, such should be the words of that other:—

Suppose the sick man should have a longing for his parents. Then if the sick man say, "I have a longing for my parents," the other should reply, "My dear good man, you are subject to death. Whether you have a longing for your parents or not, you will die. 'Twere just as well for you to abandon all longing for your parents."

And suppose the sick man say, "That longing for parents is now abandoned," then the other should say, "Yet, my good sir, you still have a longing for your children. As you must die in any case, 'twere just as well for you to abandon longing for your children."

And so also should he speak in respect of the five pleasures of sense. Suppose the sick man say, "I have a longing for the five pleasures of sense," the other should say, "My friend, heavenly delights are more excellent than the five pleasures of sense, and more choice. 'Twere well for you to remove your mind from human joys and fix it on the joys of the Four Great Deva Kings."

Again, if the sick man say, "My mind is so fixed," let the other say, "More excellent than those of the Four Great Deva Kings and more choice are the joys of the Suite of the Thirty-three . . . of the Yama Devas, of the Devas of Delight, of the Creative Devas, of the Devas who rejoice in the work of other Devas (all of whom are Worldly Devas [1]) . . . better to fix your mind on the Brahma World." And then if the sick man's mind is so fixed, let the other say:

"My good sir, even the Brahma World is impermanent, not lasting, subject to personality. Well for you, dear sir, if you raise your mind above the Brahma World and concentrate on cessation from the personal."

And if the sick man says he has done so, then I declare, Mahānāma, that there is no difference between the lay-brother who can thus aver and the disciple whose mind is freed from the *āsavas*: that is to say, so far as emancipation goes.' [2]

S.N. v. 408.

IN PRAISE OF THE MASTER

Once the Exalted One was staying near Sāvatthī, at Jeta Grove, in Anāthapindika's Park.

Now at that time the rājah of Kosala, Pasenadi,

[1] All these *devas* are termed *Bhummika* or terrestrial, as opposed to those of the subjective world of Brahmā.

[2] Lit. 'freedom by being freed.' Both Arahants and such laymen are freed from any substratum of rebirth, but apparently their state after the final life on earth is one of degree.

had just returned from a sham-fight, in which he was victorious, having carried out his object. And on reaching the Park he turned in that way. So far as the cart-road went he rode in his chariot, and then got down and went on foot through the Park.

On that occasion a number of the brethren were walking up and down in the open air. Then Pasenadi, the rājah of Kosala, went up to those brethren and thus accosted them: 'Reverend sirs, where now is the Exalted One staying, that Arahant, Buddha Supreme: for I long to behold Him?'

'Yonder, mahārājah, is His lodging, and the door is shut. Do you go up quietly, without nervousness, enter the verandah, cough, and rattle the door-bar. The Exalted One will open the door to you.'

So Pasenadi, the rājah of Kosala, went up to the lodging as he was told, coughed, and rattled the door-bar. And the Exalted One opened the door.

Then Pasenadi entered the lodging, fell with his head at the feet of the Exalted One, kissed His feet and stroked them with his hands, and announced his name, saying, 'Lord, I am Pasenadi, the rājah of Kosala: Pasenadi, the rājah of Kosala am I.'

'But, mahārājah, seeing what significance therein do you show me this profound humility and pay such affectionate obeisance to this body?'

'To show my gratitude, Lord, to show my thankfulness to the Exalted One do I show this profound humility, do I manifest this affectionate obeisance. For the Exalted One, Lord, is one who walketh for the profit of many folk, He is one who setteth many folk in the Ariyan method, which is in conformity with whatsoever is lovely and goodly. That is why, Lord, I show my reverence in this way.

Then again, Lord, the Exalted One is virtuous, hath the Buddha-virtues, the Ariyan, the goodly virtues, He is possessed of good virtues. That is another reason for this worship of mine.

And again, Lord, the Exalted One hath been a forest-dweller for many a day. He is a haunter of forest-solitudes, resorts to the solitary lodging of the forest. That is another reason for my worship.

And yet again, Lord, the Exalted One is well content with whatever offerings of robes or food, or lodging, medicines, requisites, and extra allowances He may receive. That is a further reason for my worship.

And He is worthy of respect, worthy of honour, worthy of offerings, of salutations with lifted hands, He is a field of merit unsurpassed for the world. That is another reason for this my worship.'

(*His majesty then recites all the characteristics of the Arahant, given elsewhere, in detail, concluding :*)

'Well now, Lord, I am going. I am a busy man. I have much to do.'

'Very well, mahārājah. Do what seems good to you,' said the Master.

So Pasenadi, the rājah of Kosala, rose up from his seat, saluted the Exalted One by the right hand, and went away.

Ang. Nik. v. 66–9.

CHARITY

GIFTS

'There are these two sorts of gifts, brethren: the gift of material things and the gift of the Norm. Of these two gifts, the gift of the Norm is pre-eminent.

There are two disbursements: that of things material and the disbursement of the Norm. Of these two, the disbursement of the Norm is pre-eminent.

There are two favours: that of things material and the favour of the Norm. Of these two favours, that of the Norm is pre-eminent.

There are two sacrifices: that of material things and that of the Norm. Of these two, the sacrifice of the Norm is pre-eminent.'

Such was the essence of the words of the Exalted One.

Iti-vuttaka, § 100.

The mighty sea, unmeasured mighty lake,
The fearsome home of multitudes of pearls—
As rivers, serving countless hosts of men,
Flow widely forth and to that ocean come:—

Just so, on him that giveth food, drink, clothes,
Who bed and seat and coverlet provides,
Torrents of merit flood that mortal wise,
As rivers, bearing water, reach the main.

S.N. v. 400.

CHARITY

GIFTS COMPARED

'Master Gotama, I am a giver of gifts, a lord of almsgiving: affable am I and a proper man to ask a boon of. I pursue wealth in a lawful way, and having done so I give freely of my wealth thus lawfully obtained,—I give alms to one, two, three, five, seven, ten, twenty, even up to a hundred,—nay to more than that. (Tell me this) Master Gotama, by so giving, by making such sacrifices, do I beget any merit?'

'Surely, young man, by so giving, by making such sacrifices . . . you do beget much merit! He who pursues wealth in a lawful way, and having done so gives freely of his wealth thus lawfully obtained,—by so giving, by making such sacrifices, he begets much merit.'

Sutta Nipāta, Māghasutta.

(*A brāhmin asks the Master about sacrifices.*)

'But, Master Gotama, is there any other sacrifice, not so hard and not so troublesome as this threefold sacrifice with its sixteen attributes (aforesaid), but bearing greater fruit and profit?'

'Yes, brāhmin, there is indeed another sacrifice, not so hard and not so troublesome (as yours), but bearing greater fruit and profit.'

'Pray, Master Gotama, what is that?'

'Whosoever, brāhmin, with devout heart goes for refuge to the Buddha, to the Norm, and to the Order of Brethren,—he makes a sacrifice . . . that bears greater fruit and profit.'

'But, Master Gotama, is there any other sacrifice (of such a sort)?'

'Yes, brāhmin, there is. . . . Whosoever with devout heart takes upon him the Charges, to wit: abstention from taking life, from taking what is not given, from wrong conduct in respect of lusts, from falsehood, from fermented liquor, from distilled liquor that gives rise to slothfulness,—that, brāhmin, is a sacrifice, not so hard and not so troublesome (as yours), but bearing greater fruit and profit.'

D.N. i. 145.

THE FIVE GREAT GIFTS

(When one has gone for refuge to the Three Refuges, the Buddha, the Norm, and the Order of Brethren. . . .)

'These five gifts, brethren, are great gifts, supreme gifts, long lasting, traditional, of ancient days: they were unconfounded before, they are not confounded now, nor shall be hereafter confounded with other things: they are gifts not scorned by recluses and brāhmins who are shrewd. What are the five?

Herein, brethren, the Ariyan disciple abandons taking life, is opposed to taking life. So opposed to it, brethren, the Ariyan disciple grants security to all beings in fullest measure, he grants them freedom from hate and injury. So granting to the full he is himself a sharer in such security, in such freedom from hate and injury. That, brethren, is the first of the five great gifts that are supreme, long lasting, traditional . . . not scorned by recluses and brāhmins who are shrewd. Now this, brethren, is (with the going to the Three

Refuges) the fourth thing that has meritorious results, goodly results, the support of bliss, heavenly, resulting in happiness, leading heavenwards, bringing fulfilment of what is desired, dear, delightful, profitable, and bringing happiness.

Secondly, brethren, the Ariyan disciple abandons taking what is not given, abandons wrong conduct in respect of sense-desires, abandons falsehood, abandons indulgence in liquors fermented or distilled that gives rise to neglect. Abandoning all these, brethren, he grants security to all beings in fullest measure : he grants freedom from hate and injury. So doing to the full, he is himself a sharer in such security, in such freedom from hate and injury. This, brethren, is the fifth of the five great gifts.'

Ang. Nik. iv. 246.

EARLY GIFTS TO THE ORDER

Anāthapindika, the Feeder of the Poor

Now at that time the housefather Anāthapindika was husband to the sister of the Rājagaha millionaire, and he had gone to Rājagaha on some business or other. And on that occasion the Order of Brethren, led by the Buddha, had been invited for the morrow's meal by the Rājagaha millionaire, who was giving orders to his slaves and workmen, saying : 'Now, men, be up in good time to-morrow and make rice-gruel, boil rice, make curries and sweetmeats.'

Then, Anāthapindika, the housefather, thus thought : 'In former times, when I came here, this housefather used to put aside whatever he was doing and greet me with friendly talk. But now he seems quite beside himself, ordering his slaves and workmen about, saying: "Now, men, be up early to-morrow," and so on. . . . What can be the cause of this? Is he, I wonder, taking a wife or giving a wife in marriage, or preparing for a great sacrifice, or has he invited Seniya Bimbisāra, the Magadhan, with all his court, for to-morrow's meal?'

But when the Rājagaha millionaire had given his orders to his slaves and workmen, he went up to the housefather Anāthapindika and held him in friendly talk and sat down beside him. So seated, the housefather repeated to the millionaire the thoughts that had occurred to him:

'No, housefather,' replied he, 'neither am I taking a wife nor giving one in marriage, nor have I invited the Seniyan Bimbisāra, the Magadhan, with all his court for to-morrow's meal. But I have indeed prepared a great sacrifice, for I have invited the Order of Brethren, led by the Buddha, for to-morrow's meal.'

'What! "The Buddha," said you?'

'Yes. I said "the Buddha."'

(And in amazement Anāthapindika repeated twice again his question, and got the same reply.)

'Hard indeed to find in the world is even the sound of the word "Buddha," "the Buddha!" Is it possible, housefather, at this very moment, for me to go to see that Exalted One, that Arahant, who is a Perfectly Enlightened One?'

'Just now, housefather, is not the proper time to go to see the Exalted One, but to-morrow in good time you shall go to see Him.'

Well, Anāthapindika, the housefather, that night lay down to rest with his mind so much occupied with those words: 'To-morrow, then, in good time, you shall go to see Him, the Exalted One, the Arahant who is a Perfectly Enlightened One,' that thrice did he get up, thinking it was the dawn.

Then, on the third occasion, the housefather Anāthapindika went towards the gate of Cool-Grove (where the Master was lodging), and beings not human opened the city gate for him. But as he left the city, the light vanished, darkness arose, and fear and trembling came upon him, so that every hair of his body stood on end, and he was fain to go back again. Then the Yaksha Sīvaka, though unseen, made a voice sound [which said]:

'A hundred elephants, a hundred steeds,
A hundred mules yoked to a hundred cars,
A hundred thousand maids with jewels decked,
One quarter of a quarter are not worth
Of one long stride (that's made towards the Goal).

Go on, housefather! Go on, housefather! Better for you to go on and not go back!'

Then the darkness vanished from around Anāthapindika and a light shone forth, so that his fear and trembling, whereby every hair on his body stood on end, were quelled. (And this happened twice more in the same way.)

So Anāthapindika, the housefather, came to Cool-Grove. Now at that time the Exalted One, having risen early, was walking up and down in the open air. And the Exalted One saw Anāthapindika, the housefather, while he was yet some way off. So the Exalted One left His walking-place and sat down on a seat that was ready for Him. So seated He called to Anāthapindika, the housefather, and said to him: 'Come, Sudatta!'

Then Anāthapindika said to himself: 'The Exalted One calls me by my name!' So, delighted and elated thereat, he approached the Exalted One, fell at His feet, saying: 'Hath my Lord, the Exalted One, rested happily?' And the Master replied:

Happy he ever rests, the brāhmana set free,
Whom lusts defile not, who is cooled and loosed from bonds,
Who hath all barriers burst, by taming his heart's pain.
Happy the calm one rests, reaching the Peace of Mind.

Then did the Exalted One discourse unto Anāthapindika, the housefather, with talk that led gradually on, thus: of charity and righteousness and the heaven-world; of the danger, uselessness, and defilement of the passions, and of the profit of giving up the world. And when the Exalted One saw that the heart of Anāthapindika, the housefather, was made pliable and soft and without obstruction, uplifted and calmed, then did He set forth the Norm teaching of the Buddhas, proclaimed most excellent, that is, suffering, the arising of suffering, the ceasing of suffering, and the way leading to the ceasing of suffering.

Then, just as a clean cloth that is freed from stains can readily take on the dye, even so in Anāthapindika, the housefather, as he sat there, arose the pure and spotless eye that sees the Norm, (the sight) that whatsoever is of nature to arise, all that is of nature to cease again.

Then did Anāthapindika, the housefather, behold, reach, grasp, and plunge into the Norm, so that he passed beyond doubt, left all questioning of this and that, reached confidence, and was dependent on no other in his knowledge of the Master's Message, and he said to the Exalted One: 'Excellent, O Lord! Excellent, O Lord! Even as one raises what is overthrown, or shows forth what is hidden, or points the way to him that wandereth, or holds up a light in the darkness that they who have eyes may see objects,—even so in divers ways hath the Norm been set forth by the Exalted One: so that I myself, O Lord, do go for refuge to the Exalted One, to the Norm, and to the Order of Brethren. May the Exalted One accept me as a disciple, that hath taken refuge in Him, from this day until the end of life. And may the Exalted One accept from me to-morrow's meal, along with the Order of Brethren.'

And the Exalted One accepted by His silence.

Then Anāthapindika, the housefather, seeing the acceptance of the Exalted One, rose from his seat, bowed before Him, saluted Him by the right, and went away.

Now the Rājagaha millionaire came to hear that the Order of Brethren, led by the Buddha, was bidden to the next day's meal by Anāthapindika, the housefather. And he said to him: 'I hear, housefather, that the Order, led by the Buddha, has been bidden by you to the morrow's meal. Now you are a visitor here (in Rājagaha), so I offer you, housefather, the means for providing food for the Order, led by the Buddha.'

'Not a word, housefather! I myself have the means for providing food for them.'

Then also the chief citizen of Rājagaha came to hear the news, and he came to Anāthapindika and made the same offer; and in like manner came the Seniyan Bimbisāra (rājah) of Magadha, and made the offer of help, but Anāthapindika rejected them.

Then Anāthapindika, the housefather, when that night was past, prepared at the house of the Rājagaha millionaire choice food, both hard and soft, and sent a message to the Exalted One saying: 'It is time, Lord! Ready is the meal!'

So the Exalted One, robing Himself at early dawn, took bowl and robe, and started off to the house of the Rājagaha millionaire, and reaching it sat down on a seat prepared for Him, along with the Order of Brethren.

Then Anāthapindika, the housefather, with his own hands served and satisfied the Order, led by the Buddha, with choice food, both hard and soft: and when they had finished eating and had withdrawn their hands from the bowls, he sat down at one side, and said to the Exalted One: 'May the Exalted One, I beg, consent to spend the rainy season at Sāvatthī, along with the Order of Brethren?'

And the Exalted One replied: 'The Tathāgatas, housefather, delight in solitude.'

'I see, Exalted One! I see, O Happy One!'

Then the Exalted One, when He had taught, stirred, roused, and delighted Anāthapindika, the housefather, with pious talk, rose up and went away.

Now at that time, Anāthapindika, the housefather, had many friends and acquaintances and ever a welcome word for them. So when he had finished his business at Rājagaha he departed for Sāvatthī. And on the way he gave orders to the people, saying: 'Do you, good people, prepare rest-houses, get ready lodgings, get ready offerings (of food), for a Buddha has arisen in the world, and that Exalted One has been bidden by me, and He will pass along this road!'

So the people, thus urged by Anāthapindika, the housefather, did so.

Now when Anāthapindika reached Sāvatthī, he surveyed Sāvatthī all about, thinking: 'Now where can the Exalted One dwell so that He will not be too far from a village and not too near: in a place convenient for coming and going, easy of approach for folk who wish to see Him: not too much frequented by day and free from noise and din at night: a place sheltered from the wind, remote from the haunts of men and suitable for solitude?'

Then Anāthapindika, the housefather, observed that the park of Prince Jeta had all these qualities . . . that it was not too near and not too far, and so on. . . . So he went to Prince Jeta and said: 'Young master, give me, I beg, your park to make a residence therein.'

'No, housefather, it is not for sale,' said the Prince, 'not even if you spread the purchase-money all over it.'

'It is a bargain, young master!' said the housefather.

'No, no! 'tis not a bargain, housefather.'

So they consulted the councillors whether the thing was to be taken as a bargain or not. And the councillors decided thus: 'In so far as by you, young master, a price was named, the matter of the park is a bargain.'

So the housefather Anāthapindika had the gold brought in carts, and he caused to be spread therewith the whole of Jeta Grove. But the gold that was brought at one time did not suffice to cover one small spot close by the entrance. So Anāthapindika despatched men, saying: 'Go, my men, fetch more gold and cover up this spot.'

Then thought Prince Jeta: 'This can be no ordinary matter, in that the housefather is lavishing so much gold.' So he said to him: 'Stay, housefather! Cover not that space. Give me that space. Let it be my gift.'

Then thought the housefather: 'This Jeta Prince is a man of great eminence and widespread fame. Of great influence would be such a distinguished man's belief in the Norm-Discipline.' So he gave up that space to Prince Jeta. And Prince Jeta built a gate-house there.

Then did Anāthapindika, the housefather, build lodgings, build cells, storerooms, service-halls, rooms for fires, and conveniences, lavatories, walking-places, wells and well-houses, bathrooms and dressing-rooms, and tanks and pavilions did he build therein.

Vinaya, ii, 6, 4.

[The first part is repeated at *S. N.* i. 211.]

HAPPINESS IN THE WORLD

PRECEPT

THEN did Vipassi, the Exalted One, the Arahant, a Fully Enlightened One, thus recite an obligation [1]:

Long-suff'rance is the best austerity:
Nibbāna, say the Awakened Ones, is best.

No Wanderer is he who others harms:
Who wrongs another,—he is no Recluse.

REFRAIN THYSELF FROM EVERY EVIL DEED:
STABLISH THYSELF IN GOOD: CLEANSE THINE OWN THOUGHTS:
THIS IS THE MESSAGE OF THE AWAKENED ONES,[2]

Revile not, harm not, live by Rule restrained:
Of food take little: sleep and sit alone:
In meditation keep thy thoughts controlled,—
This is the message of the Awakened Ones.

D.N. ii. 49.; *Dhammapada*, 183–5.

1 *Pātimokkha*, precept, obligation; afterwards the fortnightly confession of faults among the brethren of the Order.

2 Probably the most famous *gāthā* in the Canon (*sabba-pāpass' ākaranaṃ*, etc.). It is here ascribed by the Buddha to Vipassi, a former Buddha.

THE WAY TO HEAVEN

Faith, Modesty, and Righteous Gifts—
These things do goodly men pursue.
This is the Path that leadeth heavenward:
By this way goes one to the Deva-world.

Ang. Nik. iv. 236.

ADVICE TO A LAYMAN

(*The young householder Sigāla, after worshipping the six regions of space, asks for Ariyan Doctrine.*)

The Exalted One said:

'Now, young master, since the Four Vices of Action have been put away by the Ariyan disciple, and since he does no evil deed through the Four Motives for evil deeds, and since he does not follow the Six Openings that swallow up wealth, —he is thus one who has forsaken fourteen evil ways: *he* is the one who covers the six regions of space: he is the one equipped for the conquest of the two worlds: he is the one for whom both this world and the world beyond are assured. When body breaks up, after death he is reborn in the blissful return, the happy world.

Now what are those Four Vices of Action which he has put away?

They are these, young master:

The Vice of taking the life of creatures; of taking what is not given; of wrong practice in (sexual) acts of passion; and falsehood. These four.'

Thus spake the Exalted One. When the Happy

One had thus spoken, the Master added this further:

'Who taketh life, who steals, who telleth lies,
Who fouls another's wife,—him wise men blame.

And what are the Four Motives of Evil-doing, free from which he does no evil deed?

A man does evil deeds by going on the wrong path through desire, through hatred, through delusion, and through fear. But since the Ariyan disciple does not go on these four wrong paths, he does no evil deed through these Four Motives of Evil-doing.'

Thus spake the Exalted One. When the Happy One had thus spoken, the Master added this further:

'Who oversteps the Norm
Through lust or hate, stupidity or fear,
His good name wanes,
As in the dark fortnight waneth the moon.

Who steps not o'er the Norm
Through lust or hate, stupidity or fear,
His fame doth wax,
As in the bright fortnight waxeth the moon.

And what are the Six Openings for swallowing up wealth, which he follows not?

Young master, to be given to drinking fermented liquor and distilled liquor, which gives rise to sloth: to be given to roaming the streets at unseasonable hours: to frequent festivals: to practise gambling, which gives rise to sloth: to have evil companions: to be given to idling: such are the Six Openings which swallow up wealth.

(*a*) Now, young master, there are these six disadvantages of indulging in intoxicants: loss of wealth, increase of quarrelling, liability to sickness, loss of good name, immodest acts, weakening of brain-power. These six.

(*b*) Now, young master, there are these six disadvantages of roaming the streets at unseasonable hours: One is off one's guard and unprotected, one's wife and children are unprotected, one's property likewise: one is suspected of evil doings: false rumours about one have weight: one is exposed to many states of ill. These are the six.

(*c*) Now, young master, there are these six disadvantages of frequenting festivals. (One keeps thinking) "Where is the dancing? Where is the singing? Where is the music? Where is the recital? Where is the tambour-playing? Where are the tam-tams?" These are the six.

(*d*) Now, young master, there are these six disadvantages of being given to gambling: If one wins, he wins a foe. If he lose, he has to lament his loss. Gone is his visible means of subsistence. He goes to the Mote-Hall, but his word has no weight there. Friends and ministers of state treat him with contempt. He is not sought after by those who give and take in marriage: for they say "A gambler is not competent to support a wife." Such are the six disadvantages of being given to gambling.

(*e*) Now, young master, there are these six

disadvantages of bad companions. All the rogues, drunkards, topers, cheats, frauds, and rowdies are his friends and boon companions. These are the six.

(*f*) Now, young master, there are these six disadvantages of idling. (The idler says) "It's too cold," and does no work: or "It's too hot," and does no work: or "It's too early," and does no work: or "It's too late," and does no work: or "I'm too hungry," and does no work: or "I'm too full," and does no work. So, as he lives with all these excuses about work, the wealth that has not yet come to him does not arise, and the wealth that has come goes to destruction.'

Thus spake the Exalted One.

D.N. iii. 181.

NOT OUTWARD WASHINGS

1

Once the Exalted One was staying near Vesāli at Great Grove in the house with the peaked gable.

Then Nandaka, a dignitary of the Licchavi, came to the Exalted One, saluted Him, and sat down at one side. As he thus sat the Exalted One said this to Nandaka, the dignitary of the Licchavi:

'The Ariyan disciple, Nandaka, possessed of four things, is a Stream-winner, saved from the Downfall, assured, bound for enlightenment. What four?

Herein, Nandaka, the Ariyan disciple is possessed of certain faith, thus: "He it is, the Exalted One, the Arahant, Buddha supreme, [and so forth] . . . is possessed of certain faith in the Norm, and in the Order of Brethren. He is possessed of the virtues beloved by the Ariyans and keeps them unbroken . . . so that they conduce to balance of mind. These are the four, Nandaka.

Moreover, endowed with these four qualities, an Ariyan disciple is blessed with long life both heavenly and human, blessed with beauty, blessed with happiness, blessed with good name, and blessed with sovereignty, both human and divine.

This, Nandaka, I do know, not by hearsay from any recluse or brāhmin, but I have ascertained it for myself, seen it for myself, understood it for myself, and so do I tell it you.'

Just then someone came up to Nandaka, the dignitary of the Licchavi, and said to him, 'It is time for your bath, my lord.'

'Enough of that, good fellow!' said Nandaka. 'Enough of this outward washing! This inner washing shall be enough for me, to wit, this faith in the Exalted One.'

S.N. v. 389.

2

Once the Exalted One was dwelling at Sāvatthī. And the brāhmin Sangarava also dwelt there. Now he was a cleanser by water, and practised cleansing by water. Night and day he abode given to the habit of going down to bathe.

Now the venerable Ānanda, robing himself at an early hour and taking outer robe and bowl, went forth to Sāvatthī to beg. And when he had gone his rounds in Sāvatthī and had eaten his meal upon his return, he went to the Exalted One, saluted Him, and sat down at one side. So seated, the venerable Ānanda said:

'Lord, there is here a brāhmin, one Sangarava dwelling at Sāvatthī, a cleanser by water, one who practises cleansing by water. Night and day does he abide given to the habit of going down to bathe. Well were it, Lord, if the Exalted One would pay a visit to the brāhmin Sangarava, out of compassion for him.'

And the Exalted One consented by His silence.

So next day at an early hour the Exalted One robed Himself, and taking outer robe and bowl went to the dwelling of the brāhmin Sangarava, and when He got there He sat down on a seat made ready.

Then the brāhmin Sangarava came to the Exalted One and greeted Him, and after the exchange of mutual courtesies sat down at one side.

As he thus sat the Exalted One said this to the brāhmin Sangarava: 'Is it true, brāhmin, as they say, that thou art a cleanser by water, that thou dost practise cleansing by water, abiding night and day given to the habit of going down to bathe?'

'True it is, Master Gotama.'

'Now, brāhmin, seeking what profit dost thou so practise the habit of going down to bathe, and so forth?'

'It is in this way, Master Gotama. Whatsoever evil I do by day, I get it washed away that very evening by my bathing. Whatsoever evil I do by night I get it washed away next morning by my bathing. That is the profit I am looking for in being a cleanser by water and so forth.'

Then said the Exalted One:

The Norm it is the Pool, the brāhmin is the bathing ghāt.
'Tis clear and undefiled, by good men unto good men praised.
Hither when they have come to bathe, the masters of the lore
Are cleansed in every limb, and pass unto the Further Shore.

Whereupon the brāhmin Sangarava said to the Exalted One: 'Excellent it is, Master Gotama! . . . May the Master Gotama accept me as His follower, from this day forth so long as life doth last, as one who has taken refuge in Him.'

S.N. i. 183.

HONOUR OLD AGE

Now at that time the disciples of the Band of Six had gone on ahead of the Order of Brethren, led by the Buddha, and appropriated the lodgings and sleeping places, saying: 'This lodging is for our superior, this for our teachers, and this for ourselves.' Thus the venerable Sāriputta, who came after the Order of Brethren, led by the Buddha, finding the pavilions occupied, the beds occupied, and all spaces filled, getting nowhere to lie, sat down at the root of a tree [and there passed the night].

Now the Exalted One at early dawn came out and cleared His throat. The venerable Sāriputta also cleared his throat.

'Why, who's there?' said the Master.

'It is I, Lord, Sāriputta.'

'But why, Sāriputta, are you sitting here?'

So the venerable Sāriputta told Him all that business.

Then the Exalted One, on that occasion and about that matter, called together the Order of Brethren, and asked: 'Is it true, brethren, as I hear, that the disciples of the Band of Six have thus (appropriated the lodging of the elder brethren)?'

'It is so, Lord.'

Then the Exalted One reproved them (and reminded them of the rules He had already laid down about such things) and said to the brethren: 'Say now, brethren, who is the one that deserves the best lodging, the best water, and the best food?'

Then some of the brethren said, 'He who has gone forth (as a wanderer) from the Warrior's clan.' Others said, 'Nay, he who has gone forth from the Brāhmana's clan, or one who was a housefather, or else one versed in the Suttas, or versed in the Vinaya, or a preacher of the Norm.'

Others again said, 'Nay, it is he who has won the First State of Musing, or the Second or the Third or Fourth.' And others said, 'Nay! It is he who is a Stream-winner, he who is a Once-returner, he who is a Never-returner, he who is Arahant, he who is a Knower of the Three Truths, or who has the Six Abnormal Powers.'

Then said the Exalted One to the brethren: 'In former days, brethren, long, long ago, on the Himālayan slopes, close to a mighty banyan tree, there dwelt a partridge, a monkey, and an elephant. But they lived together without mutual respect, deference, and courtesy. So, brethren, it occurred to those friends, "Come now, suppose we find out which is the elder by birth among us, and let us agree to pay him honour and deference and respect, support him and do his bidding."

Accordingly, brethren, the partridge and the monkey said to the elephant: "Good elephant, say what you remember of olden days."

"Friends, when I was a baby elephant, I used to walk over this banyan tree so that it went between my legs and its topmost twig just reached up to my belly. I can remember old days so long ago as that, my friends."

Then, brethren, the partridge and the elephant asked the same question of the monkey, (who replied):

"My friends, when I was a little fellow, as I sat upon the ground, I was able to nibble the topmost shoots of this very banyan. Thus far can I remember olden days."

Then, brethren, the monkey and the elephant asked the same question of the partridge, (who replied):

"Friends, long ago there was a banyan tree in yonder clearing. I ate one of its berries and voided my excrements just here. From that grew up this very banyan tree. Therefore I must be older than the two of you."

Thereupon, brethren, the monkey and the

elephant said to the partridge: "You, friend, are the elder! Henceforth will we show you every honour, reverence, and respect. We will bow down to you and do your bidding. Do you henceforth give us all needful counsel."

Thereafter, brethren, the partridge counselled them, established them in the moralities, and himself undertook to keep the same. Thus they dwelt together in mutual honour, reverence, and respect, and on the death of the body they were reborn in heaven in the happy state. And the way of life of those three was called "the partridge Holy Life." [1]

> Skilled in the Norm are they who honour age:
> In this world praise, hereafter bliss is theirs.

Thus, brethren, since even animals can live together in mutual honour, reverence, and respect, do ye let your light so shine that ye, who have gone forth from the world under this Norm-discipline of mine so excellently proclaimed, may dwell together in mutual honour, reverence, and respect.' (And when the Master had taught them with pious talk, He enjoined that in all things respect should be paid to the elder.)

Vinaya, ii. 6 (repeated at *Jātaka*, i, 37).

[1] *Tittiriyaṃ Brahmacariyaṃ.*

ADVICE, MOSTLY TO LAYMEN

FRIENDS

(a) *False*

(Then the Exalted One said to the young householder Sigāla :)

'There are these four, young master, who are to be reckoned as foes masquerading in the garb of friends :

The out-and-out robber : the one good at mere words : the smooth-tongued : the wastrel comrade.

Now in four ways the out-and-out robber is to be reckoned as a foe masquerading in the garb of a friend. First, he is an out-and-out robber : then he desires to get much by giving little : he does his duty out of fear : he follows one for his own gain. In these four ways is he such.

In four ways the one good at mere words is so to be reckoned. He greets you with talk about his past deeds : he greets you with professions of future deeds : he ingratiates himself with empty words : but when need arises he points to his own ill-luck. In these four ways is he such.

In four ways the smooth-tongued is so to be reckoned. He is compliant in evil deeds : but he is not compliant in a good deed : he sings your praises to your face: but behind your back he speaks ill of you. In these four ways is he such.

In four ways the wastrel comrade is so to be reckoned. He is your mate in drinking liquor, fermented and distilled: he is your mate in roaming the streets at unseasonable hours: he goes along with you loafing to festivals: he is your mate in being given to gambling which leads to sloth.

(b) *The True*

These four, young master, are to be reckoned as true-hearted ones:

The friend who helps you is to be so reckoned: the one who is unchanged in weal and woe: the one who tells you what is for your good: the one who shows affection for you.

In four ways the friend who helps you is so to be reckoned. He watches over you when you are slack: he watches over your property when you are slack: he is your refuge in time of fear: when need arises he supplies you twice over. In these four ways he is such.

In four ways the one who is unchanged in weal and woe is so to be reckoned. He tells you his secrets: he keeps yours: he does not forsake you in trouble: he sacrifices his very life for your good. In these four ways.

In four ways the one who tells you what is for your good is so to be reckoned. He keeps you from wrong-doing: he puts you in the right way. he tells you what you did not know before: he shows you the way to heaven. In these four ways is he to be considered a true-hearted one.

In four ways the one who shows his affection for you is so to be reckoned. He rejoices not in your misfortune; he rejoices in your good fortune; he defends you against those who slander you; he commends those who speak well of you. In these four ways he is to be reckoned a true-hearted one.'

Thus spake the Exalted One.

D.N. (*Sigālovāda*), iii. 186–7.

THE SIX REGIONS [1]

'And how, young master, does the Ariyan disciple cover the six regions?

These should be regarded as the six regions: Mother and father are the East; teachers are the South; child and wife are the West; friends and comrades are the North; servants and workers are the Below; recluses and brāhmins are the Above.

(*a*) Now in five ways should a son regard his parents as the East. He says, "Supported by them as I was, I will support them (in my turn). I will do my duty by them. I will keep up the honour of my family. I will manage my inheritance. I will keep up the offerings due to relatives deceased."

Now in these five ways should mother and father, thus set in the East and ministered to by a son, show their affection for him:

[1] In the East, the mother comes first, and child is put before parent: e.g. 'mother and father; child and wife; woman and man; moon and sun.'

They keep him from evil; put him in the right way; get him taught a science; provide him with a proper wife; and in time hand over their fortune to him. . . . Thus is this Eastern region protected for him, safe and free from fear.

(*b*) Now in five ways, young master, should teachers be set in the South and ministered to by their private pupils: by rising up to greet them; by supporting them; by readiness to learn; by ministering unto them; by attentively grasping what they teach.

And thus do teachers, thus in five ways set in the South and ministered to by their private pupils, in five ways show their affection for them. They train them so that they are well-trained; they make them keep what they have learned; they are their good counsellors in every science and art; they praise them to their friends and comrades; they set up a guard for them on every side.

Thus in these five ways (*as before*) . . . do they show their affection for their private pupils. Thus is this Southern Region protected for the Ariyan disciple, made safe and free from fear.

(*c*) Now in five ways, young master, should a wife be set in the West and ministered to by her husband:

By showing her respect; by showing her compliance; by not committing adultery; by leaving her in charge; by supplying her with finery.

And in these five ways (thus honoured) . . . does she show her affection for him:

By doing her duties thoroughly; by good treatment of her household; by not committing adultery; by guarding what he earns; by skill and zeal in all she has to do.

Thus in five ways (*as before*). . . . Thus is this Western Region protected for him and made safe and free from fear.

(*d*) Now in five ways, young master, should friends and comrades be set in the North and ministered to by the clansman:

By charity; by kind words; by acting for their welfare; by putting them on equal terms; by keeping one's promises to them.

And in five ways (thus honoured) . . . do friends and comrades show their affection for the clansman:

They watch over him when he is slack; they watch over his property when he is slack; they are his refuge in time of fear; they do not forsake him in time of trouble; they show respect for the rest of his people.

Thus in five ways (*as before*). . . . Thus is this Northern Region protected for him and made safe and free from fear.

(*e*) Now in five ways, young master, are servants and workers set in the Below and ministered to by a true gentleman (their master): [1]

He assigns them work according to their strength, provides them with food and wage, nurses them in time of sickness, gives them a share in any extra dainty, and in due season gives them leave of absence.

Thus (in five ways honoured) . . . do servants and workers show their affection for the true gentleman (their master):

[1] A rare word, *ayirakena* for *ariyakena*.

They rise up early; late take rest; take what is given; do their work thoroughly; and sing his praises everywhere.

Thus in five ways (*as before*). . . . Thus is the Below protected for him, made safe and free from fear.

(*f*) Now in five ways, young master, should a clansman set recluses and brāhmins in the Above, and minister unto them:

By kindly action; by kindly words; by kindly thought unto them; by not closing his doors against them; by providing for their worldly needs.

And in these five ways (*as before*) do recluses and brāhmins show their affection for the clansman:

They restrain him from evil; set him in the right way; teach him what he did not know before; clarify what he had already heard; and show him the way to heaven.

Thus in these five ways (*as before*). . . . Thus is the Region Above protected for him and made safe and free from fear.'

Thus spake the Exalted One.

D.N. iii. 185–91.

THE STAGE-MANAGER

Once the Exalted One was staying near Rājagaha, in Jeta Grove, at the Squirrels' Feeding-ground.

Then Tālaputo, the stage-manager,[1] came to

[1] At Theragāthā, v. 1091, after his ordination this brother describes his experiences in striking verses, well rendered by Dr. C. A. Rhys Davids in *Psalms of the Brethren*, p. 370.

the Exalted One, saluted Him, and sat down at one side. So seated, Tālaputo, the stage-manager, said this to the Exalted One:

'I have heard, Lord, this traditional saying of teachers of old, to wit: speaking of stage-players, they said, "A player who, on the stage or in the arena, makes people laugh and delights them by his counterfeiting of the truth, when body breaks up, after death, is reborn in the company of the Laughing Devas." What says the Exalted One in this matter?'

'Enough, manager! Let be. Ask me not this question.'

(Then Tālaputo, the stage-manager, heedless of the Master's words, put his question again, and yet a third time. Then said the Exalted One:)

'True it is, I did not permit your question, saying, "Enough, manager! Let be. Ask me not that question." Nevertheless (such is your importunity) I will expound this thing to you.

In the case of those beings, manager, who aforetime were not free from lusts, but were bound with the bond of lust: who aforetime were not free from hate, but were bound with the bond of hate: who aforetime were not free from delusion, but were bound with the bond of delusion,—in such cases, a player who on the stage or in the arena brings about lustful, hateful, or delusive states of mind, so that such beings become still more lustful, still more hateful, still more deluded,—being himself drugged and slothful he drugs and makes others slothful. Such an one, when body breaks up, after death is reborn in the Purgatory of Laughter.

Now if his view of the matter is as you say, "Whatsoever player, on the stage or in the arena, makes people laugh and delights them with his counterfeiting of the truth . . . is reborn in the company of the Laughing Devas,"—then I declare his view to be perverted.

Now, manager, I declare that for one who is guilty of perverted view there are two paths open, one is Purgatory and the other is rebirth as an animal.'

At these words Tālaputo, the stage-manager, cried aloud and burst into tears. Then said the Exalted One:

'Did I not say to you, manager, "Enough, manager! Let be. Ask me not this question"?'

'Yes, Lord. I am not lamenting for that. I lament at the thought that for many a long day I have been cheated, deceived, led astray by teachers of old and their tradition, who say that a player . . . is reborn in the company of the Laughing Devas. Excellent, Lord! Excellent it is, Lord! Just as if one should raise what is overthrown, or show forth what is hidden, or point the way to him that wanders astray, or hold up a light in the darkness that they who have eyes may see objects,—even so in divers ways hath the Norm been set forth by the Venerable Gotama. To the Venerable Gotama I go for refuge, to the Norm, and to the Order of Brethren from this day forth so long as life doth last.'

S.N. iv. 305.

THE LAYMAN'S PROFIT AND LOSS

Then the Exalted One addressed the lay brethren of Pāṭaligāma :

'There are these five losses, housefathers, which attend the wicked and immoral man. What five ?

Herein, housefathers, the wicked immoral man, as the result of sloth, comes to great loss of wealth. That is the first loss.

Then again, housefathers, an evil report prevails about him. That is the second loss.

Then again, housefathers, whatever company he may enter, be it a company of the nobles, or the brāhmins, or the housefathers, or a company of recluses, he enters shyly and confused in mind. That is the third loss.

Again, housefathers, he is troubled in mind when he dies. That is the fourth loss.

And lastly, housefathers, upon the break-up of the body, after death, he is reborn in the Purgatory, the Ill-path, the Downfall, the Place of Suffering.

Such, housefathers, are the five losses that attend the wicked and immoral man.

Now there are these five profits, housefathers, that attend the righteous man who lives virtuously:

Herein, housefathers, the righteous man who lives virtuously comes by a great mass of wealth, due to his own exertions. That is the first profit.

Then again, housefathers, a good reputation prevails about him. That is the second profit.

Then again, housefathers, into whatsoever company he enters, be it of the nobles or the brāhmins or the housefathers or the recluses,—he enters bold and confident. That is the third profit.

Then again, housefathers, he makes an end with mind untroubled. That is the fourth profit.

Lastly, housefathers, on the break-up of body, after death, he is reborn in the Blissful, Happy World. That is the fifth profit.

Such, housefathers, are the five profits that attend the righteous man who lives virtuously.'

D.N. ii. 85.

RETRIBUTION

The fool in doing ill knows not his folly :
His own deeds, like a fire, the fool consume.

He who offends the harmless innocent
Soon reaches one of these ten states of woe :—

Sharp pain, disease, or bodily decay,
Grievous disaster, or a mind distraught,

Oppression by the king, or calumny,
Loss of relations, loss of all his wealth,

His house burned by a thunderbolt or fire :
At death, poor fool, he finds rebirth in Woe.

Dhammapada, 136–40.

THE DEVAS ENCOMPASS THE PRUDENT MAN

In whatsoever place the prudent man shall make
his home,
Let him support the virtuous ones who live the
holy life.

To all the devas dwelling there let him make
offerings.
Thus honoured, they will honour him: revered,
they'll him revere.

As a mother doth compassionate the child that
she hath borne,
Whom the devas do compassionate doth ever see
good luck.

D.N. ii. 88.

As in a forest vast the stately trees
Grow 'neath the shadow of a mighty rock,—
So in this world, if any be devout
And well-born, 'neath the shadow of that man,
Children and wife, his relatives and friends,
And all depending on him, grow apace.
And they, when they behold the piety,
The charity and goodness of that man,
If they be wise, soon follow his example,
And in this life do works that lead to good,
And win the bliss they long for in the heavens.

Ang. Nik. i. 152.

ADVICE, MOSTLY TO LAYMEN

TYPES OF LISTENERS

Then the Exalted One said: 'Brethren, there are these three sorts of people to be found in the world:

The empty-head, the fool who cannot see,—
Tho' oft and oft unto the Brethren going,
He hears their talk, beginning, middle, end,—
Can never grasp it. Wisdom is not his.

Better than he the man of scattered brains,
Who oft and oft unto the Brethren going
Hears all their talk, beginning, middle, end,
And seated there can grasp the very words,
Yet, rising, nought retains. Blank is his mind.

Better than these the man of wisdom wide.
He, oft and oft unto the Brethren going,
Hears all their talk, beginning, middle, end,
And, seated there, can grasp the very words,
Bears all in mind, steadfast, unwavering,
Skilled in the Norm and what conforms thereto.
This is the man to make an end of Ill.'

Ang. Nik. i. 131.

GOOD WORKS

BE NOT AFRAID OF GOOD WORKS

Thus spake the Exalted One, thus spake the Arahant (so I have heard):

'Be not afraid of good works, brethren. It is

another name for happiness, for what is desired, beloved, dear and delightful—this word "good works."

I myself, brethren, can bear witness to having reaped for many a long day the profit of good works,—a thing desired, beloved, dear and delightful. For seven years I practised kindly thought, and (as a result) I came not back into this world for seven æons of the unrolling and rolling up of the world.[1] When the æon had unrolled, brethren, I became one of the Splendid Devas. When the æon had rolled up, brethren, I was reborn in the Highest Abode.[2] There was I a Brahmā, a great Brahmā, conquering and unconquered, the all-seeing Controller.

Thirty and six times, brethren, was I Sakka, Lord of the Devas. Countless hundreds of times was I a rājah, a world-ruler, a righteous monarch, victorious over the four quarters, ruling a realm that enjoyed the blessing of security: possessed of the Seven Gems was I: (such a ruler was I) —not to speak of (mere) provincial rule.

Then, brethren, this thought came to me: "Of what deeds, I wonder, is all this the fruit? Of what deed is it the ripening, in that I am now thus prosperous and of such mighty magic power?"

Then, brethren, this thought came to me: "Of three deeds this is the fruit. Of three deeds this is the ripening, in that I am now thus prosperous and of such mighty magic power,—

[1] *Saṃvatta-vivatta,* 'involution and evolution.

[2] *Brāhma-vimāna.*

the deeds of Charity, Self-taming, and Self-control." '[1]

Such was the essence of the words of the Exalted One ; herein is said :

Whoso would merit win
Long-lasting, bringing bliss—
Let him give alms, be calmed,
And cultivate good-will.

By practice of these three,
These three bliss-bringing things,
That wise man, sorrowless,
I' the world of bliss is born.

Iti-vuttaka, § 22.

GOOD WORKS

Auspicious, festive, happy, blessed dawn !
Fair day, glad time is that when alms are given
To worthy ones : when goodly acts, words, thoughts,
Right aspirations, bring auspicious gain
To those that practise them. Happy are they
That win such gain, and prosperous in the Way !
So be ye also prosperous in the Way[2]—
Free from disease and happy with your kin.

Ang. Nik. i. § 150.

Maghavā[3] by Heedfulness attained the kingship of the gods.

Dhammapada, v. 30.

[1] Corresponding to *dāna, sīla, bhāvanā.*
[2] *Buddha-sāsana.* [3] Indra.

S.S.B.—7*

SOME SAYINGS OF THE BUDDHA

GOOD RESOLUTIONS

At Sāvatthī . . . in Jeta Grove. . . .

Then the Exalted One said this to the Brethren :

'In former times, brethren, when Sakka, Lord of the gods, was in human form, by undertaking and performing seven rules of conduct, he attained his state of sovereignty. What seven ?

[He undertook these resolutions :]

"All my life long may I support my parents. May I respect the head of my clan. May I be of gentle speech. May I speak evil of none. Clearing my heart of the stain of selfishness, may I dwell at home generous, pure-handed, delighting in giving up, may I be a proper man to ask a boon of, delighting in sharing gifts with others.

All my life long, may I speak the truth.

All my life long, may I be angerless, and, if anger arise, may I quickly check it."

Such were the seven rules, brethren, by undertaking and performing which Sakka attained his state of sovereignty.'

S.N. i. 227.

THE BUDDHA AND THE COWHERD [1]

'Cooked is my rice, milked are my kine,' said
Dhaniya the herd,
'And here on Mahī's bank I dwell with them
that are my peers.
Thatched is my hut, well-fed the fire. Rain
down, god, if thou wilt !'

[1] *Dhaniya Sutta* [*Sutta Nipāta*, vv. 18–34]. The Buddha plays upon the words of Dhaniya, giving them a contrary meaning which cannot be well expressed in a translation.

'From anger free, with every bar removed,' the Lord replied,
'A dweller here on Mahī's[1] bank I sojourn but one night.
Roofless my hut and quenched my fire. Rain down, god, if thou wilt!'

'No gadflies here are to be seen,' said Dhaniya the herd.
'Amid the marshland grasses there my kine a-roaming go.
The rain that comes they can endure. Rain down, god, if thou wilt!'

'I made a raft to cross the stream, of logs well put together.
Now have I crossed and gone beyond, by stemming of the Flood.
So now I need my raft no more. Rain down, god, if thou wilt!'

'My wife she is a loyal one—no wanton,' said the herd.
'Full many a day she's dwelt with me, and she is kind and dear.
I hear no man speak ill of her. Rain down, god, if thou wilt!'

'My mind it is a docile one, set free,' the Lord replied.
'Full many a day I tamed it down and shaped it to my will.
No evil now is found in me. Rain down, god, if thou wilt!'

[1] *Mahī*, a river, also means 'the Earth.'

'By the labour of my hands I live,' said Dhaniya the herd.
'My children, they all dwell with me, and they are stout and strong.
Of them I hear no word of ill. Rain down, god, if thou wilt!'

'I too, I am a slave to none,' the Exalted One replied,
'And by the powers I have won I roam through all the world.
I have no need for service more. Rain down, god, if thou wilt!'

'Kine have I, yea, and calves that suck,' said Dhaniya the herd,
'And cows in calf, and they shall carry on the breed for me,
And a bull, the lord of all the herd. Rain down, god, if thou wilt!'

'I have no kine, I have no calves that suck,' the Lord replied.
'I have no cows in calf to carry on the breed for me;
No bull, the Lord of all the herd. Rain down, god, if thou wilt!'

'Well-set the pegs that hold my kine: shaken they cannot be.
My tethers, made of munja grass, bran new and twisted well,
No sucking calf can break 'em. So rain down, god, if thou wilt!'

'But I, the Bull, have burst the bonds that bind,' the Lord replied,
'Have burst them as a tusker rends the twisted creeper-cords.
Never again shall I be born. Rain down, god, if thou wilt!'

Forthwith the mighty rain poured down and filled the hills and plains.
When he heard the raining of the god Dhaniya thus spake his mind:

'No little gain is ours that we the Exalted One have seen.
In Thee we take our refuge, Thou that hast the eye to see.
Be Thou our teacher, mighty sage. The goodwife and myself
Docile will live the holy life with Thee, O happy one,
And passing over birth and death an end of suffering make!'

(*Māra, the Evil One, then said:*)
'He that hath sons delights in sons,' then said the Evil One.
'He that hath kine delights in kine. Delight binds man to birth.
But he that hath no bond to bind delighteth thus no more.'

(*The Lord said:*)

'He that hath sons must sorrow have because of sons, and he
That owneth kine owns trouble. Ownership is woe to man.
Happy the man that owneth naught to bind him to rebirth!'

LIFE, DEATH, AND AFTER

RARE IS THE CHANCE OF HUMAN BIRTH[1]

Remember how the parable was told
Of purblind turtle in the Eastern Seas
Or other oceans, once, as time goes by,
Thrusting his head thro' hole of drifting yoke.
So rare as this the chance of human birth.

'Just as if, brethren, a man should throw into the mighty ocean a yoke with one hole, and then a one-eyed turtle should pop up to the surface only once at the end of every hundred years. Now what think ye, brethren? Would that one-eyed turtle push his neck through that yoke with one hole (on each occasion) when he popped up to the surface, only once at the end of every hundred years?'

'It might be so, Lord, now and again, after the lapse of a long time.'

'Well, brethren, sooner, do I declare, would that one-eyed turtle, if he were to pop up to the surface . . . thus,—sooner would he push his neck through that yoke with one hole than would a

[1] The introductory verses are from *Psalms of the Sisters*, Dr. C. A. Rhys Davids, p. 173.

The brother Abhaya (*Psalms of the Brethren*, 30) is said to have become a Stream-winner just by meditating on this parable.

fool, who has once gone to the Downfall, become a man. What is the reason for that?

It is because herein there is no living of the righteous life, no living in tranquillity, no doing of righteous deeds, no doing of meritorious deeds, but feeding on each other's flesh and feeding on the weaker sort prevails. What is the reason for that?

Owing to not seeing the Four Ariyan Truths. What Four? The Ariyan Truth of Ill, the Ariyan Truth of the arising of Ill, the Ariyan Truth of the ceasing of Ill, the Ariyan Truth of the Way leading to the ceasing of Ill.

Wherefore, brethren, thus must ye exert yourselves, holding the thought of "This is Ill, this is the arising of Ill, this is the ceasing of Ill, this is the Way leading to the ceasing of Ill."

Thus, brethren, must ye exert yourselves.'

S.N. v. 455; *M.N.* (partly), iii. 169.

To gain a birth as man is hard indeed;
'Tis hard to get one's living in the world;
Hard is the hearing of the Doctrine true;
Hardest to be an All-awakened one.

Dhammapada, v. 182.

'Brethren, just as in this Rose-apple Land, small is the part consisting of delightful parks, delightful groves, of tillage-land and water-tanks: whereas larger is the part consisting of land that runneth up and down, of rivers barring passage, of spots beset with stumps and thorns, of rough and rocky ground,—

Even so, brethren, few are those beings that are born on land: more numerous are those that are water-born: and in like manner few are those beings that are born among mankind: more numerous are they that are reborn outside the human race. . . .

Likewise, brethren, of those who decease from the human state, few are they who take rebirth among the human race, but more numerous are they who are reborn in a state of woe, among the animals and in the world of ghosts.'

Ang. Nik. i. 35–37.

A WORLD WITHOUT END IS EXISTENCE

1. Straws and Boughs

Thus have I heard. Once the Exalted One was staying near Sāvatthī at Jeta Grove in Anathāpindika's Park.

Then the Exalted One said to the brethren, 'Brethren!'

'Lord!' replied those brethren to the Exalted One. The Exalted One said:

'A world-without-end,[1] is this round of birth and death. No beginning can be seen of those beings hindered by ignorance, bound by craving, running through the round of birth and death.

Just as if a man should chop up all the straws, boughs, twigs, and leaves in this India, and piling them together should lay them in a heap, square by square, saying: "This is my mother, this is the mother of that mother of mine,"—still un-

[1] *Ana-mata 'gga*—'incalculable is the beginning.'

supplied would be the mother's mothers of that man. Nay, to supply them all, the straw, boughs, twigs, and leaves in this India would come to an end and be used up (ere that were done).

What is the cause of this? A world-without-end, brethren, is this round of birth and death. No beginning can be seen of those beings hindered by ignorance, bound by craving, for ever running through the round of birth and death.

Thus for a long time, brethren, have ye experienced Ill, experienced grievous pain, experienced misery, and swollen are the charnel-fields. So that ye may well be disgusted with, well turn away from, well be released from all the activities of existence.'

2. The Earth

... staying near Sāvatthī ... (The Exalted One said:)

'A world-without-end is this round of birth (*as before*).

Just as if a man should make this mighty earth into ball after ball of mould, of the size of kolaṭṭhis, and lay them down, saying: "This is my father, this is the father of that father of mine." Unsupplied thus would be the father's fathers of that man. Nay, (to supply them all) all the straw, boughs, twigs, and leaves in this India would come to an end and be used up (ere that were done).

What is the cause of this? (*as before*) ... the activities of existence.'

3. Tears

. . . near Sāvatthī . . . (The Exalted One said :)

'A world-without-end, brethren . . . (*as before*).

Now what think ye ? Whether is the greater, the flood of tears shed by you on this long journey, for ever running through the round of birth and death, weeping and wailing because of union with the undesired, because of separation from the desired,—or the water of the four mighty oceans ?'

'Insofar, Lord, as we understand the Norm preached by the Exalted One, greater is this flood of tears shed by us, Lord, not the water of the four mighty oceans.'

'Well said ! Well said, brethren ! Well do ye understand the Norm which I have preached to you.

Truly, greater is the flood of tears shed by you . . . (*as before*).

For a long, long time have ye experienced the death of mothers, sons, daughters, the misery of kin, the misery of wealth : for a long, long time have ye experienced the misery of disease. The flood of tears shed by you, when experiencing the misery of disease, weeping and wailing, is indeed greater than the waters of the four mighty oceans.

And what is the cause of that ? A world-without-end . . . (*as before*).

So that ye may well be disgusted with, well turn away from, well be released from the activities of existence.'

4. (Mother's) Milk

. . . near Sāvatthī . . . (The Exalted One said :)

'A world-without-end, brethren. . . .

Now what think ye, brethren ? Whether is the greater, all the mother's milk that ye have sucked in this long journey, for ever running through the round of rebirth, or the water in the four mighty oceans ?'

'Insofar, Lord, as we understand the Norm preached by the Exalted One, greater is this milk sucked by us, Lord,—not the water of the four mighty oceans.'

'Well said! Well said, brethren! 'tis well that ye thus understand the Norm which I have preached to you.

Indeed, greater is the milk sucked by you in this long journey . . . (*as before*).

And what is the cause of that ? A world-without-end . . .

So that ye may well be disgusted with . . . the activities of existence.'

5. Mountains

. . . near Sāvatthī. . . .

Then a certain brother came to the Exalted One, saluted him, and sat down at one side.

So seated, that brother said to the Exalted One : 'How long, Lord, is the æon ?'

'Long, indeed, is the æon, brother : it is not easy to reckon it in this way : "So many years, so many centuries, so many millennia, so many hundred thousand years."'

'But can an illustration be given, Lord ?'

'It can, brother,' replied the Exalted One.

'Just as if, brother, there were a mighty mountain crag, four leagues in length, breadth, and height, without a crack or cranny, not hollowed out, one solid mass of rock, and a man should come at the end of every century, and with cloth of Benares should once on each occasion stroke that rock: sooner, brother, would that mighty mountain crag be worn away by this method, sooner be used up, than the æon.

Thus long, brother, is the æon: of æons thus long many an æon has passed away, many a hundred æons, many a thousand æons, many a hundred thousand æons.'

S.N. ii. 178 ff.

But one man's bones who has *one* æon lived [1]
Might form a cairn—so said the Mighty Seer—
High as Vipulla, higher than the Peak
Of vultures, mountain-burg of Magadha.
Yet when that man with perfect insight sees
The Ariyan Truths—the Fourfold Ariyan Truth—
Even the What and Why of Ill, and how
Ill comes, and how Ill may be overpassed,
Even the Ariyan, the Eightfold Path Way
That leadeth to th' abating of all Ill—
Seven times at most that man shall wander
round,[2]
Then make an end of Ill, all bonds destroyed.

Iti-vuttaka, § 24; *S.N.* ii. 185.

[1] Cf. Mrs. Rhys Davids's *Psalms of the Sisters*, pp. 172–3, for the first four lines.

[2] On entering the Stream, one is only bound to the wheel *at most* for seven more births. Cf. sections on *the Fetters*.

WRONG VIEW

'For him that hath wrong view, Punna, one of two things is in store, I declare: either rebirth in purgatory or in the world of animals.'

S.N. iv. 307.

'Whatsoever individual, brethren, follows perverted views, perverted aim, perverted speech or acts or living, perverted effort, attention, and contemplation; whose knowledge and emancipation are perverted,—for him every action of deed, word, or thought, performed and achieved according to such perverted views; every willed act, every aspiration, every resolve, all his activities, these things one and all conduce to what is distasteful, unpleasing, repulsive, unprofitable, and painful. And why so? Because of his evil view.'

Ang. Nik. v. 212.

ACTION HAS RESULT

'Brethren, of deeds done and accumulated with deliberate intent I declare there is no wiping out. That wiping out has to come to pass either in this very life or in some other life at its proper occasion.

Without experiencing the result of deeds so done, I declare there is no making an end of Ill.

Herein, brethren, threefold is the fault and guilt of bodily action, done with deliberate intent, causing pain and resulting in pain.

Fourfold is the fault and guilt of action through

speech, done with deliberate intent, causing pain, resulting in pain.

Threefold is the fault and guilt of mental action which has these same results.'

Ang. Nik. v. 292.

LIFE IS SHORT

Short indeed is this life. This side of a hundred years it perishes. And, even if one live beyond, yet of decay he perishes at last.

It is from selfishness that people grieve. 'Not lasting are possessions in this world: all this is liable to change,'—so seeing let not a man stay in his house.[1]

By death is put away even that of which one thinks 'This is mine own.' So seeing let not one devote himself to selfishness.

As when one awakes he sees no more him whom he met in a dream, even so one sees no more the beloved one who hath died and become a ghost.

Sn. v. 804–7.

IMPERMANENCE

Then said the Exalted One to the venerable Ānanda:

'I can remember, Ānanda, how in this place my body was six times laid aside. And dwelling here as a rājah, as a world-ruler, a righteous ruler, a lord of the four quarters, a protector of

[1] The meaning of this verse is twofold. 'Let him not cling to self or body,' and 'Let him become a wanderer.'

the folk, a possessor of the seven gems,—that was the seventh time that my body was laid aside.

But I see not, Ānanda, any place in the world, together with the world of the devas, with its Māras, its Brahmās, its recluses and brāhmins, with all the host of devas and mankind,—I see not the place where the Tathāgata shall lay aside His body for the eighth time.'

Thus spake the Exalted One. When the Happy One had thus spoken, the Master added this further:

IMPERMANENT, ALAS! ARE ALL COMPOUNDED THINGS.
THEIR NATURE IS TO RISE AND FALL. WHEN THEY HAVE RISEN
THEY CEASE. THE BRINGING OF THEM TO AN END IS BLISS.

D.N. ii. 198.

DEATH CLOSETH ALL

Thus have I heard. Once the Exalted One was staying at Sāvatthī in East Park, at the storeyed house of Migāra's mother.

Now on that occasion the Exalted One, having risen at eventide from His solitude, was sitting in the westering sun, letting it warm His back.

Then the venerable Ānanda came to the Exalted One and, while chafing His limbs with his hand, thus addressed the Exalted One:

'A marvel it is, Lord! Strange it is, Lord! Now, Lord, the Exalted One's complexion is no longer clear and translucent: all his limbs are loosened and become wrinkled. Formerly His body was radiant, but now is seen a change of every organ,—of sight, hearing, smelling, savouring, and body-feeling,—all is changed, Lord!'

'Even so, Ānanda, the nature of decay is inherent in youth, the nature of sickness is in health, in the midst of life we are in death, so that now my complexion is no longer clear and translucent: all my limbs are loosed and wrinkled. Formerly my body was radiant, but now is seen a change of every organ,—of sight, hearing, smelling, savouring, and body-feeling.'

Thus spake the Exalted One; thus spake the Happy One. Having thus spoken, the Master added this further:

> Shame on thee, worthless age,
> That maketh colour fade!
> Thus the delightful form
> By age is trampled down.
>
> Who lives a hundred years
> Is natheless doomed to die.
> Naught can avoid Death's tread,
> That crusheth everything.

S.N. v. 216.

DEATH'S MESSENGERS

> Lo! thou art now a pale and withered leaf:
> Death's messengers are close at hand:
> Thou in the very gate of Death dost stand,
> And yet hast no provision for the way.

Then make thyself *an island of defence*:
Strive quick: be wise: when all thy taints
Of dirt and dust are blown away, the Saints
Shall greet thee entering the Happy Land.

Thy life has run its course: thou art come nigh
The King of Death. For thine abode
Thou hast no resting-place upon the road,
And yet hast no provision for the way.

Then make thyself *an island of defence*:
Strive quick: be wise: blow off the dust
And stains of travel: wipe away the rust.
So shalt thou see no more birth and decay.

The wise and thoughtful man attacks his faults
One after other, momently,
In order due, and rubs them all away,
E'en as a smith blows off the silver's dross.

Just as the iron rust accumulates
Self-born, and eats itself away,
So with the man who sinneth: day by day
His own deeds to destruction lead him on.

Dhammapada, vv. 235–40.

AFTER DEATH

Once the Exalted One was staying at Sāvatthi in Anāthapindika's Park.

Then Hatthaka, son of a deva, when night was waning, lit up the whole of Jeta Grove with exceeding splendour and approached the Exalted One.

Having drawn near to Him, he thought 'I will stand before the Exalted One,' but he sank down, collapsed, could not stand upright. Just as butter, or oil, when poured upon sand, sinks down, sinks in, and cannot abide, even so was Hatthaka, son of a deva, unable to stand before the Exalted One, but sank down, collapsed, could not stand upright.

Then said the Exalted One to Hatthaka, son of a deva, 'Create a body-form substantial, Hatthaka.'

'Yes, Lord!' replied Hatthaka to the Exalted One: and having done so he came to Him and stood at one side. As he thus stood the Exalted One said to him:

'Well, Hatthaka, do things go on now just the same as before, when you were in human shape?'

'Yes, Lord, they do. But there are also things now going on which I did not experience when I was in human shape. Just as, Lord, the Exalted One now dwells surrounded by brethren and sisters, by lay-brothers and lay-sisters, by royalties and ministers, by sectarians and their followers, —just so do I dwell surrounded by sons of devas. Even from a distance, Lord, do sons of the devas come saying, "We'll hear the Norm from the lips of Hatthaka, son of a deva."

Of three things, Lord, I never got enough. I died regretful of three things. What were they? I never had enough of beholding the Exalted One. I died regretting it. I never had enough of hearing the good Norm. I died regretting it. I never had enough of serving the Order of

Brethren. I died regretting it. These are the three things, Lord.' (Then he sang this verse :)

I never could be sated of delight
Of my desire to see the Exalted One,
Hear the good Norm and wait upon the Brethren.
Keeping the virtues ten, hearing the Norm,
And never sated of delight in these
Three things did Hatthaka (a deva's son) attain
Unto Aviha of the Brahma World.[1]

Ang. Nik. i. 279.

THE SICKNESS, DEATH, AND APPARITION OF ANĀTHAPINDIKA

Thus have I heard. Once the Exalted One was staying near Sāvatthī, in Jeta Grove, at Anāthapindika's Park.

Now at that time the housefather Anāthapindika was sick, afflicted with a sore disease. Then Anāthapindika the housefather called to a certain man, saying :

'Come thou, good man ! Go to the Exalted One and, coming to Him, in my name worship at the feet of the Exalted One, and say thus : "Lord, Anāthapindika the housefather is sick, afflicted with a sore disease. He worships at the feet of the Exalted One." Then go you to the venerable Sāriputta and do likewise and say the same. And say this also, "It were well, sir, if

[1] One who is born in heaven after death becomes a lodger there and is called son of a deva, *devaputto*. The Aviha is one of the highest of the subjective or formless states of the Brahma world.

the venerable Sāriputta would go to the dwelling of Anāthapindika the housefather out of compassion for him." '

'Very well, sir,' said that man, went to the Exalted One, and did as he was bid. Then he went to the venerable Sāriputta and gave the message.

Then the venerable Sāriputta consented by his silence. So he robed himself and, taking bowl and robe, with the venerable Ānanda for attendant, he set out for the dwelling of Anāthapindika the housefather. On coming there he sat down on a seat made ready, and said to Anāthapindika the housefather, 'Well, housefather, are you bearing up? Are you enduring? Do your pains abate and not increase? Are there signs of their abating and not increasing?'

'No, sir! I am not bearing up. I am not enduring. Strong pains come upon me. They do not abate. There is no sign of their abating, but of their increasing. Just as if a strong man, lord Sāriputta, with a sharp sword were crashing upon my head, so do the vital airs rack my head exceedingly. Just as if a strong man were binding a bandage of stout cord about my head, so violent are the pains in my head. Just as if a butcher or a butcher's man with a sharp knife were to rip up the belly of an ox, such are the pains that rip up my belly. Just as if two strong men were to seize a weaker man, laying hold each of an arm, and were to scorch and burn him in a pit of glowing charcoal,—such is the exceeding great burning in my body. No, master Sāriputta, I am not bearing up. I am not enduring. My pains increase. They do not abate.'

'Then, housefather, thus must you train your mind.' And the venerable Sāriputta expounded unto him the ways of controlling the faculties (*as elsewhere described*). Whereupon the housefather Anāthapindika cried aloud and burst into tears.

Then said the venerable Ānanda: 'What, housefather, does your mind cling,[1] or does it sink down, housefather?'

'No, not that, lord Ānanda! I am holding on. I don't give up. But for a long time I have sat beside the Master and a brother of trained mind: yet never did I hear such a pious talk as this of yours.'

'Of a truth, housefather, such a pious talk as this is not revealed to the house-dwellers who wear white clothes. It is to those who have gone forth that such a pious talk is revealed.'

'Then, lord Sāriputta, let it be revealed to house-dwellers who wear white clothes. There are clansmen, lord Sāriputta, with but little defilement in their nature. They perish for not hearing the Norm. They will become understanders of the Norm.'

Then the venerable Sāriputta and the venerable Ānanda, when this exhortation had been given to the housefather Anāthapindika, rose up from

[1] *Olīyasi tvaṃ, samsīdasi?* Lit. 'do you adhere, or are you giving way?' The word *olīyati* is explained at *Atthasāḷini*, p. 377, as 'hanging head-downwards, like a bat from a tree' (of mind unable to hold body together).

their seats and went away. And not long after they were gone the housefather Anāthapindika passed away, and, upon the break-up of body, after death was reborn among the company of the Happy Ones.

Then Anāthapindika, who was now the son of a deva, when the night was passing, lit up the whole of Jeta Grove with wondrous splendour and came to the Exalted One, saluted Him, and stood beside Him. So standing, Anāthapindika, son of a deva, spake unto the Exalted One in verse, saying:

> Blessed is this Jeta Grove,
> Haunted by the Band of Seers,
> Where dwells the Ruler of the Norm:
> It maketh joy arise in me.
>
> Doing, knowing, training self,
> Life in utter blamelessness,—
> Men are purified by these,
> Not by birth and not by wealth.
>
> Therefore let the wise man strive,
> Seeing his own good therein.
> Let him throughly search the Norm:
> Thereby cometh purity.
>
> Like Sāriputta, who is wise,
> Virtuous and self-controlled,
> A brother who hath passed beyond
> Thereby is equal to the best.

Thus spake Anāthapindika, son of a deva. And the Master was approving of it. Then said

Anāthapindika, son of a deva, 'The Master approves,' and saluted the Exalted One by the right and vanished there and then.

Now when the night was gone, the Exalted One called the brethren and said: 'Brethren, this night a certain deva's son, when night was waning, lit up the whole of Jeta Grove with wondrous splendour, and came to me; and so coming, saluted me and stood beside me. So standing, that deva's son spake to me in verses.' And He recited the verses. . . . 'Thus spake that deva's son, brethren, and saying, "The Master approves," saluted me by the right and vanished there and then.'

Whereupon the venerable Ānanda said to the Exalted One: 'Why, Lord, that deva's son must be Anāthapindika! For the housefather Anāthapindika, Lord, had perfect faith in the venerable Sāriputta.'

'Well said, Ānanda! Well said, Ānanda! So far as reasoning goes, you have conjectured aright. That deva's son, Ānanda, was Anāthapindika and none other.'

Thus spake the Exalted One. And those brethren were delighted at the words of the Exalted One.

M.N. iii. chap. 143.

PROGRESS IN THE HEAVEN-WORLD

'Four blessings, brethren, may be looked for as resulting from lending an ear to, from reciting with the lips, from pondering with the mind, from penetrating by insight the teachings of the Norm. What are the four ?

Herein, brethren, a brother masters the Norm (in its ninefold limbs), the discourses, the songs, the expositions, the verses, the solemn sayings, the Master's words, the birth tales, the marvels, and the book of divers teachings. He listens to them, repeats them, ponders over them, and thoroughly penetrates them by his insight. Then he dies with mindfulness confused and is reborn in a certain company of devas. There the blissful ones recite to him the stanzas of the Norm. Slow, brethren, is mindfulness to arise, but that being quickly attains pre-eminence therein.

This is the first blessing to be looked for by so doing.

Then again, brethren, a brother masters the Norm (*as before*). He dies with mindfulness confused, and is reborn in a company of devas. There the blissful ones do not recite to him the stanzas of the Norm, but maybe some brother of magic powers, who has mastered his will, expounds the Norm in that company of devas. Then that brother thinks, "Why, this is the life, this is the very Norm-Discipline according to which in my former birth I lived the life of righteousness !" Slow indeed, brethren, is the arising of mindfulness, but that brother quickly attains pre-eminence therein.

Just as a man who is skilled in distinguishing the sounds of drums,—he may be travelling along the highroad, and he hears the sound of a certain drum, and has no manner of doubt as to its being the sound of a drum, but at once comes to the conclusion, "That's the sound of a drum." Even so, brethren, does a brother master the Norm . . . (*as before*).

This is the second blessing to be looked for by so doing.

Then again, brethren, a brother masters the Norm . . . and is reborn among a certain company of devas. Then the blissful ones do not recite the stanzas of the Norm to him, nor does a brother of magic powers who has mastered his will expound the Norm in that company of devas: but some son of a deva himself expounds the Norm to the company of devas. Then that brother thinks: "Why, this is the life, this is the very Norm-Discipline according to which I lived the life of righteousness in my former birth." Slow indeed, brethren, is the establishing of mindfulness, but that brother quickly attains pre-eminence therein.

Just as one who is skilled in the sounds of chanks,—he may be travelling along the highroad, and hears the sound of chanks, and has no manner of doubt as to its being the sound of a chank, but at once concludes, "That's the sound of a chank": even so, brethren, does a brother master the Norm . . . (*as before*). This is the third blessing to be looked for by so doing.

Then again, brethren, a brother masters the Norm . . . and is reborn in the company of certain devas. Then the blissful ones do not recite to him the stanzas of the Norm: nor does a certain brother of magic powers, who has mastered his will, expound the Norm to that company of devas: nor does a son of a deva expound the

Norm to that company of devas: but some being born as an apparition [1] reminds another similarly born, thus: "Do you remember, good sir? Do you remember, good sir, how in our former birth we led the life of righteousness?" And the other replies, "Yes, good sir, I do indeed remember, I do remember it." Slow indeed, brethren, is the arising of mindfulness, but quickly does that brother attain pre-eminence therein.

Just as when two who once were playmates, making mud-pies together, meet, and one says to the other: "Friend, do you recall this? Do you recall that?" And the other answers, "Yes, friend, I do indeed remember. I do indeed remember." Even so, brethren, does a brother master the Norm . . . (*as before*).

This is the fourth blessing to be looked for by one who has so done,—who has listened to it, recited it, pondered over it, penetrated it by his insight. And these are the four blessings so to be looked for.'

Ang. Nik. ii. 185–6.

SUPPABUDDHA THE LEPER

Thus have I heard. Once the Exalted One was staying near Rājagaha, in the Bamboo Grove, at the Squirrels' Feeding-ground.

Now there lived in Rājagaha at that time a certain poor man, who was a leper, named Suppabuddha, a poor, wretched, miserable

[1] *Opapātiko*, by apparitional birth, without parents. Such an one 'just comes to be' or 'appears' in a heaven-world.

creature. And it happened at that time that the Exalted One was sitting there in the midst of a great multitude, teaching the Norm.

And Suppabuddha the leper saw from afar the multitude gathered together, and at the sight he thought: 'Without a doubt an almsgiving of food, both hard and soft, is toward yonder. Suppose I draw near to yonder crowd. I might get here somewhat to eat, soft food or hard.'

So Suppabuddha the leper drew near that crowd, and he beheld the Exalted One sitting there amid a great crowd, preaching the Norm. So, seeing the Exalted One, he thought: 'No! There is no almsgiving here of food, both hard and soft. It is Gotama the Samana preaching the Norm in the assembly. Suppose I were to listen to the teaching.'

So he sat down at one side, thinking: 'I too will listen to the teaching.'

Now the Exalted One, reading with His thought the thoughts of that whole gathering, said to Himself: 'Who, I wonder, of these present, is able to grasp the Truth?' Then He saw Suppabuddha the leper sitting in the crowd: and at the sight of him He knew, 'This one can grasp the Truth.'

So for the sake of Suppabuddha the leper, the Master preached a sermon, dealing in order due with these topics: On Almsgiving, on the Holy Life, and on the Heaven-world; and He pointed out the meanness and vileness of sensual desires and the profit of freedom from the *āsavas*.

Now when the Exalted One saw that the heart of Suppabuddha the leper was softened, pliant, set free, elated, and full of faith, then He set forth to him the Norm most excellent of the Buddhas, to wit, Suffering, the Cause of Suffering, the Ceasing of Suffering, and the Path.

Then, just as a white cloth, free from stains, is ready to receive the dye, even so in Suppabuddha the leper, as he sat there in that very place, arose the pure stainless insight of the Truth, the knowledge that whatsoever hath a beginning, that also must have an end. And Suppabuddha the leper saw the Truth, reached the Truth, perceived the Truth, plunged into the Truth, crossed beyond doubting, was freed from all questionings, won confidence, and needing nothing further, being established in the Master's teaching, sprang up from his seat and drew near to Him, and there he sat down at one side.

So seated he said to the Exalted One: 'Excellent, O Lord! Excellent, O Lord! Just as if, Lord, one should lift up the fallen, discover the hidden, point out the way to one bewildered, show a light in the gloom, saying, "Now they who have eyes to see can see shapes," even so in divers ways has the Exalted One expounded the truth. I, even I, Lord, do go for refuge to the Exalted One, to the Norm and to the Order of Brethren. May the Exalted One accept me as His follower, as one who from this time forth even to life's end gone to refuge in Him.'

Thereupon Suppabuddha the leper, being taught, established, roused, and made happy by the Exalted One's pious talk, praised and welcomed His words, gave thanks and rose up from his seat, saluted the Exalted One by the right, and went away.

And it came to pass that a young calf flung down the leper Suppabuddha and gored him to death.

Now a number of brethren went to the Exalted One, drew near, saluted Him, and sat down at one side. So seated, they said to the Exalted One: 'Lord, Suppabuddha the leper, after being taught, established, roused, and made happy by the Exalted One's pious talk, is now dead. Pray, what is his rebirth? What is his attainment?'

(Then said the Master:) 'Brethren, Suppabuddha the leper was a sage. He lived in accordance with the Norm. He did not worry me with disputings about the Norm. Suppabuddha the leper, brethren, by breaking the three Fetters is a Stream-winner. He hath escaped the Downfall. He hath won assurance. He is bound for Enlightenment.'

Upon this a brother asked the Exalted One: 'Pray, Lord, what was the condition, what was the cause that made Suppabuddha the leper a poor, mean, miserable creature?'

'Once upon a time, brother, Suppabuddha the leper was son to a rich man in this very town of Rājagaha. One day, walking through a garden, he saw Tagara-Sikhī, the Pacceka Buddha, entering the town to beg: and on seeing Him he thought, "What does this leper here?" and spat upon Him and went away. Thereafter he went to hell for many a year, for hundreds, for thousands, for many hundreds of thousands of years: and as the fruit of that deed he was reborn here in this town of Rājagaha, as a leper, a poor, mean, miserable creature. He, as soon as he came into the Norm-Discipline set forth by the Tathāgata, took on the faith, took on the holy life, the doctrine, self-sacrifice, and wisdom. Thus established, when the body was destroyed, after death he was reborn in the happy state, the blissful world, in the company of the Devas of the Thirty-three, and there does he outshine all other devas in glory and in fame.'

Thereupon the Exalted One, beholding the fitness of the theme, gave utterance to this inspired saying:

> He that hath eyes to see
> The pitfalls in his path
> Should journey stoutly on:
> So in this world of men
> The sage should put away
> All sin and wickedness.

Udāna, v. 3.

ALL MEET IN THE CENTRE

At Sāvatthī. Then the brāhmin Unnabha came to the Exalted One and gave Him friendly greeting, and, after the exchange of mutual courtesies, sat down at one side. So seated, the brāhmin Unnabha said this:

'Master Gotama, there are these five controlling faculties, of different scope, of different range, which do not mutually reap the fruit of each other's scope and range. What five? The controlling faculty of eye, ear, and so on, and body.

Now, Master Gotama, as these five controlling faculties are thus independent of each other in scope and range, what common resort is there (to which all tend) and who is he that reaps the fruit of their joint scope and range ?'

'It is as you say, brāhmin. . . . The common resort of them is mind. It is the mind that reaps the fruit of their joint scope and range.'

'But what, Master Gotama, is the resort of mind ?'

'Mindfulness, brāhmin, is the resort of mind.'

'And what, Master Gotama, is the resort of mindfulness ?'

'Release, brāhmin, is the resort of mindfulness.'

'And what, Master Gotama, is the resort of release ?'

'Nibbāna, brāhmin, is the resort of release.'

'But what, Master Gotama, is the resort of Nibbāna ?'

'That question, brāhmin, goes too far. You cannot get an answer to encompass that question. Plunged in Nibbāna, brāhmin, is the holy life lived, with Nibbāna for its goal, and ending in Nibbāna.'

Thereupon the brāhmin Unnabha was pleased with the words of the Exalted One, and he thanked Him, rose up from his seat, saluted Him by the right, and went away.

Not long after he was gone, the Exalted One said to the brethren :

'Brethren, just as in a peaked hut or a hall with a peaked gable, with a window facing east, when the sun comes up and its rays strike through the window, where do they alight ?'

'On the western wall, Lord.'

'Just so, brethren, is the faith of the brāhmin Unnabha in the Tathāgata settled, rooted, fixed, and strong, not to be pulled up by any one in the world, be he recluse or brāhmin, or deva or Māra or Brahmā.

If at this time, brethren, the brāhmin Unnabha should come to die, there is no fetter, bound by which he would come back again to this world.'

S.N. v. 217–19.

THE PATH OF HOLINESS

THE HOLY LIFE CONSISTS IN FELLOWSHIP WITH THE LOVELY

Thus have I heard. Once the Exalted One was staying among the Sakyans at Sakkara, a Sakyan township.

Then the venerable Ānanda came to the Exalted One, saluted Him, and sat down at one side. So seated, the venerable Ānanda said this:

'The half of the holy life, Lord, it is the friendship with what is lovely, association with what is lovely, intimacy with what is lovely.'

'Say not so, Ānanda! Say not so, Ānanda! It is the whole, not the half of the holy life. Of a brother so blessed with fellowship with what is lovely we may expect this,—that he will develop the Ariyan Eightfold Path, that he will make much of the Ariyan Eightfold Path.

And how, Ānanda, does a brother so blessed develop and make much of the Ariyan Eightfold Path?

Herein, Ānanda, he develops right view, which is based on detachment, on passionlessness, on cessation: which is concerned with readiness for giving up. He develops right aim, which is so based and concerned: likewise right speech, right action, right living, right effort, right mindfulness, and right contemplation, which is based on detachment, on passionlessness, on cessation; which is concerned with readiness for giving up.

That, Ānanda, is how a brother blessed with friendship with what is lovely, association with what is lovely, intimacy with what is lovely, develops and makes much of the Ariyan Eightfold Path.

This is the Method, Ānanda, by which you are to understand how the whole of this holy life consists in fellowship, association, intimacy with what is lovely. Truly, Ānanda, beings liable to rebirth are liberated from rebirth; beings liable to decay, liable to death, liable to grief, woe, lamentation, and despair are liberated therefrom because of my fellowship with what is lovely.

By the Method, Ānanda, you are to understand that the whole of the holy life consists in fellowship with what is lovely, in association with what is lovely, in intimacy with what is lovely.'

S.N. v. 2.

BEAUTY IS TRUTH, TRUTH BEAUTY

(*The Master had been accused of several heresies by different sects, among others of having taught that the universe was of fortuitous origin, a mere sport of chance. He now explains to the Wanderer, Bhaggava.*)

'Now I, Bhaggava, have attained to the topmost Knowledge. Not only do I know that, but I know it in its highest excellence. And still further, I do not misapply that knowledge. As I do not misapply it, I have seen the Calm, realizing which the Tathāgata cannot fall into error.

Now, Bhaggava, as I have thus declared (my knowledge), certain recluses and brāhmins have abused me with groundless, empty lies that have no truth in them, saying: "Gotama the recluse and his brethren have gone astray. For Gotama the recluse teaches this:

'When one reaches up to the Release, called the Beautiful, and having reached it abides therein, at such a time he regards the Whole (Universe) as ugly.'"

But I never said that, Bhaggava. This is what I do say: "Whenever one reaches up to the Release, called the Beautiful, then he knows indeed what Beauty is."'

'Then, Lord, it is they who have gone astray, they who accuse the Exalted One and His brethren of having gone astray. Assured am I, Lord, in the Exalted One. It is the Exalted One who can teach me in such a way that I too may reach up to the Release, called Beautiful, and having reached it may abide therein.'

'But it is hard for you, Bhaggava, holding other views, acquiescing in another faith, and having other inclinations, different aims, and a different system,—it is hard for you to reach up to the Release, called Beautiful, and having reached it to abide therein.

Come now, Bhaggava, as to that assurance which you have in me, do you guard it carefully!'

'Well, Lord, if it be a hard thing for me,

holding as I do other views, acquiescing in another faith, having other inclinations, a different aim, and a different system,—then I will at any rate guard carefully that assurance which I have in the Exalted One.'

Thus spake the Exalted One. And he of the Bhaggava-clan, the Wanderer, was pleased at what the Exalted One said, and took delight therein.

D.N. iii. 34–5.

'I HAVE FOUND THE MASTER'

Thus have I heard. Once the Exalted One was on his travels among the folk of Magadha and came to Rājagaha. And he drew near to the dwelling of Bhaggava the potter, and came to Bhaggava the potter and said to him :

'If it be agreeable to you, Bhaggava, I will pass one night in your shed.'

'I have no objection, sir,' said Bhaggava the potter. 'But there is also here a wanderer who has just begun to pass his first rainy season. If he consents, do you, sir, stay as long as you please.'

Now at that time there was a certain clansman named Pukkusāti, who, having faith in the Exalted One, had gone forth as a wanderer from home to the homeless life. Now he it was who had just begun to pass his first rainy season in the potter's shed.

So the Exalted One approached the venerable Pukkusāti and came to him and said : 'If it be agreeable to you, brother, I will spend one night in the shed.'

'The shed is big enough, friend! Stay as long as you please, worthy sir.'

Then the Exalted One entered the potter's shed and spread a heap of straw at one side, and sat down cross-legged, holding His body straight up, and setting mindfulness before Him as His aim. And so the Exalted One sat far into the night. Likewise the venerable Pukkusāti sat far into the night.

Now it occurred to the Exalted One: 'I wonder whether this clansman is well disposed. Suppose I question him.' So the Exalted One said to the venerable Pukkusāti:

'Having faith in whom, brother, did you go a wandering from home to the homeless life? Who is your teacher? Of whose doctrine do you approve?'

'Friend, there is a recluse called Gotama, of the Sakyan clan, one who went forth as a wanderer from the Sakyan clan. About this Gotama, the Exalted One, such is the goodly rumour that is noised abroad: "'Tis He, the Exalted One, Arahant, Fully Enlightened One, perfect in knowledge and practice, the Wellfarer, knower of the world, the charioteer of men who would be tamed, teacher of devas and mankind, the Buddha, the Exalted One!" Having faith in that Exalted One I went forth a wanderer. That Exalted One is my teacher. The doctrine of that Exalted One do I approve.'

'But where now is that Exalted One dwelling, brother, that Arahant who is a Fully Enlightened One?'

'In the northern provinces, friend, there is a

town called Sāvatthī. That is where the Exalted One is now dwelling, that Arahant who is a Fully Enlightened One.'

'Have you ever seen Him, brother? Would you know him again if you were to see Him?'

'No, friend, I have never seen that Exalted One. If I saw Him, I should not know Him.'

Then thought the Exalted One: 'So this clansman went forth as a wanderer through faith in Me. Suppose now I teach him the Norm.' Then the Exalted One said to the venerable Pukkusāti:

'I will teach you a teaching, brother. Do you listen to it. Attend carefully. I will speak.'

'Very good, friend,' replied the venerable Pukkusāti to the Exalted One.

(Then the Master expounded unto him at length the sixfold nature of man. And when He had finished He said to him:)

'This sixfold analysis of Mine, brother,—do you bear it in mind.'

Thereupon the venerable Pukkusāti exclaimed: 'I have found the Master! I have found the Wellfarer! The All-enlightened One have I found!'

And he sprung up from his seat, threw his robe over one shoulder, and with his head worshipped the feet of the Exalted One, saying:

'Mine is the fault, Lord! Mine is the offence! Such was my folly, my blindness, my stupidity, in thoughtlessly using the word "friend" in speaking to the Exalted One. Let the Exalted One accept this acknowledgement of my offence as such, for my better restraint in future time.'

'True it is, brother, that you erred in your folly, your blindness, your stupidity, in thus addressing Me. Yet inasmuch as you have seen your fault as a fault, and have acknowledged it as is right, we do now accept the same of you. For herein, brother, lies growth in the Ariyan discipline, that, when one has seen his fault as a fault, he should confess it as such and practise self-restraint in future time.'

'O Lord, may I receive full ordination from the Exalted One?'

'But, brother, is your bowl and robe complete?'

'Nay, Lord, I have not bowl and robe complete.'

'But, brother, the Tathāgatas do not give full ordination to those whose bowl and robe are not complete.'

Whereupon the venerable Pukkusāti was delighted with the words of the Exalted One, and gave thanks, and rose up again from his seat, saluted the Exalted One by the right, and went forth to search for robe and bowl.

Now while the venerable Pukkusāti was going about in search of robe and bowl, a stray cow gored him so that he died.

Then a number of brethren came to the Exalted One, approached Him, and sat down at one side. So seated those brethren said to the Exalted One: 'Lord, the clansman named Pukkusāti, who was given brief instruction by the Exalted One, has been killed. What is his lot? What is his after-death state?'

'A sage, brethren, is Pukkusāti the clansman. He walked according to the ordinances of the

Norm, and he did not vex Me with questions about the Norm. Brethren, the clansman Pukkusāti, by destroying the Five Fetters that bind to rebirth in the lower world, has come-to-be by apparitional birth (in the Brahma world), he is destined to win Nibbāna, his lot is not to return thence any more.'

M.N. iii. chap. 140.

THE DHAMMA IS PROFOUND

The Exalted One was once staying among the Kurūs at Kammāsadamma, a suburb of the Kurūs. Now the venerable Ānanda went to the Exalted One, saluted Him, and sat down at one side. So seated the venerable Ānanda said this to the Exalted One:

'Wonderful, Lord! Marvellous, Lord! How deep is this Causal Law, and how deep it seems! And yet do I regard it as quite plain to understand!'

'Say not so, Ānanda! Say not so! Deep indeed is this Causal Law, and deep it appears to be. It is by not knowing, by not understanding, by not penetrating this doctrine, that this world of men has become entangled like a ball of twine, become covered with mildew, become like munja grass and rushes, and unable to pass beyond the doom of the Waste, the Way of Woe, the Fall, and the Ceaseless Round (of rebirth).

In one, Ānanda, who dwells contemplating the enjoyment of all that is concerned with grasping, there grows up craving. Craving is the condition of grasping: grasping is the condition of becoming.

Conditioned by these are birth, decay-and-death, grief and suffering, woe, lamentation, and despair. So arises all this mass of Ill.

Just as if there were a great tree, whose roots go down and across and draw up the sap. Indeed, Ānanda, so great a tree thus fed, thus supplied with nourishment, would stand fast for a long time.

Just so, in one who dwells contemplating the enjoyment of all that is concerned with grasping, there grows up craving. And (as I told you) . . . from craving arises all this mass of Ill.

But in him, Ānanda, who dwells contemplating the misery of all that is concerned with grasping, craving ceases. By the ceasing of craving, grasping ceases: so also cease becoming, birth, decay-and-death . . . and suffering and despair. So ceases all this mass of Ill.

Suppose, Ānanda, there were a great tree, and a man comes with axe and basket and cuts down that tree at the root. He cuts it at the root and digs a trench all round and pulls out the roots, even the little roots and the fibres of them. Then he cuts it into logs, splits the logs, and cuts the logs into chips. Then he dries the chips in wind and sun, burns them with fire, collects them into a heap of ash, winnows the ashes in a strong wind, or lets them be carried away by a swift-flowing stream.

Surely that great tree, thus cut off at the roots, would be made like a stump of a palm-tree, become nothing, become unable to sprout again in future time.

Just so, Ānanda, in him who dwells contemplating the misery of all concerned with grasping, craving ceases. And with the ceasing of grasping cease also becoming, birth, decay-and-death, grief, sorrow, woe, lamentation, and despair. Such is the ceasing of this whole mass of Ill.'

S.N. ii. p. 92.

FETTERS

(*Mahāli asks the Master about the object of the holy life or brahma-cariya.*)

'Then, Lord, is it for the sake of realizing the practice of contemplation that the brethren live the holy life under the Exalted One ?'

'No, indeed, Mahāli. It is not for the sake of this that the brethren live the holy life under my guidance. There are other higher and more excellent things, Mahāli, for the realization of which the brethren live the holy life under my guidance.'

'And what, Lord, are those higher and more excellent things . . . ?'

'Herein, Mahāli, (in this discipline) a brother, by the utter destruction of the Three Fetters (of belief in the reality of bodyhood, doubt in the Master and His Teaching, belief in the value of rites and ceremonies), becomes a Stream-winner, saved from the Downfall, assured of attaining to the perfect wisdom. That, Mahāli, is one thing higher and more excellent. . . .

Then again, Mahāli, a brother by the utter destruction of the Three Fetters and by wearing thin (the Fetters) Lust, Ill-will, and Delusion, becomes a Once-returner,—yea, only once more returning to this world he makes an end of woe. That, Mahāli, is a thing higher and more excellent.

Then again, Mahāli, a brother by the utter destruction of the Five (last) Fetters that bind to rebirth in the lower worlds becomes spontaneously (in the Formless Worlds), thence to pass utterly away, being of a nature never to return. That, Mahāli, is a thing higher and more excellent. . . . Then again, Mahāli, a brother even in this very life, by the destruction of the *āsavas*, having realized by his own abnormal powers the taintless heart-release, the wisdom-release, having so won it abides therein. This, Mahāli, is a thing yet higher and more excellent, for the sake of realizing which brethren live the holy life under my guidance. Such are these other things. . . .'

'But, Lord, is there a path, is there a Way leading to the realization of these things.'

'There is indeed a Path, Mahāli. There is indeed a Way so leading.'

'What is that Path, Lord? What is that Way so leading?'

'Verily it is this Ariyan Eightfold Path, to wit: Right View, Right Aim, Right Speech, Right Action, Right Living, Right Effort, Right Mindfulness, Right Contemplation. This, Mahāli, is the Path, this is the Way leading to the realization of these things.'

D.N. i. 155.

THE FIVE FETTERS

Cut off the Five: desert the Five: the Five subdue.
That mendicant who from the Fetters Five
Hath freed himself at last, by men is called
A Crosser of the Stream.

Dhp. v. 369.

THE FIVE LOWER FETTERS AND THEIR ABANDONING

Thus have I heard. Once the Exalted One was dwelling at Sāvatthī, in Jeta Grove, at Anāthapindika's Park. Then the Exalted One called to the brethren, saying, 'Brethren!' 'Yes, Lord,' replied those brethren to the Exalted One. The Exalted One thus spake:

'Do ye bear in mind, brethren, the Five Fetters that bind to the lower world, as taught by me?'

Whereupon the venerable Mālunkyaputta said this to the Exalted One:

'I, Lord, bear in mind those Five Fetters.'

'And how, Mālunkyaputta, do you bear them in mind?'

'I bear in mind, Lord, the view of bodyhood, as taught by the Exalted One, and wavering, and the moral taint of dependence on rite and ritual, the excitement of sensual delight, and malevolence, taught by the Exalted One as fetters that bind to the lower world. These are the Five Fetters that I bear in mind, Lord.'

'As taught for whom, Mālunkyaputta, do you bear in mind these Five Fetters? Will not the wanderers of other views reproach you, using the parable of a tender baby-boy for their reproach and saying thus:

"But, Mālunkyaputta, there can be no bodyhood for a tender baby-boy, dull of wits and lying on his back. How, then, can there arise in him any view of bodyhood? Yet there is indeed latent in him a tendency to the view of bodyhood.

Likewise, Mālunkyaputta, there can be no mental conditions for a tender baby-boy, dull of wits and lying on his back. How, then, can there be in him any wavering of mental conditions? Yet there is in him a latent tendency to wavering.

So also, Mālunkyaputta, he can have no moral practice. How, then, can there be in him any moral taint of dependence on rite and ritual? Yet he has a latent tendency thereto.

Again, Mālunkyaputta, that tender babe has no sensual passions. How, then, can he know the excitement of sensual delight? But the tendency is there.

Lastly, Mālunkyaputta, for that tender babe beings do not exist. How, then, can he harbour malevolence against beings? Yet the tendency thereto is in him."

Now, Mālunkyaputta, will not those wanderers of other views thus reproach you, using for their reproach the parable of the tender baby-boy?'

When this was said, the venerable Ānanda thus addressed the Exalted One: 'Now is the time, Exalted One! O Wellfarer, now is the time for the Exalted One to set forth (the meaning of) the Five Fetters that bind to the lower world. Hearing the Exalted One the brethren will bear it in mind.'

'Then, Ānanda, do you listen and apply your mind carefully. I will speak.'

'Even so, Lord,' replied the venerable Ānanda to the Exalted One. Then the Exalted One thus spake:

'In this matter, Ānanda, the untaught manyfolk, who discern not those who are Ariyans, who are unskilled in the Ariyan discipline, who are untrained in the Ariyan discipline, who discern not those who are worthy ones, who are unskilled in the worthy Doctrine, untrained in the worthy Doctrine,—these remain with minds obsessed by, possessed by the bodyhood view: and when this view of bodyhood has arisen they know not fully, as it really is, the escape from that view. That view of bodyhood which is engrained in them and not driven out of them, is a fetter that binds to the lower world.

And the same may be said of each of the other four Fetters.

But the well-taught Ariyan disciple, he who discerns those who are Ariyans, who is skilled in the Ariyan discipline, trained in the Ariyan discipline, who discerns those who are worthy ones, who is skilled in the worthy Doctrine, trained in the worthy Doctrine,—such an one does not remain with mind obsessed by, possessed by the view of bodyhood. When this view has arisen he fully knows, as it really is, the escape from it. In him the latent tendency to that view is abandoned.

And the same may be said of each of the other four Fetters.

Now, Ānanda, as to the Path, the Approach to the abandoning of these Five Fetters that bind to the lower world. It is impossible to suppose that anyone will know or see or abandon those Five Fetters without entering on that Path, that Approach to the abandoning of those Fetters.

Just as, Ānanda, no man will get at the sound

timber of a great upstanding tree, full of sound timber, without cutting away its outer back and its outer pith ; so is it impossible to get at those Five Fetters without entering on the Path, the Approach to the abandonment of them.

But as, Ānanda, a man will get at the sound timber of a great upstanding tree, full of sound timber, by cutting away its outer bark and outer pith . . . so with those Five Fetters.

Likewise, Ānanda, just as the River Ganga flows on full of water, brimful, so that even a crow can drink therefrom : and then some man who is a weakling comes saying, " I will cleave with my arm this Ganga's flood and so cross safely to the farther shore,"—but he could not do so : even so, Ānanda, in whomsoever the heart leaps not up, is not calmed, established, and released when the doctrine for the ceasing of bodyhood is shown,—even as that weakling should such be regarded.

But suppose, Ānanda, that when the River Ganga is flowing, full of water, brimful, so that a crow could drink therefrom, and a strong man comes saying, " I will cleave this Ganga's stream with my arm and go safe to the farther shore,"—he could do so. Just so, Ānanda, when the doctrine for the ceasing of bodyhood is shown, he whose heart leaps up within him, is calmed, established, and set free,—like that strong man is such to be regarded.

Now, Ānanda, what is the Path, what the Approach for the abandonment of the Five Fetters that bind to the lower world ?

In this matter, Ānanda, a brother by insight into the substrates (of rebirth), by the abandonment of evil things, by the calming down in every way of unchastity, aloof from sensuality, aloof from states that are evil, enters on the First Musing, which is accompanied by thought directed and sustained, which is born of solitude, easeful and zestful, and abides therein.

Then he regards all things concerned with body, feeling, perception, the activities, and consciousness, in the light of impermanence and suffering, as a plague, an imposthume, a dart, as an evil thing, as ill-health, as alien, as corruptible, void, without the Self. Of such things he cleanses his heart. So cleansing his heart of them he disposes his heart for the nature of the Ambrosial, thinking, "This is the good, this is the excellent, this calming of all activities, this laying down of all the substrates (of rebirth), this destruction of craving, passionlessness, ceasing, Nibbāna."

Thus established he wins destruction of the *āsavas* (even if he do not win destruction of the *āsavas*), yet by that very thirsting after righteousness, lured by that lure of righteousness, by that destruction of the Five Fetters that bind to the lower world, he is reborn without parents (in the Brahma world), from that world to pass away for good and never to return.

Such, Ānanda, is the Path, such the Approach to the abandonment of these Five Fetters.

Again, Ānanda, a brother, by the calming down of thought directed and sustained, enters on the inward calm, that single-mindedness of will, apart from thought directed and sustained, born of mental balance, zestful and full of ease, which is the Second Musing . . . and so reaches the Third Musing, and the Fourth Musing . . . and abides therein. Such, Ānanda, is the Path, the Approach to the abandonment of these Five Fetters.

In like manner, Ānanda, a brother, passing beyond all perception of objects, making an end of objectivity, by not attending to perception of the diversity of things, (thinking) "boundless is space," reaches the conception of the boundlessness of space, and so abides . . . (*as before*) . . . and so reaches the sphere of the infinity of consciousness and abides therein . . . and so reaches the sphere of nothingness and abides therein.

Then he regards all things concerned with feelings, perception, the activities, and consciousness also in the light of impermanence, suffering, and as a plague, an imposthume, a dart, as an evil thing, as ill-health, as alien, as corruptible, void, and without the Self. Of such things he cleanses his heart . . . (*as above*). . . .

Such, Ānanda, is the Path, the Approach to the abandoning of the Five Fetters that bind to the lower world.'

'If this, Lord, be the Path, the Approach . . . how, then, are some brethren released by emancipation of heart, others by the release of wisdom ?'

'That, Ānanda, I declare to be due to a difference of faculties.'

Thus spake the Exalted One. And the venerable Ānanda was delighted by His words.

M.N. i. chap. **64.**

THE PATH OF HOLINESS

THE SELF

Then Vacchagotta the Wanderer came to the Exalted One and greeted Him in friendly wise, and after the exchange of mutual courtesies sat down at one side. So seated he said to the Exalted One:

'Master Gotama, what have you to say about the existence of the Self?'

At these words the Exalted One was silent.

'How now, Master Gotama? Is there no such thing as the Self?'

At these words the Exalted One was silent.

Then Vacchagotta the Wanderer (in disgust) rose up from his seat and went away. Not long after he was gone the venerable Ānanda said to the Exalted One:

'How is it, Lord, that the Exalted One made no reply to the question asked by Vacchagotta the Wanderer?'

'If, Ānanda, when asked "Does the Self exist?" I had replied to him, "The Self exists," then, Ānanda, that would be to side with all those recluses and brāhmins who are eternalists.

But if, Ānanda, when asked the question, "Does the Self not exist, then?" I had replied, "No! The Self does not exist," that would be to side with those recluses and brāhmins who are annihilationists.

Again, Ānanda, if when asked by Vacchagotta the Wanderer "Does the Self exist?" I had replied, "The Self does exist," would that reply be consistent with My knowledge that all things are impermanent?'

'No, Lord, it would not.'

'Again, Ānanda, when asked "Then does not the Self exist?" if I had replied "No! it does not exist," it would have added to the bewilderment of Vacchagotta the Wanderer, already bewildered. For he would have said, "Formerly I had a self, but now I have one no more."'

S.N. iv. 400.

'THIS LITTLE BODY HOLDETH ALL'

Once the Exalted One was dwelling near Sāvatthī, in Jeta Grove, in the Park of Anāthapiṇḍika, the Feeder of the Poor.

Now at that time one Rohitassa, who was son to a deva, when the night was far spent, lit up the whole circuit of Jeta Grove with a wondrous radiance, and came to the Exalted One and, greeting Him, stood at one side.

So standing, Rohitassa, son to a deva, thus spoke: 'Is there, O Lord, anywhere, whither going one can reach to where there is no birth, no ageing, no decaying, no falling away to rise up again elsewhere in rebirth? Can one, O Lord, by going thither know the end or see the end or reach the end of the world?'

'No, friend! I declare that there is nowhere whither going one would find no birth, no ageing, no decay, no falling away to rise up elsewhere in rebirth. By going I declare one cannot know the end, see the end, reach the end of the world.'

'Wonderful, O Lord! A marvel, O Lord! How well said is this saying that is uttered by the Exalted One! In former days, Lord, I was a sage, called Rohitassa. Son of Bhoja I was. I had the magic power of flying through the air Such speed I had—it was even as when a mighty archer, well trained and skilled in archery, with a light arrow and slight effort, speeds a shaft far beyond the limits of the shadow cast by a palm-tree.[1] So mighty was the stride of my feet that it was even as the stretch between the Eastern and the Western Oceans. To me, Lord, possessed of such speed and of such a mighty stride, there came this longing: "By going I will reach the end of the world."

And so, Lord, even as I was, unfed by food or drink, without resting or even performing nature's needs, without waiting to dispel my weariness by sleep—though in those days man's span of life was a hundred years,—yet a hundred years I journeyed on. But I never reached it. I never came to the end. I died before I reached world's end!

Wondrous it is, O Lord, that hath been so well spoken by the Exalted One, to wit: "Thou canst not by going reach that place wherein there are no birth, no ageing, no decaying, no falling away, no rising up elsewhere in rebirth. Thou canst not by going come to such a place!"'

'Even so. Nevertheless, my friend, I do not say that without reaching the world's end an end of woe cannot be made (for you can end it here and now). For, my friend, in this very body, six feet in length, with its sense-impressions and its thoughts and ideas, I do declare to you are the world, and the origin of the world, and the ceasing

[1] About two hundred yards at sunrise and sunset.

of the world, and likewise the Way that leadeth to the ceasing thereof.'

(So saying the Master summed up what He had said in these verses :)

Not to be reached by going is world's end.
Yet is there no release for man from woe,
Unless ye reach world's end. Yea verily
He that is wise and lives the holy life,
He knows the world. He goeth to world's end.
Calmed is he, for he knows. He hankereth
Neither for this world nor for any world.

Ang. Nik. ii. 46.

CONSCIOUSNESS (1)

(The Exalted One said :)

'Owing to two things, brethren, consciousness comes to pass. What two things? Owing to eye and shape arises eye-consciousness. Eye is transient, changeable, becoming other: shapes are transient, changeable, becoming other. So this duality is mobile and transitory, transient, changeable, becoming other, and eye-consciousness is of a like nature.

Whatsoever the condition and whatsoever the relation of the arising of eye-consciousness, that condition and that relation are transient, changeable, becoming other. Thus, happening because of a transient relation, is eye-consciousness. How, then, can it be enduring?

Now, brethren, that collision, coincidence, encounter of these three things (eye, shape, eye-consciousness) is called visual contact.

Visual contact also is transient, changeable,

becoming other. Whatsoever the condition and whatsoever the relation of the arising of visual contact, that condition and relation are transient, changeable, becoming other. Thus, happening because of a transient relation is visual contact. How, then, can it be enduring ?

Contacted, brethren, one feels, contacted one is aware, contacted one perceives. So these things also are mobile and transitory, transient, changeable, becoming other.

And the same may be said of ear, nose, tongue, body, and mind.

Thus owing to two things consciousness comes to pass.'

S.N. iv. 67.

OCEAN

(The Exalted One said :)

' " The ocean, the ocean," brethren, say the untaught manyfolk.

But in the Ariyan discipline, brethren, that is not ocean, but a great mass of water, a great pool of water.

The eye of a man, brethren, is an ocean. Its motion is of shapes. Whoso overcomes that motion made of shapes, he is called " crosser over." He who has crossed over, gone beyond the ocean of eye, with its waves, its inlets, its sharks and goblins (which are lusts), that brāhmin stands upon the further shore.

So likewise a man's tongue, brethren, is an ocean : and made of taste is its motion. He who conquers taste . . . so crosses over.

Man's mind, brethren, is an ocean. Its motion

is made of ideas. He who conquers mind . . . stands upon the further shore.'

Thus spake the Exalted One. . . .

Whoso hath crossed this monster-teeming sea,
With devils and fearsome waves impassable,
'Versed in the lore,' 'a man of saintly life,'
'Gone to world's end,' and 'gone beyond' he's called.

S.N. iv. 157 (*verses also at Iti-vuttaka*, § 69).

THE ALL

The Exalted One said :

'Brethren, I will teach you the All. Do you listen to it.

And what, brethren, is the All ?

It is eye and visible object : ear and sound : nose and scent : tongue and taste : body and tangibles : mind and ideas. This, brethren, is called the All.

Now, brethren, he who should say, "Rejecting this All, I will proclaim some other All,"—such might be the substance of his talk, but when questioned he would not be able to make good his boast, and he would come by disappointment besides. What is the cause of that ? Because, brethren, it would be beyond his powers to do so.'

S.N. iv. 15.

CONTROL OF FACULTIES

He meets with ill, brothers, who hath not tamed
The sixfold impact of the sphere of sense.
They who have learned the mastery of these,
With faith for comrade, they dwell free from lust.

THE PATH OF HOLINESS

Beholding with the eye delightful things
Or things unlovely, let him restrain his bent
To lust for loveliness, and let him not
Corrupt his heart with thoughts of 'O 'tis dear.'

And when, again, sounds sweet or harsh he hears,
Not led astray by sweetness, let him check
The error of his senses : let him not
Corrupt his heart with thoughts of 'O 'tis sweet.'

If some delightful fragrance meet the nose,
And then again some foul malodorous stench,
Let him restrain repugnance for that stench,
Nor yet be led by lust for what is sweet.

Should he taste savours that are sweet and choice,
And then again what's bitter to the tongue,
He should not greedily devour the sweet,
Nor yet feel loathing for the bitter taste.

By pleasures' impact not inebriate,
Nor yet distracted by the touch of pain,
To pleasure and to pain indifferent,
Let him be free from likings and dislikes.

Obsessed (by lusts) are others : so obsessed
They know, and so they fare. But he dispels
All the world's vulgar fashionings of mind,
And treads the path of sacrifice of self.

By contact of these Six, if mind be trained,
The heart is never shaken any more.
O'ercome these two, O brethren,—Lust and Hate.
Pass ye beyond the bounds of birth and death.

S.N. iv. 70–1.

S.S.B.—9

UNTROUBLED AND RELEASED

Then the venerable Mālunkya's son came to the Exalted One, saluted Him, and sat down at one side. So seated the venerable Mālunkya's son said this to the Exalted One:

'Well for me, Lord, if the Exalted One were to teach me a doctrine in brief, hearing which doctrine from the Exalted One I might dwell alone, remote, earnest, ardent, and resolute.'

'As to this request of yours, Mālunkya's son, what is the use of my teaching youthful brethren (to no purpose)[1] if, now that you are old, of ripe age, full of years, far gone in years, come to the end of your life, you now ask me for a doctrine in brief?'

'But, Lord, though I am old . . . and well stricken in years, let my Lord the Exalted One teach me a doctrine in brief. Maybe I can understand what is said by the Exalted One. Surely I might become an inheritor of the words of the Exalted One.'

'Now what think you, Mālunkya's son? As to those shapes cognizable by eye, which you have not seen, which you have never seen before, which you do not see now, which you have no desire to see in future,—have you any partiality, any passion, any affection for such shapes?'

'Not so, Lord.'

'As to those sounds, cognizable by ear, which

[1] The commentary says this old brother had wasted his opportunities in youth, and now asks for a private teaching.

you have not heard, which you have never heard before, which you do not hear now, which you have no desire to hear in future time,—have you any partiality, any passion, any affection for such sounds ?'

'Not so, Lord.'

'As to those scents cognizable by nose; those tastes cognizable by tongue; those tangibles cognizable by body;—which you have not smelt, tasted, or contacted before, do not smell, taste, or contact now, and do not wish to do so in the future,—have you any partiality, any passion, any affection for such scents, tastes, or touches ?'

'Not so, Lord.'

'As to those things cognizable by mind, things not cognized, never cognized before, things which you do not cognize now, and do not wish to cognize in future,—have you any partiality, any passion, any affection for such things ?'

'Not so, Lord.'

'Then in these cases, as regards things visible, audible, sensible, and cognizable, you will simply have the sight of the thing seen, the sound of the thing heard, the sense of the thing sensed, and the idea of the thing cognized. Now, Mālunkya's son, since this is so, as I have just said, and since *thereby* and *therein* you will have no partiality, no passion, no affection, either in this life or that beyond, or in the intermediate state, just this is the end of suffering.'

'Of this teaching, Lord, given me in brief by the Exalted One, I understand the meaning in detail.'

(Whereupon the venerable Mālunkya's son in

stanzas enlarges on this teaching, with the approval of the Master, who repeats his stanzas.[1])

Thereupon the venerable Mālunkya's son, rejoicing in the words of the Exalted One, thanked Him, rose from his seat, saluted Him by the right, and went away.

Then the venerable Mālunkya's son, abiding alone, remote, earnest, ardent, and resolute, in no long time attained that Goal to gain which the clansmen duly wander forth from home to the homeless, that unsurpassed life of holiness, realizing it for himself in that very life by his own abnormal powers, and abode therein: so that he realized 'Destroyed is rebirth, lived is the holy life, done is what I had to do, there is no more existence for me in conditions such as these.'

And the venerable Mālunkya's son was yet another of the Arahants.

S.N. iv. 72 ff.

THE PARABLE OF THE EVER-SMOULDERING ANT-HILL

Thus have I heard. Once the Exalted One was staying near Sāvatthī, at Jeta Grove, in Anāthapindika's Park. Now at that time the venerable Kumāra-Kassapa was staying in Dark Grove. Then a certain deva of wondrous radiance, when night was waning, lit up the whole of Dark Grove with splendour and came to the venerable Kumāra-Kassapa, and drew near and stood at one side.

[1] Which may be read in *Theragāthā*, *Psalms of the Brethren*, trans. by Dr. C. A. Rhys Davids, pp. 308–9.

As he thus stood, that deva said this to the venerable Kumāra-Kassapa: 'Brother, brother, this ant-hill smoulders by night and bursts into flame by day (*and spake this parable unto him*). "And the brāhmin said: 'Dig, O wise one, taking thy tool.' And the wise one took his tool and dug and came upon a crowbar, and said, 'Sir, here is a crowbar.'

Then said the brāhmin, 'Throw down the crowbar. Take thy tool, wise one, and dig.' And he did so and came upon a bladder, and said, 'Sir, here is a bladder.'

Then said the brāhmin, 'Throw down the bladder. Take thy tool and dig.' And he did so and came upon a two-pronged fork, and said, 'Sir, here is a two-pronged fork.'

Then said the brāhmin, 'Throw down the two-pronged fork, wise one. Take thy tool and dig.' And he did so and came upon a casket, and said, 'Sir, here is a casket.'

Then said the brāhmin, 'Throw down the casket. Take thy tool and dig, wise one.' And he did so and came upon a tortoise, and (in like manner) a knife-blade, then a lump of meat, then a snake.

Then said the brāhmin, 'Throw these away, but let be the snake. Slay not the snake; do honour to the snake.'"

'Now, brother' (said the deva), 'do you take these questions to the Exalted One. Ask Him of them and bear in mind the explanation given by the Exalted One, for I see none other in this world, brother, and in the world of the devas with its

Māras, its Brahmās, and all its hosts of recluses and brāhmins, of devas and mankind,—I see none other who will establish one's heart by giving the answer to these questions, save only the Tathāgata, a disciple of the Tathāgata, or one who has learned from them.'

Thus spake that deva, and, so saying, vanished there and then.

Thereupon the venerable Kumāra-Kassapa, when that night was gone, approached the Exalted One, and coming to Him, saluted Him and sat down at one side. So seated he described to the Exalted One what had happened and the words of that deva, and he asked the Exalted One:

'What, Lord, is the ant-hill? What is that which smoulders by night? What is that which bursts into flame by day? Who the brahmin, who the wise one, what the tool, what the digging, what the crowbar, the bladder, the two-pronged fork, the casket, the tortoise, the knife-blade, the lump of meat, and what the snake?'

'"The ant-hill," brother, is a term for this body, of the four elements compounded, begotten of parents, fed on rice, on gruel and soup, a thing impermanent, liable to destruction, liable to be crushed, of nature to break up and be scattered. Whatsoever, brother, is thought over and pondered at night concerning one's daily needs,—that is the smouldering by night. Whatsoever, brother, after pondering and thinking it over by night, one puts into action by day in thought, word, and deed,—that is the bursting into flame by day.

"The brāhmin," brother, is a name for the Tathāgata, the Arahant, the Fully Awakened One.

"The wise one," brother, is a name for a brother who is yet a learner.

"The tool," brother, is a name for the Ariyan insight.

"Digging," brother, is a name for earnest application.

"The crowbar," brother, is a name for ignorance. "Throw away the crowbar" means "banish ignorance." "Dig, wise one" means "use your tool."

"The bladder," brother, is a name for anger and the state of being angry. "Throw away the bladder" means "cast aside anger and the state of being angry." That is the meaning of "Dig, wise one, taking thy tool."

"The two-pronged fork," brother, is a name for wavering. "Throw away the fork" means "abandon wavering." That is the meaning of the saying.

"The casket," brother, is a name for the Five Hindrances: the hindrances of sensual lust, enmity, sloth and torpor, worry and flurry, and wavering. Thus "Throw away the casket" means abandon the Five Hindrances. . . .

"The tortoise," brother, is a name for the Five Grasping-groups, of body, of feeling, of perception, of the activities, of consciousness. "Throw away the tortoise" means "abandon the Five Grasping-groups." . . .

"The knife-blade," brother, is a name for the five strands of Sensual Delights, to wit: of shapes perceived by the sense of sight, delightful, pleasing, attractive, dear, pleasure-giving, and lustful. Likewise those perceived by the ear, the nose, the tongue, and those tangible by body. "Throw away the knife-blade" means "abandon the five strands of Sensual Delight." . . .

"The lump of meat," brother, is a name for the Lust of Enjoyment. "Throw away the lump of meat" means abandon that. . . .

"The snake," brother, is a name for the brother who has destroyed the *āsavas*. "Let be the snake, slay not the snake, do honour to the snake," that is the meaning of it.'

Thus spake the Exalted One, and the venerable Kumāra-Kassapa was pleased at the words of the Exalted One and heard them gladly.

M.N. i. chap. 23.

'THERE IS ONE AMONG YOU'

Now at that time the Exalted One was dwelling near Sāvatthī, in East Park, at the house of Migāra's mother. And on that occasion He was seated surrounded by the Order of Brethren, and it was the Sabbath.[1]

Then the venerable Ānanda, as the night advanced and the first watch was passing, arose from his seat, put his outer robes over one shoulder, and, bowing towards the Exalted One with folded palms, said to the Exalted One:

'Lord, the night is far advanced. The first watch is passing. Long hath the Order of Brethren been sitting here. Let my Lord the Exalted One recite the Obligations[2] to the

[1] *Uposatha*, the days of full, new, and quarter moon.
[2] *Pātimokkha*, also a confession of faults.

brethren.' At these words the Exalted One was silent.

Then a second time, when the second watch was passing, the venerable Ānanda arose and made the same request. But the Exalted One was silent.

And yet a third time, when the third watch was passing, the venerable Ānanda rose from his seat and made the same request. Then the Exalted One said: 'The assembly is not perfectly pure, Ānanda.'

Then thought the venerable Moggallāna the Great: 'Concerning what person, I wonder, does the Exalted One say this?' And the venerable Moggallāna the Great surveyed in mind the whole Order of Brethren, reading their thoughts with his.[1] And the venerable Moggallāna the Great beheld that person, one of evil conduct, of wicked nature, an impure and suspicious liver, one who covered up his deeds, one who was no recluse though claiming to be one, one who was unchaste though claiming to be chaste, inwardly foul, full of lusts, a sink of filth,—sitting there amid the Order of Brethren. And, beholding him, he rose from his seat, went up to him and said: 'Rise up, friend! You are seen by the Exalted One! You have no part nor lot with the brethren!'

But at these words that man was silent.

Then did the venerable Moggallāna the Great repeat his words, and again a third time. But a third time also that man was silent.

Then the venerable Moggallāna the Great took

[1] M. had the *iddhi*-power of clairvoyance.

that man by the arm, and put him outside the door and drew the bolt, went to the Exalted One and said: 'Lord, that person is put out. Quite pure is the assembly, Lord. Let my Lord the Exalted One recite the Obligations to the brethren.'

'Strange it is, Moggallāna! Wonderful it is, Moggallāna, that that infatuated person (so I call him) should wait till taken by the arm!'

Then the Exalted One addressed the brethren, saying: 'From this time forth, brethren, I myself will not observe the Sabbath, I will not recite the Obligations. Do ye, brethren, henceforth observe the Sabbath and recite the Obligations. It is not fitting, brethren, it is inopportune for the Tathāgata to observe the Sabbath and recite the Obligations when the assembly is not perfectly pure.'

(*The Master then recited the Eight Wonders of the mighty ocean*, *pp.* 249 *ff*.)

Udāna, v. 5.

EXCESS OF ZEAL

(One Soṇa Kolivisa, a rich man's son, obtained ordination and full orders from the Master.)

Now the venerable Soṇa, not long after being fully ordained, was dwelling in Cool Grove. And he, through excess of zeal in walking up and down (while striving for the Goal), lacerated his feet, and the place where he walked up and down was dabbled with blood like a butcher's shambles. Then to the venerable Soṇa, as he dwelt apart in solitude, there came a train of thought like this:

'Here am I, one of those disciples of the Exalted One who dwell in earnest zeal: yet is not my heart released without clinging from the *āsavas*.[1] Now great possessions await me at home. That wealth I may employ and do good deeds with it. How now if I were to return to the (layman's) lower life, employ my wealth, and do good deeds with it?'

Now the Exalted One read with His own mind the thoughts that were in the mind of the venerable Soṇa, and, just as a strong man stretches out his arm and draws back his arm stretched out, even so did He vanish away from the mountain Vulture's Peak and appeared in Cool Grove. Then with a number of brethren the Exalted One went His rounds from lodging to lodging and came to where the venerable Soṇa was walking up and down.

Now when the Exalted One saw that place dabbled with blood like a butcher's shambles He said to the brethren: 'Whose is this walk, brethren, all dabbled with blood like a butcher's shambles?'

And they said to Him: 'Lord, the venerable Soṇa, through excess of zeal in walking up and down, has lacerated his feet, so that his walking-place is in this state.'

Then the Exalted One went to the lodging of the venerable Soṇa and sat down on a seat that was ready for Him. And the venerable Soṇa

[1] The *āsavas*, literally 'floods, fluxes, intoxicants' of life. There are four, viz.: *kāma* (sensuality), *bhava* (coming to be), *ditthi* (views and speculation), *avijjā* (ignorance). To be freed utterly from these four makes one Arahant, Saint, Superman.

saluted the Exalted One and sat down at one side. As he thus sat the Exalted One said to the venerable Soṇa: 'Is it not true, Soṇa, that this train of thought occurred to you as you dwelt apart in solitude: "Here am I, one of those disciples of the Exalted One who dwell in earnest zeal. Yet is not my heart released from the *āsavas* without clinging to them. Now great possessions await me at home. That wealth I may employ and do good with it. How now if I were to return to the (layman's) lower life, employ my wealth, and do good deeds with it?"'

'It is so, Lord.'

'Now how say you, Soṇa? Formerly when you dwelt at home, were you not skilled in playing stringed music on the lute?'

'Yes, Lord.'

'Now how say you, Soṇa? When your lute strings were over-taut, did your lute then give out a sound, was it fit to play upon?'

'No, Lord.'

'Now how say you, Soṇa? When your lute-strings were neither over-taut nor over-slack, but evenly strung, did your lute then give out a sound; was it fit to play upon?'

'It was, Lord.'

'Even so, Soṇa, excess of zeal makes one liable to self-exaltation, while lack of zeal makes one liable to sluggishness. Wherefor do you, Soṇa, persist in evenness of zeal, master your faculties, and make that your mark.'

'Even so, Lord,' said the venerable Soṇa, and attended to what was said to him by the Exalted One.

And the Exalted One, having thus exhorted the

venerable Soṇa with these words, as a strong man stretches out his arm or draws back again his arm outstretched, even so did He vanish from the sight of the venerable Soṇa in Cool Grove, and appeared again on the mountain Vulture's Peak.

Thereupon the venerable Soṇa persisted in evenness of zeal, mastered his faculties, and made that his mark. And the venerable Soṇa, living alone, remote, earnest, ardent, and resolute, in no long time came to realize for himself in that very life, by his own powers of mind, that Goal unsurpassed of holy living, to win which the clansmen duly wander forth from home to the homeless life, so that he knew for sure: 'Destroyed is rebirth (for me), lived is the holy life, done is my task: there is no more life for me on terms like these.'

Thus did the venerable Soṇa become yet another of the Arahants. *Vinaya*, i. 5. § 13.

GOOD SHOOTING

Once the Exalted One was staying at Vesāli, in Great Grove, at the Hall with the peaked gable.

Now on that occasion the venerable Ānanda robed himself early and taking robe and bowl entered Vesāli to beg. Then the venerable Ānanda beheld a number of youths of the Licchavi in the mote-hall, making practice at archery, shooting an arrow from a good distance through a small keyhole, and splitting the arrow (in front) shot after shot, without ever a miss.

On seeing this he thought, 'Good shots in sooth are these young fellows of the Licchavi, well skilled in sooth are these young fellows of the Licchavi, for even from a distance they can split an arrow, shooting through a small keyhole, shot after shot, without ever a miss.'

Then the venerable Ānanda, having gone his rounds in Vesāli, came back and ate his meal, then went to the Exalted One, and sat down at one side. So seated he told the Exalted One what he had seen and what he had thought about it. Then said the Exalted One:

'Now what think you, Ānanda? Which is the harder task, which is the harder thing to achieve, to shoot thus through a small keyhole at a distance and so split an arrow, or with the tip of a hair to split the hundredth part of a hair tip?'

'A much harder task, Lord, much harder to achieve is the latter.'

'Yes, Ānanda, a still harder task do they achieve who pierce through in very truth the meaning of "This is Ill, this is the arising of Ill, this is the ceasing of Ill, this is the approach to the ceasing of Ill."

Wherefore, Ānanda, do you apply yourself to realize the truth of this.'

S.N. v. 453.

THE MONKEY AND THE PITCH-TRAP

'In Himālaya, king of mountains, brethren, there is a tract of land that is rough and hard to cross, where neither monkeys nor humans do resort. Likewise there is a tract where monkeys resort, but not humans.

There are tracts, brethren, in Himālaya, tracts

of level country, delightful spots, where both monkeys and humans do resort.

In those spots, brethren, hunters set traps of pitch in the monkeys' tracks to catch the monkeys. Now, brethren, those monkeys who are free from folly and greed, on seeing that pitch-trap, keep far away from it. But a greedy foolish monkey comes up to the pitch and handles it with one paw, and his paw sticks fast in it. Then, thinking "I'll free my paw," he seizes it with the other paw: but that too sticks fast. To free both paws he seizes them with one foot, and that sticks fast. To free both paws and one foot, he lays hold of them with the other foot, but that too sticks fast. To free both paws and both feet, he lays hold of them with his muzzle, and that sticks fast.

So, brethren, that monkey, thus caught in five ways, lies down and howls, a prey for the hunter to work his will upon him. So the hunter spits him and prepares him for eating there and then over a charcoal fire, and goes off at his pleasure.

Just so it is, brethren, with one who roams in wrong pastures that are beyond his range. Wherefore do ye not so roam; for Māra seizes him who roams in pastures that are beyond his range: Māra seizes his chance, Māra seizes his opportunity.

Now what, brethren, is a brother's wrong pasture and range? It is the fivefold strand of sensual delight, to wit: shapes cognizable by eye, shapes desirable, charming, delightful, and dear. Also shapes tangible by body, shapes desirable, charming, delightful, and dear, endowed with pleasantness and prompting to desire. That, brethren, is the wrong pasture that is beyond a brother's range.

Do ye, brethren, roam in pastures that are your own, keep ye to your ancestral bounds: for, so roaming, Māra does not seize a man. Thus Māra does not get a chance, gets no opportunity.

And what, brethren, is that pasture that is your own ancestral range?

It is the Four Stations of Mindfulness. What four? Herein, brethren, a brother abides contemplating body, ardent and self-possessed, mindful and restraining the covetousness and discontent that are in the world. And so does he abide contemplating feelings, mind, and ideas. That, brethren, is a brother's pasturage, his own ancestral range.'

S.N. v. 148.

CONSCIOUSNESS (2)

Thus have I heard. Once the Exalted One was dwelling near Sāvatthī, in Jeta Grove, in Anāthapindika's Park. Then on that occasion in the mind of a certain brother Sāti, Fisher's Son, there had arisen such a wrong perverted view as this:

'As I understand the doctrine taught by the Exalted One, this same consciousness it is that goes travelling through the round of births and deaths, this and none other.'

Now a number of brethren heard of this wrong perverted view held by the brother Sāti, Fisher's Son, and they went to him and asked him, saying: 'Is it true, friend Sāti, as we hear, that you hold such a wrong perverted view as this: "As I understand the doctrine taught by the Exalted One, this same consciousness it is that goes travelling through the round of births and deaths,—this and none other"?'

And the brother Sāti, Fisher's Son, replied, 'It is so.'

Then those brethren, desirous of converting the brother Sāti, Fisher's Son, from that wrong perverted view, entered on a talk with him, questioned him closely, and remonstrated with him, saying: 'Say not so, friend Sāti! Do not misrepresent the Exalted One! It is ill done to misrepresent the Exalted One! Surely the Exalted One would never say such a thing! Surely in divers ways the Exalted One has taught that consciousness is a thing that arises by way of occasion. Without an occasion there can be no coming-to-be of consciousness.'

But the brother Sāti, Fisher's Son, though thus argued with and questioned and reasoned with by those brethren, stubbornly persisted in that wrong perverted view, to wit: 'As I understand the doctrine . . .' and so forth.

Now when those brethren could not convert the brother Sāti, Fisher's Son, from his wrong perverted view, they went to the Exalted One, saluted Him, and sat down at one side. So seated those brethren told the Exalted One the whole matter, of their ill-success and of the cause of their coming thither.

Then the Exalted One called to a certain brother, 'Come thou, brother! In my name bid hither brother Sāti, Fisher's Son, saying: "Friend Sāti, the Master calls for you."'

'Even so, Lord,' replied that brother to the Exalted One, and delivered the message.

So the brother Sāti, Fisher's Son, came to the Exalted One, saluted Him, and sat down at one side. Thus seated, the Exalted One questioned him about what had been said of him, saying: 'Is it true, Sāti, as I hear, that you do hold this wrong perverted view . . . ?'

'It is true, Lord, that I hold it.'

'Now what is consciousness, Sāti?'

'Lord, it is that speaker, that feeler who experiences the fruit of deeds done here and there, of deeds both good and bad.'

'What, misguided man! Whence heard you that such a doctrine was taught by Me? Have I not declared in divers ways that consciousness arises by occasion: that without occasion there is no coming-to-be of consciousness? But you, misguided man, through wrongly grasping My teaching do thus misrepresent Me and dig a pit for yourself, and have wrought demerit that shall be to your loss and suffering for many a long day.'

Then the Exalted One called to the brethren, and said: 'Now what think ye, brethren? Has this brother Sāti, Fisher's Son, been warmed [1] in this Norm-Discipline?'

'Not so, Lord.'

Then at these words the brother Sāti, Fisher's Son, sat in silence, confused, huddled up, and hung his head and sat downcast, unable to reply.

[1] *Usmī-kato*, used only here. It seems to refer to the action of a hen hatching eggs.

Thereupon the Exalted One, seeing his dejected condition, thus addressed Sāti, Fisher's Son:

'You shall be shown up, misguided man, by this same wrong perverted view of yours. Herein I will question the brethren.'

Then the Exalted One addressed the brethren, saying:

'And have ye, brethren, thus understood the Norm taught by Me as this brother Sāti, Fisher's Son, by wrongly grasping it, has done, and thus misrepresents Me and digs a pit for himself to fall into, and works demerit thereby, which shall be to him loss and suffering for many a long day?'

'Surely not, Lord. For in divers ways it has been said by the Exalted One that owing to occasion arises consciousness, and that without occasion is there no coming-to-be of consciousness.'

'Well said, brethren! Well do ye understand the doctrine taught by Me! But this brother Sāti, by so wrongly grasping My teaching, misrepresents Me and digs a pit for himself, and has wrought demerit that shall be to his loss and suffering for many a long day.

Now, brethren, consciousness arises in dependence on a condition, and is reckoned just according to that condition. Thus, dependent on eye and object arises consciousness, and is reckoned as eye-consciousness. And so on with ear-, nose-, tongue-, body-tangibles-, and mind-consciousness, which arises conditioned by mind and ideas.

Now, just as fire blazes up conditioned by whatever cause (as fuel), it is reckoned thereby.

Thus we have wood-fire, stick-fire, grass-fire, cowdung-fire, chaff-fire, and rubbish-heap fire. Just so, brethren, is a name given to consciousness.

This has become, do ye see, brethren ?'

'Yes, Lord.'

'Become because of such and such nutriment. Do ye see, brethren ?'

'Yes, Lord.'

'By ceasing of that nutriment, what has become is of nature to cease. Do ye see, brethren ?'

'Yes, Lord.'

'When one doubts whether "this has become," brethren, wavering arises, does it not ?'

'Yes, Lord.'

'When one doubts whether "it has become owing to that nutriment" wavering arises, does it not ?'

'Yes, Lord.'

'When one doubts whether "what has so become is of a nature to cease," wavering arises, does it not ?'

'Yes, Lord.'

'But you may say, "perhaps it has not become," or "it has not become owing to that nutriment," or "it does not cease with the ceasing of that nutriment": then wavering arises, does it not ?'

'Yes, Lord.'

'But when one sees, as it really is, by the perfect wisdom, "this has become. It originated owing to that nutriment. It ceases with the ceasing of that nutriment,"—then there is more wavering.'

'It is so, Lord.'

'Now, brethren, are ye sure "this has become: it became through that nutriment: it ceases with the ceasing of that nutriment"? Do ye clearly understand, as it really is, by perfect wisdom that these things are so?'

'Surely, Lord.'

'Then, brethren, if this view, perfectly purified and made clear, is yours: if ye cleave to it, treasure it up, value it as a possession, call it yours, would ye then be understanding it according to my Parable of the Raft, by which I taught ye the Doctrine, as something to be left behind and not to be retained?'

'Surely not, Lord.'

'But if ye do not so cleave to this view, perfectly purified and made clear, then would ye rightly understand it, as it really is, according to my Parable of the Raft, as something to be left behind and not to be retained.'

'Surely we should, Lord.'

M.N. i. 259–61 (omitting repetitions).

PROGRESS ON THE PATH IS GRADUAL

'Just as, brethren, the mighty ocean deepens and slopes gradually down, hollow after hollow, not plunging by a sudden precipice,—even so, brethren, in this Norm-Discipline the training is gradual, progress is gradual, it goes step by step, there is no sudden penetration to insight.

Now since this is so, brethren, this is the first marvel and wonder of this Norm-Discipline, seeing which again and again brethren take delight therein.

Again, brethren, just as the mighty ocean is by nature established and passes not its bounds, even so, brethren, the charge[1] which I have delivered to My disciples, that charge they do not overpass, even at the cost of life.

That, brethren, is the second marvel and wonder . . . seeing which again and again the brethren take delight in the Norm-Discipline.

Just as, brethren, the mighty ocean hath no part nor lot with a dead body, for whatsoever dead body is put into the mighty ocean, straightway it washes it ashore and throws it up on dry land: even so, brethren, whatsoever person there be,—of evil conduct, of wicked nature, an impure and suspicious liver, one who covers up his deeds, one who is no recluse though claiming to be one, one who is unchaste though claiming to be chaste, one inwardly foul, full of lusts, a sink of filth,—with such an one the Order of Brethren hath no part nor lot, but straightway, on meeting with him, rejects him. Though seated amid the Order of Brethren, yet far is he from the Order, and far is the Order from that person.

Inasmuch, then, as such a person is rejected . . . this is the third marvel and wonder of this Norm-Discipline, seeing which again and again brethren take delight therein.'

NO CASTE OR CHANGE IN THE ORDER

'Just as, brethren, the great rivers, namely, Ganga, Yamunā, Aciravati, Sarabhu, and Mahī, on reaching the mighty ocean renounce their former names and lineage and one and all are

[1] *Sikkhāpadaṃ.*

reckoned as the mighty ocean, even so, brethren, do the four castes, the Nobles, the Brāhmins, the Vessas, and the Suddas, go forth from home to the homeless life under the Norm-Discipline of the Tathāgata and renounce their former names and lineage, and are reckoned just as recluses, sons of the Sakyan. . . . Inasmuch as this is so . . . this is the fourth marvel and wonder, brethren, of the Norm-Discipline.

Just as, brethren, all the streams in the world reach the mighty ocean, and all rain from the sky falls into it; yet is no emptying or filling thereof seen: even so, brethren, though many brethren pass away with that passing away [1] which hath no condition of rebirth remaining, yet thereby no emptying nor filling of that passing away is seen:—even so, brethren, this is the fifth marvel and wonder of the Norm-Discipline. . . .'

RELEASE IS THE GOAL

'Just as, brethren, the mighty ocean hath but one savour, the savour of salt, even so, brethren, hath the Norm-Discipline but one savour, the savour of release. Since this is so . . . this is the sixth marvel and wonder of the Norm-Discipline . . .'

THE GEMS

'Just as, brethren, the mighty ocean has many a gem of divers sorts, such as the pearl, the diamond, catseye, chank, rock-crystal, coral, silver, gold,

[1] *Parinibbāna.*

ruby, emerald,—even so, brethren, hath this Norm-Discipline many a gem of divers sorts, to wit,—the Four Earnest Contemplations, the Four Best Efforts, the Four Ways of Will Power, the Five Controlling Faculties, the Five Powers, the Seven Limbs of Wisdom, the Ariyan Eightfold Path. Insofar, brethren, as the Norm-Discipline is such . . . this is the seventh marvel and wonder of this Norm-Discipline.'

THE FRUIT

'Just as, brethren, the mighty ocean is the haunt of mighty creatures, such as these: the leviathan, the whale, the great fish, the sea-gods, the sea-serpents, and the mermaids: just as in the mighty ocean there are monsters whose being[1] spreads for one, two, three, four, five hundreds of yojanas: even so, brethren, this Norm-Discipline is the haunt of mighty ones, amongst them these:—the Stream-winner and the Winner of the Fruits of a Stream-winner: a Once-returner and the Winner of the Fruits of a Once-returner: a Never-returner and the Winner of the Fruits of a Never-returner: an Arahant and the Winner of the Fruits of the Arahant. Since this is so . . . this is the eighth marvel and wonder of this Norm-Discipline, seeing which again and again brethren take delight therein.'

Thereupon the Exalted One, seeing the reality of all that, uttered thrice these inspired words:

Through the thatched roof the rain it goes,
But not through what is open.

[1] *Atta-bhāvo.*

Then open what is covered up,
And rain shall reach thee not.[1]

The whole section is from
Udāna, v. 5, and *Vin*. ii. 9.

THE FOREST-DWELLER

Thus have I heard . . . staying near Rājagaha in the Bamboo Grove.

Then the venerable Kassapa the Great came to the Exalted One, saluted Him, and sat down at one side. So seated the Exalted One said to the venerable Kassapa the Great:

'You are grown old, Kassapa. Burdensome are these coarse, cast-off, patchwork robes. Therefore, Kassapa, don the robes of the householder, enjoy their invitations, and take up your dwelling near to me.'

'For a long, long time, Lord, have I been a forest-dweller and a praiser of the forest-life: an almsman and a praiser of the almsman's life: rag-robed and a praiser of rag-robes: wearing but three robes and a praiser of three robes: contented and a praiser of contentment: secluded and a praiser of seclusion: loving solitude and a praiser of solitude: of ardent energy and a praiser of its exercise.'

[1] These riddling verses refer to the guilty brother who covered up his faults. [Cf. *Dhaniya and the Buddha*, p. 174, for the metaphor.] The commentator says that the Master sent His disciples to a poor man to ask for firewood. He gave them the timber off his roof. Then, though it rained all round, his house (like Gideon's Fleece) was dry.

'Seeing what profits therein, Kassapa, have you so long been a forest-dweller in this way?'

'Seeing, Lord, a twofold profit therein have I been so long a forest-dweller.

Seeing therein my own comfort in this present life and having compassion for the men of future times: for it may be that men of future times will be subject to wrong beliefs, thus: "'Tis said that those who, next to the Enlightened One, were the first to become enlightened, were for a long, long time forest-dwellers and praisers of the forest life" (*as before*). Thus they will shape their course according to these ways, and it shall be for their profit and happiness for a long, long time.

These, Lord, are the two significances which I behold in my being for a long, long time a forest-dweller.'

'Well said! Well said, Kassapa! For the benefit of many folk, out of compassion for the world, for the welfare, the profit, the happiness of devas and men it will have been done.

Wherefore, Kassapa, do you continue to wear these coarse, patchwork robes, this cast-off clothing: and go your rounds to beg for alms and live on in the forest.'

S.N. ii. 202.

THE PARABLE OF THE GOOD HERDSMAN

Then the Exalted One said:

'Brethren, by the possession of eleven qualities is a herdsman fitted to tend and profit by a herd of cattle. What are the eleven?

In this matter, brethren, if a herdsman be not a knower of forms, if he be unskilled in distinguishing the marks, does not remove the eggs of flies, does not cover up a sore, does not light a fire, knows not the ford, knows not the watering-place, knows not the track, is not skilled in the feeding-ground: if he milk dry, if he pay no special honour to the bulls, the fathers of the herd, the leaders of the herd,—if he have these eleven qualities, he is unfit to tend and profit by a herd of cattle.

So also, brethren, a brother failing to possess these eleven qualities is unfit to come by increase, growth, and progress in this Norm-Discipline. What are the qualities? They are (the ten I have named and this one), he pays no special honour to the elder brethren, who have known many a day in the Order, who went forth long ago, the fathers of the Order, the leaders of the Order.

And how, brethren, is a brother a knower of forms?

In this matter, brethren, a brother knows this of whatsoever form, of every form as it really is: "Form is the four great elements and based on them." Thus far is he a knower of forms.

And how, brethren, is a brother skilled in the marks?

In this matter, brethren, a brother knows as it really is: "A fool is known by the marks of his action, a wise man is known by the marks of his action." Thus far is he skilled in the marks.

And how, brethren, is a brother a remover of the eggs of flies?

In this matter, brethren, a brother does not dwell upon a train of sensual thought. When it has arisen he abandons it, restrains it, gets rid of it; he makes it become non-existent. And the same with regard to a malevolent train of thought, a hurtful train of thought. He does not dwell upon evil, unprofitable states of mind that arise from time to time, but abandons, restrains, gets rid of, and makes them become non-existent. Thus is a brother a remover of the eggs of flies.

And how, brethren, is a brother one who covers up a sore?

In this matter, brethren, a brother, on seeing a form with the eye, does not grasp at its marks in general, nor its attributes in particular, but he persists in the restraint of the sense of sight owing to which, if uncontrolled, covetousness and discontent (those evil states) might overwhelm him like a flood: but he keeps a watch on the sense of sight, reaches control of the sense of sight. Just so does he reach control of ear, nose, tongue, body, and mind. That, brethren, is how he is one who covers up a sore.

And how, brethren, is a brother one who lights a fire?

In this matter, brethren, a brother shows in detail to others the Norm which he has himself heard and learned by heart. Thus he is one who lights a fire.

And how, brethren, is a brother one who knows the ford?

In this matter, brethren, a brother from time to time approaches, questions, and inquires of learned brethren, who have received the traditions, who are supporters of the Norm, the discipline, the summaries, asking them "How is this, sir? What is the meaning of this?" Then those venerable ones unfold to him that which was closed, make plain to him that which was not plain, and on divers doubtful points of doctrine they set his doubts at rest. Thus, brethren, is a brother one who knows the ford.

And how, brethren, is a brother one who knows the watering-place?

In this matter, brethren, when the Norm-Discipline set forth by the Tathāgata is being taught, a brother gets knowledge of the meaning, gets knowledge of the Norm, gets that delight which accompanies the Norm. Thus is he one who knows the watering-place.

And how, brethren, does a brother know the track?

In this matter, brethren, a brother understands, as it really is, the Ariyan Eightfold Path. Thus is he a knower of the track.

And how, brethren, is a brother skilled in the feeding-ground?

In this matter, brethren, a brother understands, as they really are, the Four Stations of Mindfulness. Thus is he skilled in the feeding-ground.

And how, brethren, is a brother one who leaves some milk behind?

In this matter, brethren, when devoted householders bring and offer him robes, alms, lodging, requisites, and delicacies, a brother knows moderation in accepting them. Thus is he one who leaves some milk behind.

And how, brethren, does a brother pay especial

honour to the elder brethren, who have known many a day in the Order, who went forth long ago, the fathers and leaders of the Order?

In this matter, brethren, a brother treats them with kindly deeds, with kindly words, with kindly thoughts, both in public and in private. That is how he pays them special honour.

Thus, brethren, a brother possessed of these eleven qualities is fitted to gain increase, growth, and prosperity in this Norm-Discipline.'

M.N. i. chap. 33.

THE ELEPHANT

As the elephant in battle bears the arrows at him hurled,
I must bear men's bitter tongues, for very evil is the world.

Tamed, they lead him into battle: tamed, the king his back ascends:
Tamed is he the best of beings, whom no bitter speech offends.

Good are well-tamed mules, and good are Scindian steeds of lineage famed:
Good indeed the mighty tusker: best of all the man self-tamed.

Yet such mounts can nought avail us, cannot be Nibbāna's guide.
We can only reach The Pathless on the self-tamed self astride.

With the must from temples streaming, mighty
Dhanapālaka
Captive, tastes no food, but longeth to the Nāga-
Grove to go.

Sluggish, gluttonous, and sleepy, wallowing idly
to and fro,
Like a huge and grain-fed hog, a fool again to
birth must go.

Once this mind roamed as it listed, as it pleased
a-wandering went.
As the holder of the ankus checks the furious
elephant,
Now with wisdom I'll restrain it, guide it wholly
to my bent.

Take delight in earnestness: watch thy thoughts
and never tire.
Lift thee from the Path of Evil, like the tusker
sunk in mire.

Hast thou found a fellow-traveller, upright, firm,
intelligent?
Leaving all thy cares behind thee, gladly walk
with him intent.

Hast thou found no fellow-traveller, upright, firm,
intelligent?
As a king deserts his borders, by the enemy
pursued,
Like the tusker in the forest, go thy way in
solitude.

SOME SAYINGS OF THE BUDDHA

Better is the lonely life, for fools companions cannot be.
Live alone and do no evil, live alone with scanty needs,
Lonely, as the mighty tusker in the forest lonely feeds.

Dhammapada, vv. 320–30.

MAGIC POWER

At Sāvatthī. . . . Then the venerable Ānanda came to the Exalted One, saluted Him, and sat down at one side. So seated, the venerable Ānanda said:

'Does the Exalted One fully know, Lord, how to reach the Brahma-world by magic power, by means of the mind-created body?'

'I do indeed know, Ānanda.'

'Does the Exalted One fully know, Lord, how to reach the Brahma-world by means of this body which is compounded of the four great elements?'

'I do indeed know, Ānanda.'

'A strange thing it is, Lord! A marvel it is, Lord, that the Exalted One has this knowledge!'

'Yes, Ānanda. Strange indeed are the Tathāgatas and endowed with strange powers. Marvellous indeed are the Tathāgatas and endowed with marvellous powers.

Whensoever, Ānanda, the Tathāgata concentrates body in mind and concentrates mind in body, and entering on awareness of ease and buoyancy abides therein, at such time, Ānanda, the body of the Tathāgata is more buoyant, softer, more pliable, and more radiant.

Suppose, Ānanda, a ball of iron is heated all day long. It becomes lighter, softer, more pliable, and more radiant. Just so it is, Ānanda, with the body of the Tathāgata.

Now, Ānanda, at the time when the Tathāgata so concentrates body in mind and concentrates mind in body, the Tathāgata's body with but little effort rises from the earth into the sky, and in divers ways enjoys magic power, to wit: being one He becomes many, and so forth, and He has power over the body even up to the world of Brahma.

Just as, Ānanda, a ball of cotton or thistle-down, light and borne by the wind with but little effort rises from the ground into the sky . . . just so when the Tathāgata concentrates mind in body and body in mind . . . does he in divers ways enjoy magic power . . . even up to the world of Brahma.'

S.N. v. 283–4.

ABNORMAL POWERS

'I, brethren, when I so desire it, passing beyond consciousness of form, in every way, by the destruction of the impacts of sense, paying no attention to the various kinds of feeling, enter upon and abide in the sphere of boundless space, (recognizing) "It is boundless space."[1]

Kassapa, brethren, when he so desires, passing beyond consciousness. . . .

I, brethren, when I so desire it, passing wholly beyond the sphere of boundless space, enter upon

[1] See note, p. 55.

and abide in the sphere of boundless consciousness, (recognizing) " It is boundless consciousness."

Kassapa, brethren, when he so desires it, passing wholly beyond. . . .

I, brethren, when I so desire it, passing wholly beyond the sphere of boundless consciousness, enter upon and abide in the sphere of nothingness, (recognizing) " There is nothing."

Kassapa, brethren, when he so desires it, passing wholly beyond. . . .

I, brethren, when I so desire it, passing wholly beyond the sphere of nothingness, enter upon and abide in that sphere where there is neither perception nor non-perception.

Kassapa, brethren, when he so desires it, passing wholly beyond. . . .

I, brethren, when I so desire it, passing wholly beyond the sphere where there is neither perception nor non-perception, enter upon and abide in the sphere of cessation of consciousness and sensation.

Kassapa, brethren, when he so desires it, passing wholly beyond. . . .

I, brethren, when I so desire it, enjoy the possession in various ways of magic power. From being one, I become multiform: from being multiform, I become one: appearing and disappearing I pass without let or hindrance through a wall, a rampart, a mountain, as if through air: I plunge up or down through solid ground, as if through water: I walk on water without dividing it, as if on solid ground: I make the air my couch like a winged bird: with my hand I touch and feel this moon and sun, beings of mystic power though they be: I wield power with my body even to the Brahma-world.

Kassapa, brethren, when he so desires it, enjoys the possession. . . .

I, brethren, when I so desire it, with a divine faculty of hearing, clarified and surpassing that of man, can hear sounds both divine and human, sounds both far away and near.

Kassapa, brethren, when he so desires it, with a divine faculty. . . .'

RECALLING FORMER BIRTHS

'I, brethren, when I so desire it, can call to mind my various states of birth: for instance, one birth, two births, five, ten . . . a hundred thousand births: the various destructions of æons, the various renewals of æons, the various destructions and renewals of æons, thus: I lived there, was named thus, was of such a clan, of such a caste, was thus supported, had such and such pleasant and painful experiences, had such a length of days, disappeared thence and arose elsewhere: there too I lived, was named thus, was of such a clan, of such a caste (*as before*)—thus can I call to mind in all their specific details, in all their characteristics, in many various ways, my previous states of existence.

Kassapa, brethren, when he so desires it, can call to mind . . .

I, brethren, when I so desire it, can behold with the divine vision, clarified and surpassing that of men, beings falling and rising again, both mean and excellent, fair and foul, gone to a happy state, gone to a woeful state, according to their deeds, (so as to say): "Alas, sirs! these beings, given to the practice of evil deeds, of evil words, of evil thoughts, scoffing at the Noble Ones, of perverted views and reaping the fruits of their perverted views,—these beings, on the dissolution of the body, after death arose again in the Waste, the Woeful Way, the Downfall, and the Constant Round. Ah, sirs! and these beings, given to the practice of good deeds, of good words, good thoughts, not scoffing at the Noble Ones, of sound views and reaping the fruits of their sound views,—these beings, on the dissolution of the body, after death arose again in the Happy Way, the Heavenly World."

Thus with divine vision, clarified and surpassing that of men, do I behold beings (*as before*) . . . according to their deeds.

Kassapa, brethren, when he so desires it, can so behold with the . . .

And I, brethren, by the destruction of the *āsavas*, have entered on and abide in that emancipation of mind which is free from the *āsavas*, having realized it by mine own super-knowledge even in this present life.

Kassapa, brethren, by the destruction of the *āsavas* . . .'

THOUGHT-READING

'I, brethren, when I so desire it, know the minds of other beings, of other persons, grasping them with my mind. I know the passionate mind to be passionate, the dispassionate mind to be dispassionate: the hating mind I know to be hating, the mind confused to be confused: the mind intent I know to be intent, the vacillating mind to be vacillating: the exalted mind I know to be exalted, the humble to be humble, the superior to be superior, the inferior to be inferior: the concentrated mind I know to be concentrated, the emancipated to be emancipated, the unemancipated to be unemancipated.

Kassapa, brethren, when he so desires, knows the minds of other beings . . .'

S.N. ii. 213.

THE APPROACH TO THE GOAL

At Sāvatthī. Then the Exalted One addressed the brethren thus:

'I, brethren, am no approver of perverted view, whether in a layman or in a wanderer. One who walks in a perverted view, be he layman or wanderer, owing to the occasion and cause of his wrong behaviour does not attain the Method, the Norm, the Good.

And what, brethren, is the perverted approach? It is perverted view, perverted aim, speech, action, living, effort, attention, and contemplation. That is the perverted approach. I approve not of it, brethren, whether in a layman or in a wanderer: for such do not attain the Method, the Norm, the Good, owing to the occasion and cause of their perverted behaviour.

But, brethren, I do approve of the perfect approach, whether in a layman or in a wanderer. For both of them, walking perfectly aright, do attain the Method, the Norm, the Good, by reason of the occasion and cause of perfect behaviour. And what is that perfect approach ?

It is right view, right aim, and so forth . . . that is the perfect approach. And I do approve of it whether in a layman or in a wanderer. For both do attain the Method, the Norm, the Good, by reason of the occasion and cause of their perfect behaviour.'

S.N. v. 18.

THE BURDEN

At Sāvatthī. . . . Then the Exalted One said :

'I will teach you the burden, brethren, the taking hold of the burden, the lifting of it up and the laying of it down. Do ye listen. . . .

What, brethren, is the burden ?

"It is the mass of the five factors of grasping," should be the reply. What five ? The mass of the body factors of grasping, of the feeling factors, the perception, activities, and consciousness factors of grasping. This, brethren, is called "the burden."

And what, brethren, is "the laying hold of the burden" ?

"It is the person," should be the reply : "that venerable one of such and such a name, of such and such a family." This, brethren, is called "the laying hold of the burden."

And what, brethren, is "the taking up of the burden" ?

It is that craving that leads downward to rebirth, along with the lure and the lust that linger longingly now here, now there; namely, the craving for sensation, the craving for rebirth, the craving to have done with rebirth. That, brethren, is called "the taking up of the burden."

And what, brethren, is "the laying down of the burden"?

It is the utter passionless ceasing of craving, the giving up of craving, the renouncing of, the release from, the absence of longing for this craving. That, brethren, is called "the laying down of the burden".'

So spake the Exalted One. The Wellfarer having thus spoken, the Master said this yet further:

> The burden is indeed the fivefold mass:
> The seizer of the burden, man:
> Taking it up is sorrow in this world:
> The laying of it down is bliss.
>
> If a man lay this heavy burden down,
> And take not any other burden up:
> If he draw out that craving, root and all,
> No more an-hungered, he is free.

S.N. iii. 25.

REALIZATION

Once the Exalted One was staying near Sāvatthī, at Jeta Grove, in Anāthapindika's Park.

Now on that occasion the venerable Khema and the venerable Sumana were also staying near Sāvatthī in Dark Wood. Then the venerable Khema and Sumana approached the Exalted One, saluted Him, and sat down at one side. So seated, the venerable Khema said this to the Exalted One:

'Lord, a brother who is Arahant, destroyer of the *āsavas*, one who has lived the life, done his task, laid down the burden, won his own salvation, who has burst the bonds that bind to becoming, who is by knowledge perfectly set free,—such an one does not think, "Better am I," or "Worse am I," or "Equal am I" in respect of others.'

So said the venerable Khema, and the Master approved of his words. Whereupon the venerable Khema, saying, 'The Master approves,' rose up, saluted by the right, and went away.

Not long after he had gone the venerable Sumana addressed the Exalted One in the same words, and the Master approved of his words. Whereupon the venerable Sumana, saying, 'The Master approves,' rose and saluted the Exalted One by the right, and went away.

Not long after those two brothers were gone, the Exalted One said to the brethren:

'Brethren, that is how clansmen testify to having realized. The gist of the thing is told, and the Self is not brought into question.

But there are some deluded creatures who are mockers herein, methinks, when they testify to having realized. Such come to discomfiture later on.'

Not swayed by thoughts of equal, high, or low
Are such as these. One thought alone is theirs,—
'Destroyed is birth, lived is the holy life,
Freed from the bonds that bind to birth are we.'

Ang. Nik. iii. 359.

THE ARAHANT

'Thus, Cunda, should you reply, concerning the Arahant, to those of other views:

"Friend, a brother who is Arahant, one in whom the *āsavas* are destroyed, who has lived the life, who has done his task, who has laid down the burden, who has reached his own welfare, who has utterly destroyed the bond that binds to becoming, who is released by the Knowledge,—such an one is incapable of behaving in nine ways, to wit:

Intentionally taking the life of a creature;
Of taking by way of theft what is not given;
Of practising the sexual act;
Of telling a deliberate lie;
Of indulging in intoxicants;
Of storing up (food) for the indulgence of appetite, as he did before when he was a householder;
Of going on the wrong path through hatred;
Of going on the wrong path through delusion;
Of going on the wrong path through fear."'

D.N. iii. 133.

HOW TO KNOW AN ARAHANT

Then the rājah Pasēnadi, the Kosalan, not long after those ascetics had gone away, went to where the Exalted One was, and drawing near saluted Him and sat down at one side. So seated, the rājah Pasēnadi said to the Exalted One:

'Are those ascetics, Lord, among those who in

this world are Arahants or who have reached the path of Arahantship?'

'It is hard for you, mahārājah, who live the household life, in the enjoyment of the pleasures of sense, living at home with your bedroom full of children, in the enjoyment of Benares sandal-wood, wearing flower-garlands and using scents and unguents, handling gifts of gold and silver,— it is hard for such as you to aver, "These are Arahants or these have reached the Path of Arahantship."

No, mahārājah, it is by living along with a man that one learns his real character; and that only after a long time, not by giving the matter a passing thought, not by paying little heed to it. It needs a man of insight and not a dullard to do so.

It is by constant intercourse with him, mahārājah, that a man's integrity is to be known: and that only after a long time, not by giving the matter a passing thought, not by paying little heed to it. . . .

It is in misfortune, mahārājah, that a man's endurance is to be known: and that only after a long time, not by giving the matter a passing thought. . . .

It is by converse with him, mahārājah, that a man's wisdom is to be ascertained: and that only after a long time: not by giving the matter a passing thought, not by paying little heed to it. It needs a man of insight and not a dullard to do so.'

Udāna, pp. 65-6.

DEVADATTA

DISAPPOINTED AMBITION

Now at that time the Exalted One was preaching, surrounded by a great company which contained the rājah and his court.

Then Devadatta,[1] rising from his seat and throwing his upper robe over one shoulder, bowed towards the Exalted One with folded palms and said: 'My Lord, the Exalted One is now grown old, is aged, far gone in years, He has come to life's end. Let now my Lord live without worry. Let Him dwell, given to such happiness as this life contains. Let Him hand over the care of the Order of Brethren unto me, and I will take charge of the Order of Brethren.'

'Enough, Devadatta! Seek not to take charge of the Order of Brethren!'

Then a second time and yet a third time did Devadatta make the same request and get the same reply. Then said the Exalted One:

'Not even to Sāriputta and Moggallāna the Great would I hand over the care of the Order of Brethren: much less to one like thee, a vile lick-spittle!'[2]

[1] The cousin of the Buddha, who formed a sect of his own, consumed with the ambition to lead. He won over Prince Ajātasattu to give him his support (see below).

[2] *Chavassa-kheḷāpakassa*, one who lives on charity got by mean ways.

Then Devadatta thought thus: 'The Exalted One, in the very presence of the rājāh and his court, refuses me, calls me "vile lick-spittle," and extols Sāriputta and Moggallāna the Great!' So, angry and annoyed, he bowed to the Exalted One, saluted Him by the right, and went away.

Now this was the first occasion of Devadatta's grudge against the Exalted One.

(Thereupon Sāriputta was appointed to excommunicate Devadatta in a formal manner. Devadatta afterwards made several attempts to kill the Buddha, but failed and came to a miserable end, having attempted the unpardonable sins: of trying to slay his own father, create a schism in the Order, and slay an Arahant.)

Vinaya, ii. 7, 2.

AMBITION

Now at one time the Exalted One was dwelling at Rājagaha on the mountain Vulture's Peak, not long after the secession of Devadatta. Thereupon the Exalted One addressed the brethren about Devadatta, saying:—

'To his own harm, brethren, did gain, favours, and flattery come to Devadatta, and led to his downfall. Even as a plantain brings forth fruit to its own loss, to its own destruction: even as a bamboo or a reed brings forth fruit to its own loss, to its own destruction: just as a mule brings forth young to her own loss, to her own destruction: even so to his own loss, to his own downfall, have gains, favours, and flattery come to Devadatta. Thus terrible, brethren, are gains, favours, and flattery: they are a bitter, painful hindrance to the attainment of the sure peace that passeth all.

Wherefore, brethren, thus must ye train yourselves: "When gains, favours, and flattery befall us, we will reject them, and when they do befall us they shall not lay hold of and be established in our hearts." '

Thus spake the Exalted One: when the Happy One had thus spoken, as Teacher He added this further:

> The plantain, bamboo, and the reed
> Are ruined by the fruit they bear.
> By homage is the fool destroyed,
> As the mule dies in bringing forth.

THE FAVOUR OF PRINCES

Once the Exalted One was staying at Rājagaha in the Bamboo Grove in the Squirrels' Feeding-ground.

At that time Prince Ajātasattu was supporting Devadatta late and early with five hundred carts, conveying therein food brought in five hundred cooking-pots. Then a number of the brethren came before the Exalted One, saluted Him, and sat down at one side, and there sitting they told all of these things to the Exalted One.

'Do ye not long for gains, favours, and flattery, brethren! So long, brethren, as Prince Ajātasattu thus supports Devadatta late and early, with five hundred carts, conveying therein food brought in five hundred cooking-pots, it is ruin, brethren, that may be expected of Devadatta, and not growth in good conditions.

Just as if, brethren, one were to crumble liver on a mad dog's nose, the dog would only get the madder,—even so, brethren, so long as Prince Ajātasattu thus supports Devadatta . . . it is ruin that may be expected of Devadatta, and not growth in good conditions. Thus terrible, brethren, are gains, favours, and flattery. They are a bitter, painful hindrance to the attainment of the sure peace that passeth all.

Wherefore, brethren, thus must ye train yourselves: "When gains, favours, and flattery befall us, we will reject them, and when they do befall us, they shall not lay hold of and be established in our hearts." '

S.N. ii. 242.

FOOLS RUSH IN

Then the Exalted One addressed the brethren and said:

'Once upon a time, brethren, there was a great pool in a forest region and elephants dwelt beside it. These, plunging into the pool, used to pull up the stalks of lotuses: they washed them clean, and when they were free from mud snatched them up and swallowed them. This practice was for them a source of health and strength. Consequent on this they did not come by death or any mortal pain.

Now, brethren, the young elephant-calves, following the example of the big elephants, likewise plunged into that pool and pulled up the lotus-stalks, but without washing them clean they snatched them up, mud and all, and swallowed them. This practice was not for them a source of health and strength. Consequent on that they came by their death, or at least came to mortal pains. Even so, brethren, will Devadatta die, the miserable man, by imitating me.

Just as the young calf-elephant—
Who imitates the mighty beast
That shakes the earth and eats the stalks
Of lotuses, and all night long
Keeps watch upon the riverside,—
Doth eat the mud (and die the death)—
So dies the wretch that copies me.'

Vinaya, ii. 7, 5, and *S.N.* ii. 268.

THE DOOM

'Devadatta, brethren, being overcome by, his mind obsessed by, eight evil conditions, is doomed to Purgatory, the state of woe, for the whole æon, without hope of remedy. What are those eight conditions ?

He is overcome, his mind obsessed by love of gain and loss of gain, by love of fame and loss of fame, by love of honour and loss of honour, by evil desires and by evil friends. Such, brethren, are the eight conditions.

Moreover, brethren, there are three evil conditions, by which overcome, his mind obsessed by which, Devadatta is so doomed. . . . What are the three ?

Because he had evil desires, because he had

evil friends, and because he turned aside (from the Path) and came to a standstill by the attainment of the lesser powers.'[1]

Vin. Pit. ii. 7, 7.

INGRATITUDE

The Jackal (1)

. . . staying near Sāvatthī. (The Exalted One said :)

'Have ye heard the jackal, brethren, that barks by night and at early dawn ?'

'Yes, Lord.'

'That, brethren, is a decrepit jackal suffering from a disease called mange. Wherever it lists, there it goes : wheresoever it lists, there it stays : wherever it lists, there it squats down : wherever it lists, there it lies, however cold be the wind that blows upon it.

Well might it be, brethren, for such and such a brother,[2] vowed to the Sakyas' son, if he should attain such a state of birth as that.

Therefore, brethren, thus must ye train yourselves : "Earnest will we dwell." Even so, must ye train yourselves.'

The Jackal (2)

. . . staying near Sāvatthī (*the same as the above*).

. . . 'Yes, Lord.'

[1] It is said that he attained the lower magic powers which led him astray.

[2] The words were said of Devadatta, according to the commentary.

'It may be, brethren, that the sense of thanks and gratitude felt by that decrepit jackal is not to be found in such and such an one, vowed to the Sakyas' son.

Therefore, brethren, thus must ye train yourselves: "Thankful will we be and full of gratitude: may not the slightest boon to us be given in vain." Even so must ye train yourselves.'

S.N. ii. 182-3.

DOCTRINES TRUE AND FALSE

THE TEST OF TRUE DOCTRINE

1

Now Mahā-Pajāpati, the Gotamid, went to the Exalted One, saluted Him, and stood at one side . . . and said :

'Well for me, O Lord, if the Exalted One would show me a teaching, hearing which from the lips of the Exalted One I might dwell alone, solitary, zealous, ardent, and resolved.'

(The Master said :)

'Of whatsoever teachings, Gotamid, thou canst assure thyself thus : "These doctrines conduce to passions, not to dispassion : to bondage, not to detachment : to increase of (worldly) gains, not to decrease of them : to covetousness, not to frugality : to discontent, and not content : to company, not solitude : to sluggishness, not energy : to delight in evil, not delight in good" : of such teachings thou mayest with certainty affirm, Gotamid, "This is not the Norm. This is not the Discipline. This is not the Master's Message."

But of whatsoever teachings thou canst assure thyself (that they are the opposite of these things that I have told you),—of such teachings thou mayest with certainty affirm: "This is the Norm. This is the Discipline. This is the Master's Message."'

Vinaya, ii. 10.

2

Once the Exalted One was staying at Bhoganagara, near the Ānanda Shrine. Then the Exalted One called to the brethren, saying, 'Brethren!'

'Lord!' replied those brethren and gave heed to the Exalted One.

The Exalted One thus spake: 'There are these four great tests,[1] brethren, which I will show you. Do ye listen carefully. Apply your minds. I will speak.'

'Even so, Lord,' replied those brethren to the Exalted One. Then He said:

'What, brethren, are the four great tests?

Herein, brethren, a brother might say thus: "Face to face, friend, I heard this from the Exalted One: face to face with Him I received it, thus: 'This is the Norm. This is the Discipline. This is the Message of the Master.'"

Well, brethren, you should neither joyfully accept that brother's words, nor should you reject them: but without either joyful acceptance or utter rejection you should carefully take those words, word by word and syllable by syllable, and lay them side by side with the *Sutta* and compare them with the *Vinaya*. And if they do not conform to the *Sutta*, do not tally with the *Vinaya*,—then you may go to this conclusion:

[1] *Mahāpadeso*—'great topic, place' (here it = orientation).

"Surely, this is not a saying of the Exalted One, the Arahant, the Perfectly Enlightened One. But it has been wrongly grasped by this brother." Thus saying, brethren, you should reject it.

Herein, again, brethren, a brother might say: "Face to face . . . (*as before*) . . ." Then if those words do conform to the *Sutta* and do tally with the *Vinaya*, you may go to this conclusion: "Surely, this is the saying of the Exalted One, the Arahant, the Perfectly Enlightened One. Rightly grasped has it been by this brother." So saying, you should accept it as such, brethren.

This is the first great test.

Then again in this connexion, a brother might say: "At such and such a residence are dwelling a company of brethren, and among them an elder, a leader of men; and face to face with them did I hear (thus and thus). . . ."

Well, brethren, you should neither joyfully accept that brother's words nor utterly reject them: but (as before said) examine them. . . . Then, if they do not conform to the *Sutta*, do not tally with the *Vinaya*, you may go to this conclusion: "Surely this is not the saying of the Exalted One, the Arahant, the Perfectly Enlightened One. It has been wrongly grasped by this brother." So saying, brethren, ye should reject it.

Herein, again, brethren, a brother might say: (*as before*) . . . and if it conform . . . ye may conclude . . . "This is a saying of the Exalted One. . . ."

This, brethren, is the second great test.

Then again, brethren, in this connexion a brother

might say: "At such and such a residence are dwelling elder brethren, of wide general knowledge, who have received the teachings, who have learned the Norm by heart, who have learned the Discipline by heart, who have learned the Summaries by heart. Face to face with those elders did I hear and receive this, thus: 'This is the Norm. This is the Discipline. This is the Master's Message.'"

Then (*as before*) . . . if it do not conform . . . reject it.

And again, brethren, if it do conform . . . ye should accept it.

This, brethren, is the third great test.

Herein again, brethren, a brother might say: "At such and such a residence dwells a single elder, of wide general knowledge, who has received the teachings, who has learned the Norm by heart, who has learned the Discipline by heart, who has learned the Summaries by heart. . . . Face to face with that elder did I hear this. . . ." Then if it conform not . . . reject it.

And in like manner . . . if it conform . . . accept it (*as before*).

This, brethren, is the fourth great test. Such are the Four Great Tests.'

Ang. Nik. ii. 167.

USE YOUR OWN JUDGEMENT

Thus have I heard: Once the Exalted One was journeying in Kosala, accompanied by a number of the Order of Brethren, and reached Kesaputta, a suburb of the Kālāma Nobles.

Now the Kālāmas of Kesaputta heard the rumour that Gotama, the Sakyans' son, who went forth (as a wanderer) from the Sakyan Clan, had come to Kesaputta. Then concerning Gotama, that Exalted One, there was noised abroad this good report:

' 'Tis He, the Exalted One, the Arahant, the Perfectly Enlightened One, He who is endowed with knowledge and right conduct, the Happy One, the Knower of the worlds, the Charioteer of beings ready to be tamed, the Teacher of Devas and Mankind, the Buddha, the Exalted One! He knows this world, together with the world of Devas, of Māras and Brahmās, He knows the host of recluses and brāhmins, of Devas and mankind, by His own abnormal powers having realized it, and doth proclaim it. He preaches a Norm that is goodly in the beginning, in its middle, and goodly in its ending: both in its spirit and in its letter entirely perfected and purified doth He set forth the holy life. Good indeed the sight of such an Arahant as that!'

Then the Kālāmas of Kesaputta came to the Exalted One and said:

'Lord, there are here some recluses and brāhmins who come to Kesaputta. They extol and magnify their own view, but the view of others they spitefully abuse, depreciate, and pluck it bare.[1]

Then, Lord, other recluses and brāhmins come to Kesaputta . . . and do the same. And as we listen to them, doubt and wavering arise in us, as

[1] *Opakkhiṃ karonti*, lit. 'pull out its feathers.'

to which of the parties is telling the truth and which is telling lies.'

'Well may ye doubt, Kālāmas; well may ye waver; for your wavering arises about a matter that is open to doubt.

Now, Kālāmas, do not ye go by hearsay, nor by what is handed down by others, nor by what people say, nor by what is stated on the authority of your traditional teachings. Do not go by reasoning, nor by inferring, nor by argument as to method, nor from reflection on and approval of an opinion, nor out of respect, thinking a recluse must be deferred to. But, Kālāmas, when you know of yourselves: "These teachings are not good: they are blameworthy: they are contemned by the wise: these teachings, when followed out and put in practice, conduce to loss and suffering"—then reject them.'

Ang. Nik. i. 188.

MISUNDERSTANDING

The Parable of the Snake

(*The brother Ariṭṭha, in a former birth a vulture-tamer, had misinterpreted the Master's teaching about the dangers of craving and the reality of the Hindrances as such.*)

Then the Exalted One addressed the brethren, saying:

'And do ye, brethren, thus understand the Norm which I have shown, as does this brother Ariṭṭha, the late vulture-tamer? For he, failing to grasp my meaning aright, misinterprets me and digs a pit for himself to fall into, and begets demerit thereby. Is it so ?'

'Surely not, Lord : for in divers ways have the Hindrances been told us by the Exalted One, and they are real Hindrances to them that prăctise them. Insatiate are lusts, as said by the Exalted One, full of woe, full of suffering. Therein is much loss. Like unto a bony skeleton are lusts, as said by the Exalted One. Like unto a scrap of meat, a blazing torch, like glowing charcoal, (baseless as) a dream, as something borrowed, like fruit on a tree, like a slaughter-house, a spear-point, like a snake's head are the lusts spoken of by the Exalted One : full of woe and suffering. Therein is much loss.'

'Well said, brethren ! Well indeed do ye understand the Norm which I have shown ye. In divers ways (as ye repeat) have the Hindrances been told by me . . . but yet this brother Ariṭṭha, the late vulture-tamer, failing to grasp my meaning aright, misinterprets me and digs a pit for himself to fall into, and begets demerit thereby. Surely that shall be for many a long day to the loss and sorrow of that misguided man. For truly, brethren, without the existence of lusts, without the awareness of lusts, without the dwelling in thought upon lusts, it cannot be that a man should practise lusts.

Now herein, brethren, certain misguided ones learn the Norm by heart, to wit : the discourses, the songs, the exposition, the verses, the solemn sayings, the words of the Master, the birth-tales, the marvels, and the miscellanies. Thus learning them by heart they do not by wisdom investigate their meaning: they do not take interest therein: just for the sake of being free from reproach they learn the Norm by heart: just for the profit of pouring out a flood of gossip. But as to the essence of the Doctrine which thus they learn by heart, they have no part nor lot in that. The teachings are ill grasped by them and lead to their loss and suffering for many a long day. Why so? Because of wrongly grasping the teachings, brethren.

Just as, brethren, a man in need of water-snakes, searching for water-snakes, going about in quest of them, sees a big water-snake and grasps it by the body or the tail: and that water-snake turns back on him and bites him in the hand or arm or some other limb, and owing to that he comes by his death or suffering that ends in death. And why? Because he wrongly grasped the snake, brethren.

Even so, brethren, in this case some misguided ones learn the Norm by heart, and come to suffering because they grasp it wrongly.'

M.N. i. 132.

THE BLIND MEN AND THE ELEPHANT

Thus have I heard. Once the Exalted One was staying near Sāvatthī at Jeta Grove, in Anāthapindika's Park. Now on that occasion a number of sectarians, recluses, and brāhmins who were wanderers, entered Sāvatthī to beg an alms: they were men of divers views, accepting divers faiths, of divers aims, and by divers opinions swayed to and fro.

Now some of these recluses and brāhmins held such views as these: Eternal is the world: this is the truth, all else is delusion. Others held: Not eternal is the world: this is the truth, all else is delusion. Others again held: The world is finite, or The world is infinite, or again, Body and soul are one and the same. Others said: Body and soul are different things. Some held: The Tathāgata exists after death: or, The Tathāgata exists not after death: or, The Tathāgata both exists and exists not after death: or, The Tathāgata neither exists nor exists not after death. And each maintained that his own view was the truth, and that all else was delusion.

So they lived quarrelsome, noisy, disputatious, abusing each other with words that pierced like javelins, maintaining, 'This is the truth, that is not the truth: that is not the truth, this is the truth.'

Now a number of the brethren, robing themselves early and taking bowl and robe, entered Sāvatthī to beg an alms, and on their return they ate their meal and came to the Exalted One, saluted Him, and sat down at one side. So seated, those brethren described to the Exalted One what they had seen and heard of those recluses and brāhmins who were sectarians. Then said the Exalted One:

'These sectarians, brethren, are blind and unseeing. They know not the real, they know not the unreal, know not the truth, know not the untruth: in such a state of ignorance do they dispute and quarrel as ye describe. Now in former times, brethren, there was a rājah in this same Sāvatthī. Then, brethren, that rājah called to a certain man, saying: "Come thou, good fellow! Go and gather together all the blind men that are in Sāvatthī!"

"Very good, your majesty," replied that man, and in obedience to the rājah gathered together all the blind men, took them with him to the rājah and said: "Your majesty, all the blind men of Sāvatthī are now assembled."

"Then, my good man, show these blind men an elephant."

"Very good, your majesty," said the man, and did as he was told, saying, "O ye blind, such as this is an elephant!"

And to one man he presented the head of the elephant, to another the ear, to another a tusk, the trunk, the foot, back, tail, and tuft of the tail, saying to each one that that was the elephant.

Now, brethren, that man having presented the elephant to the blind men, came to the rājah and said, "Your majesty, the elephant has been presented to the blind men. Do what is your will."

Thereupon, brethren, that rājah went up to the blind men and said to each, "Have you studied the elephant?"

"Yes, your majesty."

"Then tell me your conclusions about him."

Thereupon those who had been presented with the head answered, "Your majesty, an elephant is just like a pot." And those who had only observed the ear replied, "An elephant is just like a winnowing-basket." Those who had been presented with the tusk said it was a ploughshare.

Those who knew only the trunk said it was a plough. "The body," said they, "is a granary: the foot, a pillar: the back, a mortar: its tail, a pestle: the tuft of the tail, just a besom." Then they began to quarrel, shouting, "Yes-it is! No it isn't! An elephant is not that! Yes, it's like that!" and so on, till they came to fisticuffs about the matter.

Then, brethren, that rājah was delighted with the scene.

Just so are these sectarians, who are wanderers, blind, unseeing, knowing not the truth, but each maintaining it is thus and thus.'

Whereupon the Exalted One on that occasion, seeing the gist of the matter, uttered this solemn saying:

O how they cling and wrangle, some who claim
Of brāhmin and recluse the honoured name.
For quarrelling, each to his view, they cling.
Such folk see only one side of a thing.

Udāna, vi. 4.

THE BUDDHAS SHOW THE WAY

THE PIONEER

At Sāvatthī. . . . Then the Exalted One said this to the brethren:

'Now herein, brethren, what is the distinction, what is the specific feature, what is the difference between the Tathāgata who, being Arahant, is a Fully Enlightened One, from the brother who is freed by insight?'

'For us, Lord, things are rooted in the Exalted One, have the Exalted One for their guide and their resort. Well for us, Lord, if the Exalted One should reveal unto us the meaning of this saying. Hearing the Exalted One, the brethren will bear it in mind.'

'Then listen, brethren, and apply your minds closely. I will speak.'

'Even so, Lord,' replied those brethren to the Exalted One.

'The Tathāgata, brethren, who, being Arahant, is fully enlightened, He it is who doth cause a way to arise which had not arisen before: who doth bring about a way not brought about before: who doth proclaim a way not proclaimed before: who is the knower of a way, who understandeth a way, who is skilled in a way. And now, brethren, His disciples are wayfarers who follow after Him. That, brethren, is the distinction, the specific feature which distinguishes the Tathāgata who, being Arahant, is Fully Enlightened, from the brother who is freed by insight.'

S.N. iii. 66.

THE TATHĀGATA (1)[1]

Thus spake the Exalted One, thus spake the Arahant (as I have heard):

'The world, brethren, hath been fully understood by the Tathāgata: from the world the Tathāgata is set free.

The arising of the world, brethren, hath been fully understood by the Tathāgata: the arising of the world hath been put away by the Tathāgata.

The ceasing of the world, brethren, hath been fully understood by the Tathāgata: the ceasing of the world hath been realized by the Tathāgata.

The Way going to the ceasing of the world hath been fully understood by the Tathāgata: the way leading to the ceasing of the world hath been practised (traversed) by the Tathāgata.

Whatsoever in the world, brethren, and in the world of the devas, with its Māras and Brahmās, together with the host of recluses and brāhmins,—of devas and mankind,—whatsoever hath been seen, heard, sensed, known, reached, sought after, traversed by mind,—insofar as all that hath been

[1] The commentators have derived the word in many ways, of which two may be mentioned, viz.: (*a*) *tathā-gato*, 'thus gone,' (*b*) *tathā-āgato*, 'thus come' (like other Buddhas), or 'he who has come to the Reality.'

fully understood by the Tathāgata, therefore is He called Tathāgata.

Between that day, brethren, on which a Tathāgata fully understands the incomparable perfection of wisdom, and the day on which He passes away with that passing which leaves no basis for rebirth behind,[1]—(during all that time) whatsoever He utters and specifies, all that is surely so and not otherwise. Wherefore is He called Tathāgata.

As a Tathāgata speaks, so He does : as He does, so He speaks. Thus, since He does as He says, and says as He does, therefore is He called Tathāgata.

In the world, together with the world of the devas, with its Māras, its Brahmās, its recluses and brāhmins, together with all the hosts of devas and mankind, the Tathāgata is all-conquering, unconquered by any, He is the all-seeing Controller. Therefore is He called Tathāgata.'

Such is the essence of what the Exalted One said. *Iti-vuttaka*, § 112.

DOCTRINES

'There is, brethren, in the world a world-condition which the Tathāgata has thoroughly penetrated and realized. Having thoroughly penetrated and realized it, He declares, teaches, and defines it, opens it up and analyses it.

And what, brethren, is that world-condition in the world which the Tathāgata has thoroughly penetrated and realized, and, having thoroughly

[1] *Anupādisesāya nibbāna-dhātuyā parinibbāyati.*

penetrated and realized it, what does He declare, teach, define, open up, and analyse?

Body, brethren, is that world-condition in the world which the Tathāgata . . . analysis. And whosoever, brethren, understands not and sees not when the Tathāgata declares, teaches, defines, opens up, and analyses . . . him do I set at naught, brethren, as a foolish worldling, blind, unseeing, unknowing, and sightless.

Feeling, brethren, is a world-condition in the world, and perception, the activities, consciousness, is a worldly condition in the world which the Tathāgata . . . analyses. And he, brethren, who understands not when the Tathāgata declares, teaches, defines, opens up, and analyses consciousness, . . . him do I set at naught, brethren, as a foolish worldling, blind, sightless, unknowing, unseeing.

Just as, brethren, a dark-blue lotus or a white lotus, born in the water, comes to full growth in the water, rises to the surface and stands unspotted by the water,—even so, brethren, the Tathāgata, (having been born in the world), having come to full growth in the world, passing beyond the world, abides unspotted by the world.'

S.N. iii. 139.

TATHĀGATA (2)

Then the venerable Anurādha went to the Exalted One and sat down. Seated at one side, the venerable Anurādha thus addressed the Exalted One:

'I am staying here, Lord, in a forest hut not far from the Exalted One. Now a number of heretic wanderers came to me . . . and said this : "Friend Anurādha, a Tathāgata, a superman, one of the best of men, a winner of the highest gain, is proclaimed in (one of) these four ways : A Tathāgata comes to be after death : or He comes not to be after death : or He both comes to be and comes not to be after death : or He neither comes to be nor comes not to be after death." Whereupon, Lord, I said to those heretic wanderers : "Friends, a Tathāgata is spoken of in other than these four ways."

Whereupon, Lord, those heretic wanderers said of me : "This brother must be a novice, not long ordained. Or, if he be an elder, he is an ignorant fool ! " Thereupon, Lord, those heretic wanderers, after abusing me by calling me a novice and an ignorant fool, rose up and went away. Not long after they had gone, Lord, the thought occurred to me : "If these heretic wanderers were to put me another question, how, in answering, should I tell them the views of the Exalted One, without misrepresenting the Exalted One by stating an untruth ? How should I answer in accordance with His teaching, so that one who agrees with His teaching and follows His views might not incur reproach ? " '

'Now what think you, Anurādha ? Is body permanent or impermanent ? '

'Impermanent, Lord.'

'Wherefore one who thus sees, he knows. . . . "for life in these conditions there is no hereafter."

Now as to this, Anurādha, what think you ? Do you regard a Tathāgata's body as the Tathāgata ? '

'Surely not, Lord.'

S.S.B.—II

'Do you regard Him as (His) feeling, (His) perception, (His) activities, or as apart from them? As consciousness or as apart from it?'

'Surely not, Lord.'

'Now what think you, Anurādha? Do you regard Him as having no body, no feeling, no perception, no activities, no consciousness?'

'Surely not, Lord.'

'Then, Anurādha, since in this very life a Tathāgata is not to be regarded as existing in truth, in reality, is it proper for you to pronounce this of him: "Friends, He who is a Tathāgata, a superman, one of the best of beings, a winner of the highest gain, is proclaimed in other than these four ways: 'The Tathāgata comes to be after death: He comes not to be after death: He both comes to be and comes not to be after death: He neither comes to be nor comes not to be after death'"?'

'Surely not, Lord.'

'Well said! Well said, Anurādha! Both formerly and now also, Anurādha, it is just Ill and the ceasing of Ill that I proclaim.'

S.N. iii. 86.

THE FOUR CONFIDENCES OF THE TATHĀGATA

Then the Exalted One said:

'There are these Four Confidences, Sāriputta, of a Tathāgata, equipped with which the Tathāgata knows His leadership, roars His lion-roar in the companies, and sets rolling the best of wheels. What are the four?

THE BUDDHAS SHOW THE WAY

I see no ground, Sāriputta, for anyone, be he recluse or brāhmin, or deva or Māra or Brahmā, or anyone in the world, to reproach me lawfully with not having perfect comprehension of these things which I claim as All-Enlightened to comprehend. Seeing no such ground, I have reached the state of calm, of fearlessness and confidence.

Claiming to have destroyed the *āsavas*, I see no ground for anyone to reproach me lawfully with not having destroyed the *āsavas*.

What I have declared to be Hindrances are really such, nor do I see any ground for anyone . . . to reproach me lawfully (by stating) that there is no harm in practising them.

That the Norm I have declared leads him who practises accordantly to the perfect destruction of Ill . . . I see no ground for anyone to deny.

These, Sāriputta, are the Four Confidences of a Tathāgata.'

M.N. i. 71.

THE TATHĀGATA JUST SHOWS THE WAY

Thus have I heard. Once the Exalted One was staying at Sāvatthī, in East Park, at the storeyed house of Migāra's mother.

Then the brāhmin Moggallāna, the accountant, came to the Exalted One and gave Him friendly greeting, and after the exchange of courtesies sat down at one side. So seated, the brāhmin Moggallāna, the accountant, said this to the Exalted One :

'Just as, master Gotama, one gets a gradual view of this storeyed house, a progress, a graduated path, and so on right up to the last step of the stairs,—just so is the progressive training of us brāhmins: that is to say, in our course of study (in the Vedas). Just as in a course of archery, the training of archers is a progressive one, so also, master Gotama, with us brāhmins the training, the progress, the approach is step by step; for instance, in counting. When we take a private pupil we make him count thus: "Once one, twice two, thrice three, four times four, and so on up to a hundred." Now is it possible, master Gotama, for this Norm-Discipline of yours to point to a similar progressive training?'

'It is so, brāhmin. Take the case, brāhmin, of a clever horse-trainer. He takes a thoroughbred in hand, gives him his first lesson with bit and bridle, and then proceeds to the further course. Just so, brāhmin, the Tathāgata takes in hand a man who is to be trained and gives him his first lesson, thus: "Come thou, brother! Be virtuous. Abide constrained by the restraint of the obligation. Become versed in the practice of right behaviour; seeing danger in trifling faults, do you undertake the training and be a pupil in the moralities."

As soon as he has mastered all that, the Tathāgata gives him his second lesson, thus: "Come thou, brother! Seeing an object with the eye, be not charmed by its general appearance or its details. Persist in the restraint of that dejection that comes from craving, caused by remaining with the sense of sight uncontrolled, those ill states which would overwhelm one like a flood. Guard the sense of sight, win control over the sense of sight. And so do with the other organs of sense. When you hear a sound with the ear, or smell a scent with the nose, taste a taste with the tongue, or with body touch things tangible, and when with mind you are conscious of a thing, be not charmed with its general appearance or its details."

As soon as he has mastered all that, the Tathāgata gives him a further lesson, thus: "Come thou, brother! Be moderate in eating; earnest and heedful do you take your food, not for sport, not for indulgence, not for adding personal charm or comeliness to body, but do it for body's stablishing, for its support, for protection from harm, and for keeping up the practice of the righteous life, with this thought: 'I check my former feeling. To no new feeling will I give rise, that maintenance and comfort may be mine.'"

Then, brāhmin, when he has won restraint in food, the Tathāgata gives him a further lesson, thus: "Come thou, brother! Abide given to watchfulness. By day, when walking or sitting, cleanse your heart from things that may hinder you. By night spend the first watch walking up and down or sitting, and do likewise. By night in the second watch, lie down on the right side in the posture of a lion, and placing one foot upon the other, mindful and self-possessed, set your thoughts on the idea of exertion. Then in the third watch of the night, rise up, and walking up and down, or sitting, cleanse the heart of things that may hinder."

Then, brāhmin, when the brother is devoted to watchfulness, the Tathāgata gives him a further lesson, thus: "Come thou, brother! Be possessed of mindfulness and self-control. In going forth or going back, have yourself under control. In looking forward or looking back, in bending or relaxing, in wearing robes or carrying robe and bowl, in eating, chewing, tasting, in easing yourself, in going, standing, sitting, lying, sleeping or waking, in speaking or keeping silence, have yourself under control."

Then, brāhmin, when he is possessed of self-control, the Tathāgata gives him a further lesson, thus: "Come thou, brother! Seek out a secluded lodging, a forest or root of a tree, a mountain or cave or mountain-grotto, a charnel field, a forest retreat, the open air, a heap of straw." And he does so. And when he has eaten his food he sits down crosslegged, and keeping his body straight up (*as described before*) he proceeds to practise the Four Musings. . . .

Now, brāhmin, for all brothers who are pupils, who have not yet attained mastery of mind, who abide aspiring for the security unsurpassed (which is Nibbāna) . . . such is the manner of my training.

But as to those brethren who are Arahants, who have destroyed the *āsavas*, who have lived the life, done their task, laid down the burden, won their own salvation, utterly destroyed the fetters of becoming, and are released by the perfect insight,—for such as those these things are conducive to ease in the present life and to mindful self-control as well.'

When this was said, the brāhmin Moggallāna, the accountant, said to the Exalted One:

'But tell me, master Gotama. Do the disciples of the worthy Gotama, thus advised and trained by the worthy Gotama,—do all of them win the absolute perfection which is Nibbāna: or do some fail thus to attain?'

'Some of my disciples, brāhmin, thus advised and trained by me, do so attain. Others do not.'

'But what is the reason, master Gotama? What is the cause, master Gotama? Here we have Nibbāna. Here we have the Path to Nibbāna. Here we have the worthy Gotama as instructor. What is the reason, I say, why some disciples thus advised and trained do attain, while others do not attain?'

'That, brāhmin, is a question that I will not answer here. But do you answer me this, so far as you think fit. Now how say you, brāhmin? Are you well skilled in the road to Rājagaha?'

'I am, master! Skilled indeed am I in the road to Rājagaha!'

'Now how say you, brāhmin? Suppose a man should come, anxious to go to Rājagaha. He comes up to you and says, "Sir, I would go to Rājagaha. Show me the way to Rājagaha." Then suppose you say to him, "All right, my man. This is the road to Rājagaha. Go on a bit, then you'll see a village called so and so. Go on a bit farther and you'll see such and such a suburb. Go a bit farther, and you'll see the delightful park, the delightful grove, the delightful landscape, the delightful lotus-pond of Rājagaha."

Well, thus instructed by you, thus advised by you, he takes the wrong road, and off he goes with his face set to the west.

Then a second man comes up with the same request, and you give him the same instructions. He follows your advice and comes safe to Rājagaha.

Now, brāhmin, what is the reason, what is the cause? Here we have Rājagaha, here we have the road to Rājagaha, and here we have you as instructor. But after all your advice and instructions one man took the wrong road and went west, while the other man got safe to Rājagaha.'

'Is that my business, master Gotama? I am just the shower of the way.'

'Well, brāhmin. Here we have Nibbāna, here we have the way to Nibbāna, and here stand I as Instructor of the Way. Yet some of my disciples, thus advised and trained by me, do attain to Nibbāna, and others do not attain.

What do I in the matter, brāhmin? The Tathāgata is one who shows the Way.'

M.N. iii. chap. 107.

O mendicants! Just as the snow-white *vassikā*,
The jasmine, putting forth fresh blooms to-day,
Sheds down the withered blooms of yesterday,
So shed ye lust and hate.

Tranquil in body, speech, and mind, O mendicants,
Whoso in every way is well-restrained,
Who all this world's desires hath thrown aside,
He is 'the tranquil' called.

Rouse thou the self by self, by self examine self:
Thus guarded by the self, and with thy mind
Intent and watchful, thus, O mendicant,
Thou shalt live happily.

Yea! Self is guard of self and refuge takes in self.
Just as a dealer trains a thoroughbred,
A noble steed, and breaks him to the rein,—
So do thou self restrain.

That mendicant, with utter joy and gladness filled,
Firm in the teaching of the Awakened One,
Reaches the bliss where all conditions cease,
Reaches the State of Peace.

Lo, ye! a mendicant, though young he be, that strives
To grasp the teaching of the Awakened One,
Lights up the world, as, from a cloud released,
The moon lights up the night.

Dhammapada, vv. 376–81.

TATHĀGATA (3)

'The body, brethren, of the Tathāgata yet remains, but cut off is that (thread) that bindeth to existence. So long as His body lasteth do devas and mankind behold Him. Upon the breaking up of body, after the ending of this life neither devas nor mankind shall see Him any more.

Just as, brethren, when the stalk of a bunch of mangoes is cut, whatsoever mangoes that hang to that stalk go along with it, even so, brethren, does the body of the Tathāgata yet remain, but cut off is that (thread) that bindeth to existence. So long as His body lasteth do devas and mankind behold Him. Upon the breaking up of body, after the ending of this life, neither devas nor mankind shall see Him any more.'

D.N. i. 45.

BEYOND DEATH

On a certain occasion the venerable Kassapa the Great and the venerable Sāriputta were staying near Benares at Isipatana in the Deer Park.

Then the venerable Sāriputta, rising up at eventide from his solitude, went to the venerable Kassapa the Great . . . and sat down at one side.

So seated, the venerable Sāriputta said to the venerable Kassapa the Great: 'How now, friend Kassapa? Does the Tathāgata exist beyond death?'

'Undeclared is it, friend Kassapa, by the Exalted One that the Tathāgata exists beyond death.'

'How then, friend? Does the Tathāgata not exist beyond death?'

'Undeclared also, friend, is this by the Exalted One.'

'What then, friend? Does the Tathāgata both exist and not exist beyond death?'

'This also, friend, is undeclared by the Exalted One.'

'How then, friend? Does the Tathāgata neither exist nor not-exist beyond death?'

'That also, friend, is not declared by the Exalted One.'

'But why, friend, has it not been declared by the Exalted One?

'This is a question not concerned with profit or with the first principles of the holy life. It does not conduce to aversion, disgust, cessation, calm, to supernormal powers, nor yet to perfect wisdom nor to Nibbāna. That, friend, is why it is not declared by the Exalted One.'

'Then what has been declared by Him?'

'That This is Ill, friend, has been declared by the Exalted One: that This is the Arising of Ill: that This is the Ceasing of Ill: that This is the Way leading to the Ceasing of Ill,—that is what has been declared by the Exalted One.'

'And why, friend, has it so been declared?'

'Because this is concerned with profit and the first principles of the holy life: because it conduces to aversion, to disgust, to cessation, to calm, and to supernormal powers, to perfect wisdom and to Nibbāna. Therefore has it been declared by the Exalted One.'

S.N. ii. pp. 222–3.

THEORIES AND FACTS

Thus have I heard. Once the Exalted One was dwelling at Sāvatthī, in Jeta Grove, at Anāthapindika's Park.

Then to the venerable Mālunkyaputta, aloof and solitary, there arose this train of thought:

'As to those holdings of views, left undeclared and rejected by the Exalted One, such as: "Eternal is the world: not eternal is the world: finite is the world: infinite is the world." Or again, "What is the life, that is the body: one thing is life, another thing is body." Or again,

"The Tathāgata is beyond death: the Tathāgata is not beyond death: the Tathāgata both is and is not beyond death: the Tathāgata neither is nor is not beyond death": as to these views, the Exalted One does not declare them to me. It does not commend itself to me. I myself will approach the Exalted One and ask Him this question: "If the Exalted One will declare the truth of these things to me, then I will follow the holy life under the Exalted One. If the Exalted One will not declare them to me, then I will give up the training and go back to the lower life (of the world)."'

So the venerable Mālunkyaputta, rising at eventide from his solitude, approached the Exalted One, drew near to Him, saluted Him, and sat down at one side. So seated, the venerable Mālunkyaputta described to the Exalted One his thoughts (as above described) and said:

'If the Exalted One will declare these things to me, I will follow the holy life under the Exalted One. But if the Exalted One will not so declare them to me, then will I give up the training and go back to the lower life (of the world).

Now, if the Exalted One knows, "Eternal is the world," let Him declare it to be so. If He knows, "Not eternal is the world," let Him so declare it to me. And so with regard to the other views that I have mentioned. But if the Exalted One does not know, does not see which theory is true, the straight thing is to say out, "I know not, I see not." And so with regard to the other views which I have named.'

'Now, Mālunkyaputta, did I say to you,

"Come thou, Mālunkyaputta, follow the holy life under me, and I will declare to you 'Eternal is the world' or 'Not eternal is the world,'" and so forth?'

'Not so, Lord.'

'And did you, Mālunkyaputta, say to Me, "Lord, I will follow the holy life under the Exalted One, and the Exalted One will declare to me, 'Eternal is the world, or not eternal is the world,'" and so forth?'

'Not so, Lord.'

'Then it is true, as you say, Mālunkyaputta, that I never said to you, "Come thou, Mālunkyaputta, follow the holy life under Me," and so forth: and it is true that you did not say to Me, "I will follow the holy life under the Exalted One, and the Exalted One will declare these things to me." This being so, misguided man, who are you and whom do you thus disallow? He who should say, Mālunkyaputta, "I will not follow the holy life under the Exalted One, until the Exalted One declare to me whether the world be eternal or not" . . . "whether the Tathāgata is beyond death or not," and so forth,—such an one, Mālunkyaputta, would come to an end, but that question of his would still remain unanswered by the Tathāgata.

Suppose, Mālunkyaputta, a man were pierced with an arrow well steeped in poison, and his close friends and relatives were to summon a physician, a surgeon. Then suppose the man says, "I will not have this arrow pulled out until I know, of the man by whom I was pierced, both his name and his clan, and whether he be tall or short or of middle stature: till I know him whether he be a black man or dark or sallow-skinned: whether he be of such and such a village or suburb or town. I will not have the arrow pulled out until I know of the bow, by which I was pierced, whether it was a long-bow or a cross-bow.

I will not have the arrow pulled out until I know of the bow-string by means of which I was pierced, whether it was made of creeper, or of reed, or of tendon, or of hemp, or of sap-tree.

. . . Till I know of the arrow by which I have been pierced, whether it be a reed-shaft, or of a sapling.

. . . Till I know of the feathers of it, whether they be feathers of a vulture or a heron, or of a kite or peacock, or of a hook-bill.

. . . Till I know of the arrow that has pierced me, whether it is bound with the tendon of an ox or of a buffalo or a deer or a monkey.

. . . Till I know whether the arrow which has pierced me be just an arrow, or a razor-edge, or a splinter, or a calf-tooth, or a javelin-head, or a barb-headed arrow."

Well, Mālunkyaputta, that man would die, but still that matter would not be found out by him.

Just so, Mālunkyaputta, he who should say, "I will not follow the holy life under the Exalted One until He declare unto me whether the world be eternal or not: whether what is the life, that is the body: whether one thing is the life, another thing is the body: whether the Tathāgata is beyond death or not: whether the Tathāgata both is and is not beyond death: whether the Tathāgata neither is nor is not beyond death,—such an one would come to his end, but that thing would not be declared by the Tathāgata."

Now, Mālunkyaputta, to say that the very existence of the holy life should depend on those two opposing views, to wit: that the world is eternal or not eternal, and so forth,—that is not the way.

But I am one who declares thus: Whether the world be eternal or not, nevertheless there is birth, there is decay, there is death, there are sorrow and grief, woe, lamentation, and despair: and it is the destruction of these things that I do declare.

And so with the other views, the infinity of the world . . . that the life is the body . . . that the Tathāgata is beyond death, and so forth . . . and their opposite views.

Wherefore, Mālunkyaputta, do you bear in mind that what I have declared is declared, and what I have not declared is not declared. Bear that in mind.

And what, Mālunkyaputta, have I not declared? That the world is eternal or otherwise . . . that the Tathāgata is beyond death or otherwise, and so forth.

And why, Mālunkyaputta, have I not so declared?

Because this thing is not concerned with profit: because it is not a principle of the holy life: because it does not lead to repulsion, to aversion, to cessation, to calming, to the super-knowledge, to the supreme wisdom, to Nibbāna. That is why I have not declared it.

And what, Mālunkyaputta, have I declared ?

I have declared, " This is suffering, This is the arising of suffering, This is the ceasing of suffering, This is the Way leading to the ceasing of suffering."

And why, Mālunkyaputta, have I so declared ?

Because it is concerned with profit : because it is a principle of the holy life : because it leads to repulsion, to aversion, to cessation, to calming, to the super-knowledge, to the supreme wisdom, to Nibbāna. That, Mālunkyaputta, is why I have declared it.

Wherefore, Mālunkyaputta, do you bear in mind what I have declared as undeclared : and what I have declared as declared.'

This spake the Exalted One, and the venerable Mālunkyaputta was delighted with what was said by the Exalted One.

M.N. i. chap. 63.

WHAT IS REVEALED ?

Once the Exalted One was staying at Kosambī, in Simsapa Grove. Then the Exalted One, taking up a handful of simsapa leaves, said to the brethren :

'Now what think ye, brethren ? Which are more, these few simsapa leaves that I hold in my hand, or those that are in the simsapa grove above ?'

'Few in number, Lord, are those simsapa leaves that are in the hand of the Exalted One : far more in number are those in the simsapa grove above.'

'Just so, brethren, those things that I know

by my super-knowledge, but have not revealed, are greater by far in number than those things that I have revealed. And why, brethren, have I not revealed them ?

Because, brethren, they do not conduce to profit, are not concerned with the holy life, they do not tend to repulsion, to cessation, to calm, to the super-knowledge, to the perfect wisdom, to Nibbāna. That is why I have not revealed them.

Then what, brethren, have I revealed ? That This is Ill, brethren, has been revealed by me: that This is the arising of Ill: that This is the ceasing of Ill: that This is the approach to the ceasing of Ill. And why have I so revealed it ? Because, brethren, it conduces to profit . . . to Nibbāna.

Wherefore, brethren, do ye exert yourselves to realize " This is Ill, this is the arising of Ill, this is the ceasing of Ill, this is the approach to the ceasing of Ill." '

S.N. v. 437.

THE GUIDE

THE SHIP

As the gods worship Indra, so should one
Worship the man from whom he learns the Norm.
The teacher, being honoured, pleased thereat,
From his deep knowledge doth expound the
Norm.

Knowing its value and observing it,
The wise disciple walks accordantly.
Sage he becomes, experienced and shrewd,
If earnestly he follow such a guide.

But if one serve a mean man, or a fool,
A jealous one that hath not reached the Real,—
In this world, never having grasped the Norm,
He comes to death with all his doubts unsolved.

Just as a man who steps into a stream
Of swollen waters, muddy and swift flowing,
Is carried downward by the rushing flood—
How can he ferry other men across ?

Just so, if one hath never grasped the Norm,
Not heeding wise men's teaching, but himself,
Is ignorant, with all his doubts unsolved,—
How can a man make others understand ?

THE GUIDE

Just as a ferryman boards his stout ship,
With oars and steering-gear fully equipped,
And ferries many other folk across—
A shrewd, skilled pilot he, who knows his task—

So he who knows, he who is well-composed,
Full of deep learning and unshakeable,
He surely will make others understand
Who sit beside and listen heedfully.

Well may one therefore serve a goodly man,
Full of deep learning and of wisdom ripe:
For he who knows the Real and walks aright,
He penetrates the Norm, he wins to bliss.

Sn. vv. 316–22.

CROSSING THE FLOOD

Thus have I heard. Once the Exalted One was dwelling among the Vajji at Ukkācela on the banks of Ganga. Then the Exalted One called to the brethren, saying, 'Brethren!' 'Yes, Lord,' replied those brethren to the Exalted One. The Exalted One said:

'In former times, brethren, there was a herdsman of Magadha, a fellow of small wits. In the last month of the rains, in autumn time, without proper study of the hither bank or further bank of Ganga, he sent his cattle across the stream to the further bank, belonging to the Suvidehas, just where there was no ford.

Well, the cattle got huddled together in midstream and came to destruction. Why so? Just because that herdsman, a fellow of small wits, in the last month of the rains, in autumn time, without proper study of the hither bank or further bank of Ganga . . . sent his cattle across just where there was no ford.

Just so, brethren, whatever recluses or brāhmins are ignorant of this world, of the world beyond, of the realm of Māra, of the realm beyond Māra, of the realm of Death, of the realm beyond the realm of Death,—those who think they ought to listen to and trust in such as these, they will find it to their loss and suffering for many a long day.

Now in former times also, brethren, there was a herdsman of Magadha, who was a shrewd fellow, and he sent his cattle across stream (on a similar occasion) after proper study of the hither and further bank of Ganga's stream, to the land of the Suvidehas, just there was a ford: in this way:

First he sent over the bulls, the fathers of the herd, the leaders of the herd. These crossed Ganga's stream and came safe to the further shore.

Next he sent across the sturdy kine and young bullocks, and they too came safe to the further shore.

Next he sent across the young steers and kine, and they too crossed Ganga's stream and came safe to the further shore.

Then he sent across the sucking calves, slim young things, and they too crossed Ganga's stream and came safe to the further shore.

Now on that occasion, brethren, there was a tender sucking calf being carried along, just born of its lowing dam, and it too crossed Ganga's stream and came safe to the further shore. Now how was this? Just because, brethren, that cowherd had his wits about him.

Just so, brethren, whatsoever recluses and brāhmins are skilled in this world and in the world beyond this world, in Māra's world and the world beyond Māra's, in the realm of Death and the realm beyond Death,—those who think such as these should be listened to and trusted in will find it to their profit and happiness for many a long day.

Now, brethren, just as those bulls, the fathers of the herd, the leaders of the herd, crossed Ganga's stream and came safe to the further shore, even so have those brothers who are Arahants, destroyers of the *āsavas*, who have lived the life, done their task, laid down the burden, reached their own salvation, burst the bonds that bind to rebirth, who are released by the perfect insight,—these are they that have crossed Māra's stream and gone safe to the further shore.

And just as those sturdy kine and bullocks crossed Ganga's stream and came safe to the further shore, even so those brothers who, by the bursting of the Five Bonds that bind to the lower things of life, who have been reborn in the heaven-worlds without parents and pass utterly away thence without return to this world, they too shall pass beyond Māra's stream and shall come safe to the further shore.

And just as those crossed Ganga's stream and came safe to the further shore, so also, brethren, those brothers who, by the destruction of three bonds and by the wearing thin of lust, anger, and illusion, are Once-returners,—when they have once more come back to this world, they shall make an end of sorrow. They too shall cross Māra's stream and come safe to the further shore.

And just as those sucking calves, slim young things, crossed Ganga's stream . . . even so those brothers, who by destruction of three bonds are Stream-winners, saved from the Downfall, assured of reaching the perfect wisdom . . . they too shall cross Māra's stream and come safe to the further shore.

And just as that tender sucking calf, just born of its lowing dam, and carried along, crossed Ganga's stream . . . even so those brothers who follow the Norm and walk in faith, they too shall cross Māra's stream and come safe to the further shore.

Now I, brethren, am the one that is skilled in this world and skilled in the world beyond, in Māra's realm and that beyond, in the realm of Death and that beyond Death. I am He, brethren, to whom, if men think fit to lend an ear and put trust in Him, it shall be to their profit and happiness for many a long day.'

M.N. i. chap. 34.

'They who yield to their desires
Down the stream of craving swim:
As we see the spider run
In the net himself hath spun.
Wise men cut the net and go
Free from craving, free from woe.

THE GUIDE

Loose all behind, between, before :
  Cross thou to the other shore.
With thy mind on all sides free
  Birth and death no more shalt see.

Dhammapada, 347–8.

THE RAFT

(i)

Then the Exalted One went unto the River Ganges. Now at that time the River Ganges was full, up to the banks, so that a crow might drink therefrom. Then some men, desirous of crossing to the other shore, began to hunt for a boat, while others hunted for a log-raft, and yet others began to tie reeds together.

But just as a strong man stretches out his arm and then draws back his arm outstretched, even so did the Exalted One vanish from this side of the River Ganges and stood on the further shore along with the Order of Brethren.

Now the Exalted One saw that some men . . . were hunting for a boat, others were hunting for a log-raft, while yet others were tying reeds together. Then the Exalted One, seeing the truth of the thing, uttered these inspired words :

They who cross the Ocean's deeps
Make a bridge and leave the swamps.
Other folk tie reeds together :
But the wise have crossed the Stream.

D.N. ii. 89.

(ii)

'Using the figure of a raft, brethren, will I teach you the Norm, as something to leave behind, not to take with you. Do you listen to it. Apply your minds. I will speak.'

'Even so,' Lord, replied those brethren to the Exalted One.

The Exalted One said: 'Just as a man, brethren, who has started on a long journey sees before him a great stretch of water, on this side full of doubts and fears, on the further side safe and free from fears: but there is no boat to cross in, no causeway for passing over from this side to the other side. Then he thinks thus: "Here is a great stretch of water . . . but there is no boat. . . . How now if I were to gather together grass, sticks, branches, and leaves, bind them into a raft, and resting on that raft paddle with hands and feet and so come safe to the further shore?"

Then, brethren, that man gathers together sticks . . . and comes to the further shore. When he has crossed over and come to the other side he thinks thus: "This raft has been of great use to me. Resting on this raft and paddling with hand and foot I have come to the further shore. Suppose now I were to set this raft on my head or lift it on to my shoulders and go my ways?"

Now what think ye, brethren? Would that man in so doing have finished with that raft?'

'Surely not, Lord.'

'Doing what then, brethren, would that man have finished with that raft? Herein, brethren, that man who has crossed and gone to the further shore should think thus: "This raft has been of great use to me. Resting on it I have crossed to the further shore. Suppose now I haul up this raft on the shore, or sink it in the water and go my ways!" By so doing, brethren, that man would have finished with that raft.

Even so, brethren, using the figure of a raft have I shown you the Norm, as something to leave behind, not to take with you. Thus, brethren, understanding the figure of the raft, *ye must leave righteous ways behind, not to speak of unrighteous ways.*'

M.N. i. 134.

METTEYYA BODHISATTA [THE COMING BUDDHA]

Now in those days,[1] brethren, there shall arise in the world an Exalted One by name Metteyya (the Kindly One), an Arahant, a Fully Enlightened One, endowed with wisdom and righteousness, a Happy One, a World-knower, the peerless Charioteer of men to be tamed, a Teacher of the devas and mankind, an Exalted One, a Buddha like myself.

He of his own abnormal powers shall realize and make known the world, and the worlds of the devas, with their Māras, their Brahmās,

[1] When human beings live for 80,000 years, and in the reign of Sankha, the King of Righteousness. This is the only reference in the Buddhist Canon to the Lord Metteyya.

the host of recluses and brāhmins, of devas and mankind alike, even as I do now.

He shall proclaim the Norm, lovely in its beginning, lovely in its middle, and lovely in the end thereof. He shall make known the wholly perfect life of righteousness in all its purity, both in the spirit and in the letter of it, even as I do now.

He shall lead an Order of Brethren numbering many thousands, even as I do now lead an Order of Brethren numbering many hundreds.

D.N. iii. 76.

NIBBĀNA DEFINED

THE MESSAGE OF NIBBĀNA

'It is even as some rājah's border-town, strongly built with walls and towers, and having six gates thereto. This town hath a wise and watchful Warden of the Gates, who keeps out enemies and welcomes friends. From the East there comes a pair of swift Messengers, and they say unto the Warden of the Gates: "Friend, where is the Lord of this town?"

And he replies: "Yonder he sits in the midst where the Four Ways meet."

Then those twin Messengers deliver unto the Lord of that town the Message of Truth, and go their ways by the Path by which they came.

Likewise also from the West and from the North there comes a pair of swift Messengers, and they say unto the Warden of the Gates: "Friend, where is the Lord of this town?" And in like manner he replies, and they deliver unto the Lord of that town the Message of Truth and go their ways.

Now, brethren, have I told ye a parable: and for the interpretation of the parable, it is this:

The Town is this body, of the Four Great Elements compounded, of parents born, fed on food, corruptible, and doomed to perish utterly.

The Six Gates thereof are the six avenues of Sense.

The Warden of the Gates, it is the Conscience.

The Pair of Swift Messengers, they are Calm and Insight.

The Lord of the Town, it is the Mind.

The Four Crossways meeting in the midst are the Elements of Earth and Water, Fire and Air.

The Message of Truth they bring, it is Nibbāna, the Unconditioned.

And the Path by which they come and go, it is the Ariyan Eightfold Path, to wit: Right View, Right Aim, Right Speech, Right Action, Right Living, Right Effort, Right Mindfulness, Right Contemplation.'

S.N. iv. 194.

THE UNMANIFESTED

The Exalted One said:

'In former days, brother, some ocean-faring merchants used to take with them a bird that could see the land, and launched out into the deep upon their ship. Now when the ship was out of sight of land, they used to set free the land-sighting bird. And the bird would fly east, would fly south, and west and north and up aloft, and to the other quarters. And if it sighted land around, off it would fly thither. But, if it saw no land around, back it would fly to the ship.

Even so, brother, you, having failed to get an answer to your question, though searching right up to the world of Brahmā,—you come back to Me again. But that question of yours, brother, was not put in the right way, to wit: "Where, Lord, do these four great elements[1] of earth, water, fire, and air cease to exist without leaving any trace of them?" This is how you should put the question:

> Where do water, earth and fire,—
> Where does air no footing find?
> Where do long and short, and fine,
> Likewise gross, pure and impure,
> Mind and body, cease to be,
> Leaving not a wrack behind?

Now the answer to this question is this: "It is that state of intellect[2] which is invisible, boundless, the landing-stage from everywhere."[3]

> There do water, earth and fire,
> There does air no footing find.

[1] It should be observed that Buddhism does not mean by 'the four great elements' merely the four visibles, but the forces, of which the four are the result, viz. the element of *extension*, of *cohesion*, of *expansion or heat*, and that of *vibration*. At *Sam. Nik.* i. 15, where part of these verses occurs, Dr. C. A. Rhys Davids has well turned the words (*apo, paṭhavi, tejo, vāyo*):

> Where the four elements that cleave and stretch
> And burn and move, no further footing find.

[2] *Viññānaṃ,* the Arahant's consciousness of Nibbāna.

[3] *Pahaṃ,* according to Buddhaghosa, is here 'the steps up and down to a riverside.' At *Dialogues of the Buddha,* ii. 283, Professor Rhys Davids translates, '(The Arahant's intellect) accessible from every side.' Cf. *Udāna,* p. 9. Nibbāna is therefore a state beyond mind-consciousness. In its ordinary sense *viññānam* is perishable, as one of the five *skandhas.*

There do long and short and fine,
Likewise gross, pure and impure,
Mind and body, cease to be,
Leaving not a wrack behind.
By ceasing of the conscious mind
There do all these cease to be.'

D.N. i. 222.

THE UNCOMPOUNDED

'I will teach you, brethren, the Uncompounded and the way going to the Uncompounded. Do ye listen to it.

Now what, brethren, is the Uncompounded? The destruction of lust, of hatred, of delusion, brethren, is called the Uncompounded.

And what, brethren, is the way going to the Uncompounded? It is mindfulness relating to the sphere of body that is so called. Thus, brethren, have I shown ye the Uncompounded and the way going to it.

Whatever can be done by a teacher desirous of the welfare of his disciples, out of compassion for them, that have I done for you, brethren.

Here, brethren, are the roots of trees, here are lonely dwelling-places. Do ye keep pondering, be ye not remiss, be not remorseful hereafter. This is my instruction unto you.' [1]

S.N. iv. 359.

[1] The section following of this *sutta* adds the other factors, viz.: calm, thought, concentration of mind without object, the establishing of mindfulness, the four best efforts, the four bases of power, the five controlling faculties, the five powers, the seven factors of wisdom, and the Path.

NIBBĀNA DEFINED

THE TWO PATHS

At Sāvatthī. . . . in the Park.

Now at that time the venerable Tissa, nephew to the Exalted One's father, thus spoke to a number of brethren :

'Truly, friends, my body has become as if drugged : the four quarters are become dim to my eyes, and the teachings are no longer clear to me. Sloth and torpor possess my heart : joyless to me is the righteous life, and I waver in the teachings.'

Thereupon a number of brethren went to the Exalted One, saluted Him, and sat down at one side.

So seated, those brethren said to the Exalted One : 'Lord, the venerable Tissa, nephew to the Exalted One's father, speaks thus to a number of brethren : "Truly, friends, my body is become as if drugged. The four quarters are dim to my eyes, and the teachings are no longer clear to me. Sloth and torpor possess my heart : joyless to me is the righteous life, and I waver in the teachings." '

At that, the Exalted One called to a certain brother :

'Come thou, brother, and in my name bid hither brother Tissa, saying : "Friend Tissa, the Master would speak with you." '

'Even so, Lord,' said that brother in reply to the Exalted One, and went to the venerable Tissa and said to him : 'Friend Tissa, the Master would speak with you.'

'Even so, brother,' said the venerable Tissa in reply to that brother, and came to the Exalted One, saluted Him, and sat down at one side.

As he thus sat the Exalted One thus spake unto the venerable Tissa: 'Is it true, as they say, Tissa, that you said this to a number of brethren: "Truly, friends, my body is become as if drugged . . . and so on . . . and I waver in the teachings"?'

'True, Lord.'

'Now as to that, what think you, Tissa? In a body that is not rid of lust, rid of desire, of love, of thirst, of fever and craving,—in such a body do there arise states of change and instability? Do sorrow and grief, woe, lamentation, and despair arise?'

'Yes, Lord.'

'Well said! Well said, Tissa! And is it so likewise with feeling . . . with perception, with the activities, and with consciousness?'

'Yes, Lord.'

'Well said! Well said, Tissa! So it is likewise with consciousness that is not rid of lust, of desire, of love, thirst, craving, and fever: in such consciousness there do arise sorrow and grief, woe, lamentation, and despair. Now what think you, Tissa? In a body that is rid of all these, in such a body do there arise sorrow and grief, woe, lamentation, and despair?'

'Surely not, Lord.'

'Well said! Well said, Tissa! So also with feeling, perception, the activities, do they arise?'

'Surely not, Lord.'

'Well said! Well said, Tissa! So it is with

consciousness that is rid of lust. Now what think you, Tissa? Is body permanent or impermanent?'

'Impermanent, Lord.'

'Is feeling, is perception, the activities,—is consciousness permanent or impermanent?'

'Impermanent, Lord.'

'Wherefore, he who seeth this is repelled by body, is repelled by feeling, by perception, by the activities. He is repelled by consciousness. Being repelled by it he lusts not after it: not lusting he is set free: in this freedom comes insight that it is a being-free. Thus he realizes: "Rebirth is destroyed, lived is the righteous life, done is my task, for life in these conditions there is no hereafter."

Suppose now, Tissa, there be two men, one unskilled and the other skilled in wayfaring. And the one who is unskilled asks the way of the other who is skilled in that way. And that other replies: "Yes. This is the way, good man. Go on for a while and you will see the road divide into two. Leave the path to the left and take the right-hand path. Go on for a little and you will see a thick forest. Go on for a little and you will see a great marshy swamp. Go on for a little and you will see a steep precipice. Go on for a little and you will see a delightful stretch of ground."

Such is my parable, Tissa, to show my meaning: and this is the meaning thereof. By "the man who is unskilled in the way" is meant the many-folk. By "the man who is skilled in the way" is meant a Tathāgata, an Arahant, a Fully

Enlightened One. By "the divided way," Tissa, is meant "the state of wavering." The "left-hand path" is a name for this false eightfold path, to wit: the path of wrong views, wrong intention, and so forth. The "right-hand path," Tissa, is a name for this Ariyan Eightfold Path, to wit: Right Views, and so forth. The "thick forest," Tissa, is a name for ignorance. The "great marshy swamp," Tissa, is a name for the feeling-desires. The "steep precipice," Tissa, is a name for vexation and despair. "The delightful stretch of level ground," Tissa, is a name for Nibbāna.

Be of good cheer, Tissa! Be of good cheer, Tissa! I to counsel! I to uphold! I to teach!'

S.N. iii. 106.

NIBBĀNA

At Sāvatthī. The venerable Rādha came to the Exalted One and sat down. Seated at one side the venerable Rādha thus addressed the Exalted One:

'A being! A being! they say, Lord. Pray, Lord, how far can one be called a being?'

'That desire, Rādha, that lust, that lure, that craving which is concerned with body,—entangled thereby, fast entangled thereby, therefore is one called a being.

That desire, that lust, that craving, that lure which is concerned with feeling, with perception, the activities, consciousness,—entangled thereby, fast entangled thereby, therefore is one called a being.

NIBBĀNA DEFINED

Just as when, Rādha, boys or girls play with little sand-castles. So long as they are not rid of lust, not rid of desire, not rid of affection, thirst, feverish longing and craving for those little sand-castles, just so long do they delight in them, are amused by them, set store by them, are jealous of them.

But Rādha, as soon as those boys or girls are rid of lust, of desire and affection, are rid of thirst, feverish longing, and craving for those little sand-castles, straightway with hand and foot they scatter them, break them up, knock them down, cease to play with them.

Even so, Rādha, do you scatter body, break it up, knock it down, cease to play with it, apply yourself to destroy craving for it.

So also with feeling, perception, the activities, consciousness . . . do you scatter consciousness, Rādha, break it up, knock it down, cease to play with it, apply yourself to destroy craving for it.

Verily, Rādha, *the destruction of craving is Nibbāna.*'

S.N. iii. 188.

CROSSED OVER

Whoso hath trod the hard and muddy road of births,
Hath crossed delusion, reached the other shore:
Nor lusts, nor doubts, nor grasps, is calm,—
Him I deem a Brāhmana.

Dhammapada, v. 412.

NIBBĀNA IS RELEASE

Then the venerable Rādha came to the Exalted One. Having done so he saluted the Exalted One and sat down at one side. So seated the venerable Rādha thus addressed the Exalted One :

'They say, "Māra ! Māra !" Lord. Pray, Lord, how far is there Māra ?'

'Where a body is, Rādha, there would be Māra or things of the nature of Māra, or at any rate what is perishing. Wherefore, Rādha, regard the body as Māra : regard it as of the nature of Māra : regard it as perishing, as an imposthume, as a dart, as pain, as a source of pain. They who regard it thus do rightly regard it.

And the same may be said of feeling, of perception, of the activities, of consciousness.'

'But rightly regarding, Lord, — for what purpose ?'

'Rightly regarding, Rādha, for the sake of disgust.'

'But disgust, Lord,—for what purpose is it ?'

'Disgust, Rādha, is to bring about dispassion.'

'But dispassion, Lord,—for what purpose is it ?'

'Dispassion, Rādha, is to get release.'

'But release, Lord,—what is it for ?'

'*Release, Rādha, means Nibbāna.*'

'But Nibbāna, Lord,—what is the aim of that ?'

'This, Rādha, is a question that goes too far. You can grasp no limit to this question. Rooted in Nibbāna, Rādha, the holy life is lived. Nibbāna is its goal. Nibbāna is its end.'

S.N. iii. 187.

NIBBĀNA THE END OF WOE

Thus have I heard. On a certain occasion the Exalted One was staying near Sāvatthī in Anáthapindika's Park at Jeta Grove. Now on that occasion the Exalted One was instructing, stirring, firing, and gladdening the brethren with a pious talk about Nibbāna, and those brethren understood its meaning, paid attention to it, grasped with their minds the whole teaching, listened to the teaching with ready ears.

Then on that occasion the Exalted One, seeing the application of it, uttered these solemn words:

'There is, brethren, a condition wherein there is neither earth, nor water, nor fire, nor air, nor the sphere of infinite space, nor the sphere of infinite consciousness, nor the sphere of the void, nor the sphere of neither perception nor non-perception: where there is no "this world" and no "world beyond": where there is no moon and no sun. That condition, brethren, do I call neither a coming nor a going nor a standing still nor a falling away nor a rising up: but it is without fixity, without mobility, without basis. THAT IS THE END OF WOE:

Hard to behold THE SELFLESS, so 'tis called.
Not easy is it to perceive the Truth.
But craving is pierced through by one who knows:
He who sees all clings not to anything.'

And again, on that occasion, the Exalted One uttered these solemn words:

'There is, brethren, an unborn, a not-become,

a not-made, a not-compounded. If there were not, brethren, this that is unborn, not-become, not-made, not-compounded, there could not be made any escape from what is born, become, made, and compounded.

But since, brethren, there is this unborn . . . therefore is there made known an escape from what is born, become, made, and compounded.'

And again, on that occasion, the Exalted One uttered these solemn words:

'In him who depends (on others), there is wavering. In him who is independent, there is no wavering. Where there is no wavering, there is tranquillity. Where there is tranquillity, there is no passionate delight. Where there is no passionate delight, there is no coming and going (in rebirth). Where there is no coming and going (in rebirth), there is no falling from one state to another. Where there is no falling from one state to another there is no "here," no "beyond," no "here-and-yonder." THAT IS THE END OF WOE.'

Udāna, p. 80, cap. viii.

THE CEASING OF BECOMING IS NIBBĀNA.

S.N. ii. § 68.

THE ISLE OF REFUGE

'In midstream standing, in the fearsome flood,
For those o'erwhelméd by decay and death,
O tell me of an island,' Kappa said,
'O tell me of an island, worthy sir,
Where all these things shall be no more!'

'In midstream standing, in the fearsome flood,
For those o'erwhelméd by decay and death,
I'll tell thee of an island, Kappa (said
The Exalted One)—I'll tell thee of an isle,
Where all these things shall be no more.

Possessing naught, and cleaving unto naught—
That is the isle, th' incomparable isle.
That is the ending of decay and death.
Nibbāna do I call it, Kappa (said
The Exalted One)—that is the isle.

They who know this, who in this very life
Have steadfast grown, who have become serene—
They are not Māra's subjects or his slaves.
(That is the island,' said the Exalted One,
'Where all these things shall be no more.')

Sn. v. 1091–4.

'Wherefore, Ānanda, do ye abide islands unto yourselves, refuges unto yourselves: taking refuge in none other: islanded by the Norm, taking refuge in the Norm, seeking refuge in none other.

And how, Ānanda, doth a brother abide an island to himself, a refuge to himself, taking refuge in none other, islanded by the Norm, taking refuge in the Norm, seeking refuge in none other?

Herein, Ānanda, a brother dwells contemplating body as a compound, ardent, mindful, and self-possessed by restraining the covetousness and discontent that are in worldly things. Likewise in feelings, he dwells contemplating feelings, ardent, mindful, and self-possessed by restraining covetousness and discontent in worldly things. Likewise in his mind a brother so dwells . . . and in his states of mind he dwells contemplating his states of mind, ardent, mindful, and self-possessed, by restraining covetousness and discontent in worldly things.

That, Ānanda, is how a brother abides an island unto himself, a refuge unto himself. . . . And whosoever, Ānanda, either now or when I shall have passed away, shall abide islands unto themselves, refuges unto themselves, taking refuge in none other: islanded by the Norm, taking refuge in the Norm, seeking refuge in none other,—these, Ānanda, shall be out of the darkness [1] whatsoever brethren shall be desirous of learning.'

D.N. ii. 101.

[1] *Tama-t-agge*—lit. ' at the top of the gloom,' according to the interpretation of *Commentary*: but I would prefer to translate, with Mrs. Rhys Davids, ' on the Peak of the Undying,' reading the Pāli as *t'amat'agge*. There is a Burmese reading (at *S.* v. 163) *tad-amatagge*: and a Sinhalese (*S.* v. 154) *tamata-magge*.

LAST DAYS

ĀNANDA'S OBTUSENESS

At the Cāpāla Shrine. Then the Exalted One said to the venerable Ānanda:

'In whomsoever, Ānanda, the Four Ways of Power[1] are practised, fully developed, made into a vehicle, made into a basis, gathered into one, fully mastered for use,—such an one, if he so desire, may abide for the world-period or for the rest of the world-period.[2]

In the Tathāgata, Ānanda, the Four Ways of power are practised, fully developed, made into a vehicle, made into a basis, gathered into one, fully mastered for use. He, if He so desire, may abide for the world-period, or for the remainder of the world-period.'

Now although such a broad hint, such a broad illuminating remark was made by the Exalted One, yet could not the venerable Ānanda penetrate it: so that he did not beg of the Exalted One, 'O Lord, let the Exalted One abide for the world-period: let the Happy One abide for the world-period, for the profit, for the bliss of many, out of compassion for the world, for the welfare,

[1] *Chando* (urge), *viriya* (energy), *citta* (thought), *vimamsā* (investigation).

[2] Certain sects among the early Brethren held that *kappa* here meant the period of human life.

for the bliss of devas and mankind.' To such a degree was his mind misguided by the Evil One.

(Then did the Exalted One thrice more repeat these words, but Ānanda said nothing.)

Then said the Exalted One to the venerable Ānanda:

'Go, Ānanda! Do what you think seasonable.'

Whereupon the venerable Ānanda rose from his seat, in obedience to the Exalted One, saluted Him by the right, and departed, and not long after sat down at the root of a tree.

Then Māra, the Evil One, not long after the departure of the venerable Ānanda, came to the Exalted One and stood at one side. So standing, Māra, the Evil One thus addressed the Exalted One:

'Let my Lord the Exalted One pass utterly away now. It is time, Lord, for the Exalted One to pass utterly away. For thus was it spoken by the Exalted One: "I will not pass utterly away, O Evil One, until I have brethren as disciples who shall be trained and disciplined, wise, of wide knowledge, knowing the Norm by heart, walking according to the ordinances of the Norm, walking dutifully, living in accordance with the Norm: so that, having of themselves grasped their Master's teaching, they may proclaim, teach, show forth, establish, open up, analyse, and make it plain: so that they may refute any wrong view arising, after convicting it by the help of the Norm, and thus show forth the miracle of the Norm. . . . I will not pass utterly away till I shall have sisters, lay-brethren, lay-sisters as my disciples . . . who shall be so trained and disciplined . . . to show forth the miracle of the Norm."

And now, I say, O Lord, the brethren who are disciples of the Exalted One, the sisters, the lay-brothers, and the lay-sisters of the Exalted One are (thus equipped as I have said) . . . therefore let the Exalted One pass utterly away, let the Happy One pass utterly away, according to the word of my Lord, the Exalted One. . . .

For thus spake the Exalted One unto me: "I will not pass utterly away, O Evil One, until this righteous life shall be powerful, prosperous, widely spread, and multiplied, so far as it is well proclaimed by devas and mankind."[1] And now these things are so . . . wherefore let my Lord, the Exalted One, pass utterly away. Let the Happy One pass utterly away. It is time now for the utter passing away of the Exalted One!'

At these words the Exalted One replied unto Māra, the Evil One:

'Rest content, Evil One! In no long time shall be the utter passing away of the Tathāgata. At the end of three months from now shall be the utter passing away of the Tathāgata.'

Thus did the Exalted One, at Cāpāla Shrine, mindful and self-possessed, reject the aggregate of life. And when the aggregate of life had been rejected by the Exalted One, there was a mighty earthquake, and a fearful hair-raising thundering

[1] Reading *yāva deva-manussehi* for the usual *yāvad eva manussehi*, cf. *Sam. Nik.* ii. 107 (*Kindred Sayings*, ii. 75 n.).

burst forth.[1] And seeing the meaning of it, the Exalted One thrice uttered these solemn words :

In all its parts, both small and infinite,
His own life's compound did the Sage reject.
With inward calm composedly He burst,
Like shell of armour, all that makes the self.

D.N. ii. 104–7.

(The Master then related the request of Māra to Ānanda.)

Whereupon the venerable Ānanda said to the Exalted One :

'O Lord, let the Exalted One abide for the world-period. Let the wellfarer abide for the world-period . . . !'

'Enough, Ānanda ! Ask not that of the Tathāgata. The time is now past, Ānanda, for asking that of the Tathāgata.'

Then a second time and yet a third time did Ānanda make the same request, and on the third occasion the Exalted One said :

'Ānanda, dost thou believe in the wisdom of the Tathāgata ?'

'Yes, Lord.'

'Then why dost thou importune the Tathāgata, even to asking Him a third time ?'

[1] After this the Buddha explains to Ānanda the causes of such an earthquake. Earthquakes take place from natural causes, and from the magic of adepts. But there are six other sorts of earthquake, viz. : when the *Bodhisattva* decides to be reborn for the last time ; when He is so reborn ; when He attains Enlightenment ; when He sets rolling the Wheel of the Norm ; when He decides on the final passing away ; when He finally passes away.

'But, Lord, face to face with the Exalted One I had these words: "Whosoever has developed . . . the Four Ways of Power, and so forth . . . can, if he so desire, abide for the world-period or for the remainder of the world-period. . . ." Now the Exalted One hath so done. . . . Therefore He could, if He so desired, thus abide.'

'Ānanda, dost thou believe?'

'Lord, I believe.'

'Then, Ānanda, thine is the fault and thine the transgression, insofar as, when so broad a hint was given, when such an illuminating remark was made by the Tathāgata, thou couldst not penetrate it, so as to ask the Tathāgata: "Let the Exalted One abide for the world-period, let the Wellfarer abide for the world-period, for the profit of many, for the bliss of many, out of compassion for the world, for the welfare, for the profit, for the bliss of devas and mankind!" For if, Ānanda, thou hadst begged twice, the Tathāgata might have rejected thy petition: yet at the third time of asking He might have consented. Therefore, Ānanda, thine is the fault and thine is the transgression.' [1]

D.N. ii. 115.

'IT IS TIME FOR ME TO GO'

Then the Exalted One called to the brethren and said:

'Come now, brethren, I do remind you: Subject to decay are all compounded things. Do ye

[1] After the Master's death, the Order accused Ānanda of this offence.

abide in heedfulness. In no long time shall be the utter passing away of the Tathāgata. After the lapse of three months from now shall the Tathāgata pass utterly away.'

Thus spake the Exalted One. Thus spake the Wellfarer. Having thus spoken the Master added this further :

Ripe is My age, and short My span of life.
Rejecting it, self-refuged, I go hence.

Brethren, be earnest, mindful, virtuous,
And steadfast in your aim. Guard ye your
thoughts.

Whoso shall earnest dwell in this Norm-Rule,
He shall cast off the round of birth and death,
And thereby make an end of Suffering.

D.N. ii. 120.

THE CLOSED FIST OF THE TEACHER

Now when the Exalted One had thus begun to keep the rainy season, there came upon Him a grievous sickness: strong pains racked Him, like to end in death. But the Exalted One, mindful and self-possessed, endured those pains unflinchingly. Then this thought came to the Exalted One:

'It is not fitting that I should pass utterly away without warning My supporters, without taking leave of the Order of Brethren. Suppose now I were to hold down this sickness by an effort and stay on by holding fast to the aggregates of life.'

So the Exalted One held down that sickness and stayed on, holding fast to the aggregates of life.

Then that sickness of the Exalted One was calmed down, and He arose from His sickness, and not long after so arising He went out of His lodging, and sat in the shadow of the lodging on a seat prepared for Him.

Then the venerable Ānanda approached the Exalted One, came up to Him, saluted Him, and sat down at one side. So seated the venerable Ānanda thus addressed the Exalted One:

'Lord, I have seen the Exalted One in health, and I have seen Him in endurance: and though my body, Lord, became as if drugged, and my bearings were confused, though things were no longer clear to me because of the sickness of the Exalted One, yet, Lord, I had thus much of comfort in the thought, "Surely the Exalted One will not pass utterly away until He has made some pronouncement concerning the Order of Brethren."'

'What, Ānanda, does the Order of Brethren expect of me? I have taught you the Norm, Ānanda, by making it without inner or outer. There is no closed fist of the teacher[1] in a Tathāgata, Ānanda.

If, then, Ānanda, anyone thinks, "*I* will lead the Order of Brethren" or, "On *me* the Order of Brethren depends,"—let him make some pronouncement. As for Me, Ānanda, I am now a broken-down old man, aged, far gone in years, I have reached the journey's end. I am come to

[1] *Ācariya-muṭṭhi.*

life's limit. My age is turning now eighty years. Just as, Ānanda, a worn-out cart is kept going by being tied together with helps,[1] even so, methinks, Ānanda, the Tathāgata's body is kept going by helps.

Only at times when the Tathāgata withdraws His attention from all externals, by the ceasing of His several feelings, by entering on and abiding in the objectless concentration of mind,—only at such times, Ānanda, is the Tathāgata's body at ease.'

D.N. ii. 99.

CUNDA'S OFFERING

Now at that time the Exalted One was staying at Pāvā, in the mango grove of Cunda, of the metal-workers' caste.

Now Cunda of the metal-workers' caste heard the rumour: 'They say that the Exalted One, while going His rounds among the Mallas, has come to Pāvā together with a great company of the brethren, and is staying in my mango grove.' So Cunda of the metal-workers' caste came to the Exalted One, saluted Him, and sat down at one side. So seated, the Exalted One instructed, stirred, fired, and gladdened Cunda with pious talk. Then Cunda, thus instructed, stirred, fired, and gladdened, addressed the Exalted One, saying: 'Let my Lord, the Exalted One, accept from my hands to-morrow's meal, together with

[1] *Vega-missakena*, by wrapping round with ropes; cf. St. Paul's sea voyage in which the ship is 'frapped' by 'helps' or ropes passed round.

the Order of Brethren.' And the Exalted One accepted by silence.

Then Cunda, seeing the acceptance of the Exalted One, rose from his seat, bowed before the Exalted One, and saluting Him by the right, departed.

Now when the night was gone, Cunda of the metal-workers' caste in his own house made ready choice food, both hard and soft, together with a quantity of fat hogsflesh, and sent a message as to the time to the Exalted One.

Then the Exalted One rose at early dawn and robed Himself, and, taking outer robe and bowl, started off for the house of Cunda the metal-worker, attended by the Order of Brethren. When He got there He sat down on a seat made ready. There sitting the Exalted One called to Cunda and said: 'Cunda, as to that fat hogsflesh which you have prepared, serve Me with it, but serve the brethren with whatsoever food, both soft and hard, you have prepared.'

'Very well, Lord,' said Cunda in reply to the Exalted One, and did accordingly.

Then the Exalted One called to Cunda and said: 'Cunda, whatever of the fat hogsflesh is remaining, bury that in a hole in the ground. For I can see no one in this world, Cunda, together with the world of the devas, with its Māras, its Brahmās, and all the host of recluses and brāhmins, of devas and mankind,—I can see no one by whom that food when eaten can be digested, save only by the Tathāgata.'

'Very well, Lord,' replied Cunda, and went and buried the remainder of that fat hogsflesh in a hole in the ground; then came to the Exalted One, saluted Him, and sat down at one side. As he thus sat, the Exalted One, having instructed, stirred, fired, and gladdened Cunda with pious talk, rose from His seat and went away.[1]

Now when the Exalted One had eaten the food given by Cunda, of the metal-workers' caste, a grievous sickness came upon Him, a dysentery, and strong pains set in, like to end in death. Those pains did the Exalted One endure unflinchingly, calm and composed. Then the Exalted One called to the venerable Ānanda, saying: 'Let us go, Ānanda, towards Kusinārā.' 'Even so, Lord,' replied the venerable Ānanda to the Exalted One.

The Sage, when He had eaten Cunda's food,—
Cunda the metal-worker's—so I heard,
Came by dire sickness, like to end in death.

When He had eaten of the fat hogsflesh,[2]
Within the Master a dire sickness rose.

When He had purged, the Exalted One exclaimed:
'Now go I unto Kusinārā Town.'

[1] A similar case of burying remnants of food is at *Sam. Nik.* i. 168.

[2] 'Fat hogsflesh' (*sūkara-maddava*). Much has been written about this incident. The commentator (Dhammapāla on *Udāna*, loc. cit.) merely says: 'In the Great Commentary it is written: "*Sūkara-maddava* is flesh that has become soft and fat. But some say it is not hogsflesh, but young bamboo-shoots trampled by hogs. Others, that it is the snakeshood

Then the Exalted One, stepping aside from the road, came to the root of a certain tree, and on coming there He called to the venerable Ānanda, saying: 'Come now, Ānanda! Prepare My robe by folding it in four. I am weary. I will sit down.'

'Even so, Lord,' said the venerable Ānanda, and folded the robe into four.

Then the Exalted One sat down on that seat prepared. Having sat down He said to the venerable Ānanda: 'Come now, Ānanda! Do you bring me water to drink. I am thirsty. I would drink, Ānanda.'

Whereupon the venerable Ānanda said to the Exalted One: 'Just now, Lord, as many as five hundred carts have gone across (the stream). That water is stirred up by the wheels, and being shallow it flows foul and muddy. But not far from here, Lord, is this river Kukutthā, with its clear, pleasant water, cool and translucent, easy of access and delightful. Herein the Exalted One can drink water and cool His limbs.'

Then a second time, and yet a third time did the Exalted One make the same request, and the venerable Ānanda made the same reply,

(mushroom), which grows in a place frequented by hogs. Yet others say it is a term for a curry-sauce."

It should be added that, whether the food was flesh or vegetable, the Buddha was not a vegetarian Himself, according to numerous passages of the Canon, nor did He enjoin it on His disciples, who are bidden to eat whatever is offered in charity, for beggars cannot be choosers. (See a valuable article, *Ahiṃsa and Vegetarianism*, by Dr. Otto Schrader, *Ceylon National Review*, 1910.)

and on the third occasion he replied, 'So be it, Lord,' to the Exalted One, and taking the bowl went down to the stream.

Now that stream was stirred up by the cart-wheels, and being shallow it was flowing foul and muddy. But as soon as the venerable Ānanda reached it, it was flowing clean and clear and free from mud.

Whereupon this thought came to the venerable Ānanda: 'A wonder indeed! A marvel indeed! Great is the magic art and power of the Tathāgata! For this stream, which was stirred up by the cart-wheels . . . now flows free from mud upon my approach to it.'

So taking water in the bowl he went to the Exalted One and exclaimed: 'A wonder indeed, Lord! A marvel, indeed, Lord! Great is the magic art and power of the Tathāgata. . . . Let the Exalted One drink the water! Let the Happy One drink the water!'

D.N. ii. 126; *Udāna*, viii. 5.

CUNDA'S MERITORIOUS DEED

Then said the Exalted One to the venerable Ānanda:

'It may happen, Ānanda, that someone might stir up regret in Cunda the metal-worker by saying: "It is no gain to you, friend Cunda; it is an ill-gotten thing for you, friend Cunda, that the Tathāgata passed away after eating His last meal at your hands." Any regret (so arising), Ānanda, in Cunda the metal-worker, should be banished by saying to him: "It is a gain to you, friend Cunda, it is a thing well-gotten for you, Cunda, that the Tathāgata passed away after eating His last meal at your hands. Face to face, friend Cunda, with the Exalted One did I hear it said, face to face I received the saying: 'These two meals are of like fruit and result, far exceeding any other meal in fruit and result. What two are they? That meal after eating which the Tathāgata was enlightened with the Supreme Enlightenment: and that meal after eating which the Tathāgata passed away with that utter passing away which leaves no basis (for rebirth). These two meals are of like fruit, of like result, far exceeding any other meals in fruit and in result.' A deed hath been stored up by the worthy Cunda, a deed which results in length of days, which results in beauty of person, which results in happiness, in the heaven-world, in fame, which results in power."

With such words, Ānanda, should be banished any regrets that may arise in Cunda the metal-worker.'

Then the Exalted One, seeing the meaning of the thing, thrice uttered these inspired words:

For him that giveth, merit comes to growth.
In one self-curbed no hate accumulates.
The righteous man casts wickedness away.
When Lust and Anger and Bewilderment
Are rooted out, that man hath come to Peace.

D.N. ii. 135–6; *Udāna*, viii. 5.

SOME SAYINGS OF THE BUDDHA

THE DEATHBED OF THE MASTER

Then the Exalted One called to the venerable Ānanda and said: 'Come now, Ānanda, let us go to Kusināra across the river, to the branch-road that goes to the Sāla Grove of the Mallas.'

'Even so, Lord,' replied the venerable Ānanda to the Exalted One.

So the Exalted One went thither, and (when He had reached the Sāla Grove) He said to the venerable Ānanda: 'Look you, Ānanda! Get ready a couch between the twin Sāla trees. I am weary, Ānanda. I will lie down.'

'Even so, Lord,' replied the venerable Ānanda, and did as he was bidden. Then the Exalted One lay down on His right side in the posture of a lion, with one foot resting on the other, calm and composed.

TRUE WORSHIP

Then said the Exalted One to the venerable Ānanda:

'See, Ānanda! All abloom are the twin Sāla trees: with untimely blossoms do they shower down upon the body of the Tathāgata, they sprinkle it, cover it up, in worship of the Tathāgata. Moreover, heavenly frankincense comes falling from the sky, showers down upon the body of the Tathāgata, sprinkles it and covers it up, in worship of the Tathāgata. And heavenly music sounds in the sky, in worship of the Tathāgata, and heavenly songs are wafted from the sky in worship of the Tathāgata.

Yet not thus is the Tathāgata truly honoured, revered, respected, worshipped, and deferred to. Whosoever, Ānanda, be he brother or sister, or lay-brother or lay-sister,—whosoever dwells in the fulfilment of the Norm, both in its greater and in its lesser duties,—whosoever walks uprightly in accordance with the Norm,—he it is that truly honours, reveres, respects, worships, and defers to the Tathāgata in the perfection of worship.

Wherefore, Ānanda, saying, "We will dwell in the fulfilment of the Norm, in its greater and in its lesser duties, walking uprightly in accordance with the Norm,"—thus must ye train yourselves.'

D.N. iii. 138.

DISPOSAL OF THE BODY

And the venerable Ānanda asked the Exalted One: 'How, Lord, are we to deal with the body of the Tathāgata?'

'Worry not about the body-rites of the Tathāgata, Ānanda. Look you, Ānanda! Strive for your own welfare, apply yourselves to your own welfare: dwell heedful, ardent, and resolute. There are discreet nobles, discreet brāhmins and housefathers, Ānanda, believers in the Tathāgata. They will see to the body-rites of the Tathāgata.'

'THESE FOUR PLACES'

Then the Exalted One said:

'There are these four places, Ānanda, which the believing clansman should look upon with emotion. What four?

Saying, "Here was the Tathāgata born," Ānanda, should the believing clansman look upon the birthplace of the Tathāgata.

Saying, "Here did the Tathāgata reach supreme Enlightenment," Ānanda, should the believing clansman look upon the place (of the Bodhi Tree).

Saying, "Here did the Tathāgata set rolling the unsurpassed wheel of the Norm," Ānanda, should the believing clansman look upon the place.

Saying, "Here did the Tathāgata pass away with that utter passing away which leaves no remnant for rebirth," Ānanda, should the believing clansman look upon this place. Such are the Four Places.

There will come, Ānanda, believing brethren and sisters, lay-brothers and lay-sisters, and so will they speak of these four places.

And whosoever, Ānanda, shall make an end with peaceful heart, while wandering on pilgrimage to (such) shrines, upon the breaking up of body all such shall be reborn beyond death in the blissful heaven-world.'

D.N. ii. 141.

THE BELOVED DISCIPLE

Now the venerable Ānanda went to the residence and stood leaning against the door-bar and wept, saying, 'Alas! I am still a pupil with much yet to be done, and my Master will be passing utterly away, He who was kind to me!'

Then the Exalted One called to the brethren, 'Brethren, where is Ānanda?'

'The venerable Ānanda is here, Lord,' they replied. 'He has gone into the residence and is leaning against the door-bar, weeping and saying: "Alas! I am still a pupil with yet much to be done, and my Master will be passing utterly away. He who was kind to me!"'

Then the Exalted One called a certain brother and said to him: 'Go thou, brother, and say to Ānanda in My words: "Friend Ānanda, the Master calls you."'

'Even so, Lord,' replied that brother and went to the venerable Ānanda, and said: 'Friend Ānanda, the Master calls you.'

'Very well, friend,' replied the venerable Ānanda to that brother, and he went in to the Exalted One, saluted Him, and sat down at one side.

As he thus sat the Exalted One said to the venerable Ānanda:

'Enough, Ānanda! Sorrow not, lament not! Have I not said to you ere now, Ānanda, "In all things dear and delightful there is the element of change, of separation, of otherness." How then can it be possible, Ānanda, that what is born, what has come to be, what is put together, what is of nature to crumble away, should fail to crumble away! It cannot be.

For many a long day, Ānanda, the Tathāgata has been waited on by you with kindly body-service, that is profitable, ease-giving, undivided, and unstinted; waited on with kindly service of speech, that is profitable, ease-giving, undivided, and unstinted; with kindly service of thought, that is profitable, ease-giving, undivided, and unstinted. You have done meritorious deeds,

Ānanda. Apply yourself to effort! Soon shall you be made perfect.'

Then the Exalted One called to the brethren: 'Brethren, whatsoever Arahants, Fully Enlightened Ones, have been in times past, all of those Exalted Ones had body-servers just such as Ānanda has been to me. Whatsoever Arahants, Fully Enlightened Ones, shall be in the future, all of those Exalted Ones shall have body-servers just such as Ānanda has been to me.

A wise man, brethren, is Ānanda. He knows "This is the proper time for coming to see the Tathāgata. This is the time for brethren, this is the time for sisters, for lay-brothers, for lay-sisters to come to see the Tathāgata." He knows "This is the proper time for rājahs, for great ministers, for the teachers of other views, and for their disciples."

There are four wonderful, strange things about Ānanda, brethren. What four? If a company of brethren come to see Ānanda, they are well pleased at the sight of him. Then Ānanda gives them a teaching, and so long as he is speaking they are pleased thereat, but that company of brethren is displeased only when Ānanda makes an end of speaking.

Again, brethren, if a company of sisters, of lay-brothers, or of lay-sisters come to see Ānanda, they are well pleased at the sight of him, delighted to hear him speak, and ill-pleased when he makes an end of speaking.

So also there are these four wonderful, strange things about a monarch who is a world-ruler. What four?

If, brethren, a company of nobles, of brāhmins, of housefathers, of recluses, come to see a monarch who is a world-ruler, they are well pleased at the sight of him: and so long as he is speaking they take delight in what is spoken by him, and are displeased when he makes an end of speaking.

Even so, brethren, there are these four wonderful, strange things about Ānanda . . . as I have told you.'

D.N. ii. 143.

THE LAST CONVERT

Now at that time Subhadda the Wanderer was staying at Kusināra. And Subhadda the Wanderer heard the rumour, 'This very day, 'tis said, in the last watch of the night will be the final passing away of Gotama the recluse.' Then this thought came to Subhadda the Wanderer:

'Thus have I heard it said by other wanderers who are old and far gone in years, both teachers and disciples: "Rarely, rarely do Tathāgatas arise in the world, they who are Arahants, Fully Enlightened Ones." And here to-night, in the last watch, will be the final passing away of Gotama the recluse. Now a doubt has arisen in my mind and I am assured of Gotama the recluse. Gotama the recluse can show me a teaching, so I that may dispel this doubting state of mine.'

Then Subhadda the Wanderer went towards the branch-road to the Sāla Grove of the Mallas, where the venerable Ānanda was, and coming there he said to the venerable Ānanda what he had thought to himself (*as before*), and he exclaimed: 'O master Ānanda! If only I could get a sight of Gotama the recluse!'

At these words the venerable Ānanda said to Subhadda the Wanderer: 'Enough, friend Subhadda! Trouble not the Master! The Exalted One is wearied.'

Then a second and yet a third time did Subhadda the Wanderer make the same request, and got the same reply.

Now the Exalted One overheard this talk between the venerable Ānanda and Subhadda the Wanderer. And He called to the venerable Ānanda, saying, 'Enough, Ānanda! Prevent not Subhadda. Let Subhadda be permitted to see the Tathāgata. Whatsoever Subhadda shall ask of Me, he will ask it all from a desire to know, not from a desire to trouble Me. And whatever I shall say in answer, that will he quickly understand.'

So then the venerable Ānanda said to Subhadda the Wanderer, 'Go you in, friend Subhadda. The Exalted One gives you leave.'

So Subhadda the Wanderer went in to the Exalted One, and coming to Him greeted Him pleasantly, and after the exchange of friendly compliments he sat down at one side. So seated, Subhadda the Wanderer thus addressed the Exalted One:

'Master Gotama, all those recluses and brāhmins who have followings and companies of listeners, who are teachers of companies, well known, renowned founders of sects, esteemed as holy men by the multitude, men like Pūraṇa Kassapa, Makkhali of the Cow-pen, Ajita of the hairshirt, Kacchāyana of the pakudha tree, Sañjaya son of Belaṭṭhi, and Nigaṇṭha of the Nātha clan,—have all these, as they say, realized by their own knowledge the truth of things, or have they not one and all so realized, or have some realized and others not realized it, by their own knowledge?'

'Let be, Subhadda! Trouble not yourself about such things, as to whether one and all or some have realized or not. I will show you the Norm, Subhadda. Do you listen carefully. Apply your mind. I will speak.'

'Even so, Lord,' said Subhadda the Wanderer, and gave heed to the Exalted One. Then the Exalted One said this:

'In whatsoever norm-discipline, Subaddha, the Ariyan Eightfold Path is not found, therein also no recluse is found, either of the first, the second, or the third, or the fourth degree. And in whatsoever norm-discipline, Subhadda, the Ariyan Eightfold Path is found, herein also is found a recluse of the first, second, third, and fourth degrees. Now in this Norm-Discipline (of mine), Subhadda, the Ariyan Eightfold Path is found. Herein also is found a recluse of these four degrees. Void of recluses are the other sects of disputants. But if, Subhadda, in this one brethren were to live the perfect life, the world would not be void of arahants.

My age was nine and twenty years
When I went forth to seek the Good,

Now fifty years and more are gone,
Subhadda, since I left the world
To range the Norm of Righteousness,
Outside of which is no recluse,

no recluse, of any of the four degrees. Void of recluses, Subhadda, are the other sects of disputants. But if in this one brethren were to live the perfect life, the world would not be void of arahants.'

At these words Subhadda the Wanderer said to the Exalted One: 'Wonderful, O Lord! A marvel, O Lord!' (*exactly the same words are used as in the ordination of Sabhiya, see* p. 71).[1]

D.N. ii. 148.

LAST WORDS

Then said the Exalted One to the venerable Ānanda:

'It may be, Ānanda, that you will say: "Gone is the word of the Master! We have no longer any Master now!" But you must not so regard it, Ānanda; for the Norm and Discipline taught and enjoined by me, they shall be your teachers when I am gone.

Now, Ānanda, whereas the brethren have the habit of calling one another "friend,"—when I am gone this habit must not be followed. By an elder brother, Ānanda, a brother who is a novice should be called by his name or clan-name

[1] The compilers of this Sutta add: 'and he was the last one to be personally converted by the Exalted One.'

or by the word "friend": but by a novice, Ānanda, an elder brother should be addressed as "lord" or "your reverence."

Again, Ānanda, if the Order so desires, when I am gone, let it abolish the lesser and minor charges.

As to the brother Channa, Ānanda, let the extreme penalty[1] be applied to him when I am gone.'

'What, Lord, do you mean by "the extreme penalty"?'

'The brother Channa, Ānanda, whatever he may wish or whatever he may say, is not to be spoken to, not to be admonished, not to be instructed by the brethren.'

Then the Exalted One addressed the brethren: 'It may be, brothers, that in the mind of some one brother there is doubt or perplexity, either about the Buddha, or about the Norm, or the Order, or the Path, or the Way to the Path. If it be so, brothers, do ye ask now. Be not hereafter remorseful at the thought, "Here was our Master face to face with us, and yet we had not the heart to question the Exalted One, though we were in His very presence."'

At these words the brethren were silent.

Then a second time and yet a third time did the Exalted One address the brethren in the same words. And a third time the brethren were silent.

Then said the Exalted One: 'Maybe, brethren, it is out of respect for the Master that ye ask not. Speak to Me, then, as friends to friend, brethren.'

[1] *Brahma-daṇḍa.*

Whereat those brethren were silent.

Then exclaimed the venerable Ānanda to the Exalted One: 'Strange it is, Lord! A marvel it is, Lord! Thus assured am I, Lord, of this Order of Brethren. There is not any one brother that has a single doubt or perplexity as to the Buddha, the Norm, the Order, or as to the Path, or the Way to the Path.'

'You speak out of assurance, Ānanda. But in the Tathāgata there is knowledge of the fact—"There is not in any one brother a single doubt or perplexity as to this. Of these five hundred brethren of mine, Ānanda, even he who is the most backward is a Stream-winner, one who is assured from the Downfall, assured of reaching the Supreme Wisdom."'[1]

Then said the Exalted One to the brethren:

'*Come now, brethren, I do remind ye: "Subject to decay are all compounded things." Do ye abide in heedfulness.*'

Those were the last words of the Exalted One.

D.N. ii. 154.

[1] The commentary thinks this was to encourage Ānanda, who alone was yet unperfected.